New Highlight 4

Cornelsen

INHALT

* Fakultativ (wahlfreie Bestandteile des Lehrwerks)

Unit **6*** ist nur Pflichtstoff für den E-Kurs in Nordrhein-Westfalen.

ANHANG

1⊙2 Als Hörtext oder Song auf der Audio-CD vorhanden; die Track-Angaben beziehen sich auf die Vollfassung (Bestellnummer 344630): 1⊙2 = CD 1, Track 2.

W⊙ Zusätzliche Aufgaben auf der CD-ROM im Workbook

Kann dem Portfolio-Ordner hinzugefügt werden

Aufgaben:

○ leicht ◑ mittel ● schwierig

Interkulturell

Wiederholung

Begleitend zum Schülerbuch finden sich unter www.new-highlight.de interaktive Online-Übungen, die am Ende jeder Unit bearbeitet werden können.

* Fakultativ (wahlfreie Bestandteile des Lehrwerks)

Next stop: USA

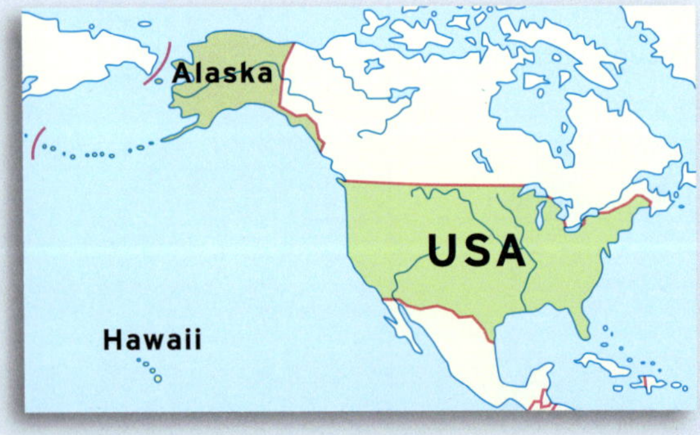

1 Songs about the USA

1 2

Listen to the songs and look at the map.
What places can you hear?
Put up your hand when you hear a name.
Then write the names on the board.

2 Places in this book

Work with a partner. Look quickly at the units in this book.
What places can you find? Can you find them on this map?

Tip:
Use the Internet. Go to:
www.new-highlight.de
Find the window for the webcode and put in:
NHL-4-7
Or look at a map.

PROJECT The USA from east to west

a) Work with a partner. Find out:

- **How many states are there in the USA?**
- **What's the capital of the USA?**
- **What's the biggest city in the USA?**
- **What's the population of the USA?**
- **What countries are the USA's neighbours?**
- **Which two states aren't near the others?**
- **How far is Los Angeles from New York City?**

b) Work in groups. Make a map of the USA for your classroom.

- **Put in the most important rivers, lakes and mountains.**
- **Put in the states, cities and towns that are in this book.**
- **Put some interesting facts on your map: capital, population, ...**

► W 2, 1–2

AMERICAN ENGLISH

1 American pronunciation

1◎3

a) British English (BE) and American English (AE) sound different. Listen to the five kids. Who's British? Who's American?

I think ... is British/American.

b) How do British people say these words? Read them out.

1◎4

c) Listen to the words in British and American English. Can you hear what's different?

1. later – better
2. park – world
3. fast – dancing
4. got – shopping
5. Tuesday – new

2 Special American words and phrases

1◎5

Listen to the conversations. Then listen again and match the phrases (1–5) with the pictures (a–e).

1. Hi, you guys.
2. Gimme five!
3. How ya doin', Ally?
4. Have a nice day!
5. Awesome!

3 British and American words

1 6 a) **Some American English words are different. Start a list in your exercise book. Look at the photos here. In your list, write the British English words for the things. Then listen and check.**

Tip:
Put new American English words in your list after every unit.

1

2

3

4

5

b) GAME
Make ten cards. Write the British English and the American English words from 3a). Mix the cards up. Can you put the right words together?

Tip:
Make cards for new AE words and play the game with a partner after every unit.

● 4 American English spelling

American spelling is sometimes different. Work with a partner. Look at the underlined words in American English spelling. Write the words in British spelling. Then check in the *Dictionary* (pages 160–179).

1 mile = 1.609 kilometers

New York T-shirts in all colors

▸W 2, 3

Unit 1

The Big Apple

1 Lower East Side

2 Chinatown

3 Little Italy

4 The Financial District

5 The Statue of Liberty and Ellis Island

1 Before you listen: Where is New York City?

It's in the east/west of the USA.

Tip: Check on the map on pages 6–7.

2 Where's what in New York?

1⊙7

You're in Manhattan at the top of the Empire State Building. Look at the photos and map on pages 10 and 11. Listen and pick the right answers.

The places on this page are north/south of the Empire State Building.
The places on page 11 are north/south of the Empire State Building.

► W 3, 1

6

The Empire State Building

7

Times Square

8

Central Park

9

Harlem

3 At the top of the Empire State Building

1 8

Listen to the tour. Are these sentences true or false?

1 Manhattan is one of the five areas of New York.
2 Lower East Side, Little Italy and Chinatown are immigrant neighbourhoods.
3 New York is the financial capital of the world.
4 About 17 million immigrants came to the USA through Ellis Island from 1890 to 1920.
5 In Central Park you can only find poor people.
6 In Times Square you can find famous theatres.
7 Harlem was famous for rap music.

4 AND YOU? Talk to a partner about the photos.

I think ... looks ...
I'd like to see ... because ...

→ beautiful • boring • busy • cheap • cool • dirty • dangerous • exciting • expensive • great • modern • good for shopping/food/sightseeing/sports/ ...

▸W 3, 2–3

SIGHTSEEING IN NEW YORK

1 Listen to the dialogue. Pick the right answers.

1◉9

1 Tyrell and Jazmin are at Central Park / the Empire State Building.
2 They're going to Ground Zero / Chinatown.
3 Then they're going to Tyrell's apartment in Harlem / Little Italy.

2 Listen again. Who ...

1◉9

1 ... has to be more careful with the traffic?
2 ... lives in Greenville and thinks New York is more exciting?
3 ... always makes dinner at 18.30?
4 ... doesn't get much pocket money?

3 At a deli: Look at the menu.

a) How much is a ham sandwich? It's ... dollars.
How much are potato chips? They're ... cents.
Which is more expensive – white bread or brown bread?

b) Listen. What does the tourist ask for?

1◉10

Make your own sandwich!

Grilled chicken	$5.00
Beef	$5.25
Black Forest ham	$5.00
Smoked salmon	$6.25
Cheese	$4.25
Egg salad	$3.75

BREAD: white, brown, roll, pita, bagel: free

Lettuce, tomato: free

Cheese	50 cents
Potato chips	50 cents

ALL DRINKS ONLY $2!!

c) Listen and read the dialogue.

1◉11

ASSISTANT Hi guys, what would you like?
JAZMIN I'll have a beef sandwich on a roll with lettuce, tomato and cheese, and potato chips. And an orange juice, please.
ASSISTANT That's $8.25.
JAZMIN My cousin is paying!
TYRELL Here you are.
ASSISTANT Thank you. Have a nice day!

d) Look at the menu. Make a new dialogue.

PROJECT Your school deli

Organize an American deli in your school for one day:

- **Write a menu.**
- **Make a list: Who's bringing what? Who's doing what?**
- **Make sandwiches and sell them at lunchtime.**
- **Everybody has to speak English!**
- **What will you do with the money?**

Look at www.new-highlight.de for help.
Put in the webcode NHL-4-12.

►W 4, 4

ON THE SUBWAY

1 **Find Chambers Street on the subway map. Listen and look at the map. Find where Tyrell lives.** 1◎12

2 **Work with a partner. Read the sentences. Your partner finds the place on the map.**

Partner A

1 From Times Square, take line 1 south to the end of the line.
2 From Central Park North, take line 2 or 3 south. Change at 42nd Street to line 7. Travel two stops.

Partner B

1 From Washington Square at W 4th Street, take line F east. Travel four stops.
2 From Grand Central, take line 4, 5 or 6 north to 86th Street. Then walk three blocks west.

3 **You're at Times Square.**
Partner A: Pick a station or a place. Tell your partner how to get there.
Partner B: Find the place on the map.

- Take line ... south/north/east/west to ...
- Change at ... to line ...
- Travel ... stops.
- Walk ... blocks north/south/east/west.

►W 4, 5

STORY

1 Who was Malcolm X?

a) Look at the photos and the quotes by Malcolm X in the boxes. Pick the right answer.

b) Read Malcom X's story. Check your answer to exercise 1a).

Malcolm X ...

a) sang rap songs **b)** helped to change history **c)** made films

The story of Malcolm X

1 13

"If you're born in America with a black skin, you're born in prison."

Malcolm Little was born in Omaha, Nebraska in 1925. He had seven brothers and sisters. In 1931, when Malcolm was six years old, his father died. The police said it was an accident. But Malcolm thought a group of white people killed him because his father often had problems with white people. Later his mother became ill, so the children had to leave their home and live in different families and children's homes. These were the most terrible years of Malcolm's life.

"Without education, you're not going anywhere in this world."

Malcolm was one of the best pupils at his school. He wanted to be a lawyer. But a teacher told him that that wasn't a job for black people. At that time, black people couldn't sit next to white people on buses or trains, or in restaurants and cafes. And black children often had to go to different schools from white children. So Malcolm left school when he was fifteen and he moved to Harlem in New York. He started to steal. In 1946 he went to prison for seven years.

In prison Malcolm read lots of books and learned about a group of black Muslims. They wanted a better life for black Americans – a life without white people. Malcolm Little changed his name to "Malcolm X" because for him "Little" was a slave name. And he started to fight for the rights of black people. He talked on the radio and on TV about freedom for black people and he wrote angry newspaper articles. For some people he was dangerous because it was OK for him to use violence to change things. But he became one of the most popular speakers in America.

"Usually when people are sad, they don't do anything. But when they're angry, they bring about a change."

In 1964 Malcolm's life changed: He travelled to Mecca and came back with a new name (El-Hajj Malik El Shabazz). Now he thought that violence was wrong. And he fought for a better life for everybody everywhere: black and white. But on February 21st, 1965, three men killed Malcolm X in Harlem. On that day America lost one of the most important men in its history – a man who helped black people to fight for their dreams.

2 When and where: Match the sentence parts.

1 Malcolm was born	**a)** when he was fifteen.
2 Malcolm's father died	**b)** in 1931.
3 Malcolm left school	**c)** in Harlem.
4 He started thinking about black rights	**d)** after his trip to Mecca.
5 Malcolm's life changed	**e)** in 1925.
6 Three people killed Malcolm	**f)** in prison.

3 Pick the right answers.

1 Malcolm had
- **a)** two different names.
- **b)** three different names.
- **c)** four different names.

2 When Malcolm was a child
- **a)** his parents died.
- **b)** things were hard for him.
- **c)** he had a happy life.

3 When Malcolm was young, black people
- **a)** had different rights from white people.
- **b)** couldn't use buses.
- **c)** had rights like white people.

4 After 1964 Malcolm X thought that violence was
- **a)** sometimes OK.
- **b)** always OK.
- **c)** never OK.

5 In his last years Malcolm wanted rights for
- **a)** American people.
- **b)** black people.
- **c)** everybody.

4 Malcolm X's life

a) Finish the sentences. Tell the class.

I think Malcolm was a/an ... man.
He had a/an ... life.

→ boring • brave • dangerous • exciting • hard • important • interesting • stupid • tough • wild

● **b) Write a summary of Malcolm X's life (about 50 words). Put your ideas together with these words:**

→ and • but • because • then

Tip:
Write only the most important things. You can use some sentences in exercises 2, 3 and 4.

▸W 5, 6–8

1 Food

a) Make lists with the class. What are the words in the pictures?

These words are on page 12.

b) Write the lists in your exercise book and put in more words.

c) What did you have for breakfast and lunch yesterday? Tell the class.

▸ Wordbank 1, p. 126

2 Money

a) What's the right word?

pocket money • cents • dollars

1 $ (American money).
2 You get it from your parents.
3 There are one hundred in $1.

b) WORD LINK Which verb can't you use?

find get kill borrow lose save spend steal win | MONEY

c) AND YOU? Talk to a partner.

1 How often do you get pocket money?
2 What do you do with your pocket money?

3 The story of Lil' Kim

Finish the story with the words and phrases from the box.

The words and phrases are all in the story pages 14–15.

fought • killed • lost • violence • was born • went to prison

Lil' Kim ... in 1975 in New York. She lived in a poor neighbourhood where there was lots of ... and other problems. She ... hard and became a rapper. Her boyfriend Notorious B.I.G. helped her, but in 1997 somebody ... B.I.G. Lil' Kim was devastated when she ... him but she worked hard and became a big star. Then in 2005 she had problems with the police: She ... for 10 months. When she came out, she said sorry to her fans.

4 WORD SEARCH The time and date

a) Write these times and dates in numbers.

They're all on pages 11–16.

1 eighteen ninety (p. 11)
2 half past six (p. 12)
3 February the twenty-first (p. 15)
4 nineteen sixty-five (p. 15)
5 two thousand and five (p. 16)

b) Write five dates or times. Say them to your partner – but don't show them! Your partner writes them. Are they right?

Tip:
1950: You say "nineteen fifty"
1998: You say "nineteen ninety-eight"
2007: You say "two thousand **and** seven"

▸ W 6, 9–11 ▸ W ⊙

1 What are they like?

a) Write the opposites.

New York	Greenville, South Carolina

1 big — small
2 … — boring
3 expensive — …
4 … — clean
5 busy — …
6 … — safe

b) Look at the photos. Talk about the girls.

I think Britney/Kimberley is …/looks … .

→ beautiful • friendly • healthy • ill • nervous • quiet • sad • shy • sporty • tired

c) AND YOU?
What's your area like? Use words in a).
What are you like? Use words in b).

2 Travel

a) Put the words from the green box in the network. Then find more words.

→ a park • presents • with friends • an amusement arcade • food • a museum • with family • car • in a holiday flat • bus • in a hotel • postcards • clothes • a church • underground/subway • plane

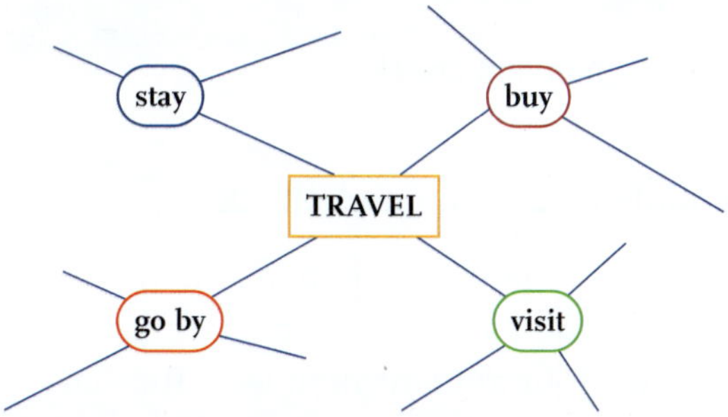

● b) Write about a trip. Use words from 2a). It doesn't have to be true!

I/We travelled to … . I went by … .
I stayed … . I visited … . I bought … .

3 SAY IT IN GERMAN

Tell your partner about the advert in German.

Tip:
Pick the most important things: What? Where? When?

▸ W 7, 12–14 ▸ W ◉

LISTENING Dates, times and places

1 Three dialogues

a) Look at the adverts, notes and cards. What are they?

1 Adverts for …
2 Notes about …
3 Appointment cards for the …

b) What's the American English word for *shopping centre*? Put it in your list.

c) Now listen to the three dialogues. Pick A, B or C. 1 14

Tip: Listen to the days, dates and times.

1 A

B

C

2 A
Jay-Z Concert
June 20th/21st
Madison Square Garden
8 p.m. $90!

B
Jay-Z Concert
June 20th/21st
Central Park
9 p.m.
$90!

C
Jay-Z Concert
June 20th/21st
Lincoln Center
8 p.m.
$80!

3 A
Jill Allen, Dentist
Your next appointment is:
September 14th
at 4:00 p.m.

B
Jill Allen, Dentist
Your next appointment is:
September 14th
at 3:30 p.m.

C
Jill Allen, Dentist
Your next appointment is:
September 14th
at 4:30 p.m.

d) Compare your answers with a partner. Then listen again and check. 1 14

2 Put in *to/at/in/on*. You can listen to the dialogues again and check. 1 14

1 On Sunday we open … 10 a.m.
2 They're … June.
3 They're … June 20th/21st.
4 … Madison Square Garden.
5 You have to go … the dentist.
6 Your appointment is … Tuesday.

3 AND YOU? Do you have any plans, appointments or invitations?

I have tickets for … / I have an invitation to …
I'm going to go to … / I'm going to meet …

on Saturday / at 3 o'clock /
at the sports club / at my house

► W 8, 15 ► W

SPEAKING Invitations

1 Brianna's invitation
1 15
- What is Brianna doing on Saturday evening?
- When should Tyrell be there?
- What can Tyrell bring?

BRIANNA Do you have any plans for Saturday night?
TYRELL No, not really.
BRIANNA I'm having a party. Do you want to come?
TYRELL That sounds great, thanks. When should I be there?
BRIANNA About 7 o'clock. There'll be some pizza and salad.
TYRELL That sounds good. Can I bring anything?
BRIANNA Yeah, can you bring some CDs? Your music is better than my music.
TYRELL OK. Thanks for the invitation. See you then.

2 Tyrell's invitation
1 16
a) Finish the dialogue.

TYRELL Do you have ... for Friday evening?
JUSTIN No, ...
TYRELL I'm having a movie night. Do you ...?
JUSTIN That ..., ... When ...?
TYRELL About 6 o'clock . There'll be lots of movies and music concerts on DVDs.
JUSTIN That ... . Can I bring anything?
TYRELL Yeah, can ... some popcorn?
JUSTIN ... . See you then.

b) Read the dialogue in a) with a partner.

3 ROLE PLAY
Partner A: Invite partner B to a party. Look at your card on page 94.
Partner B: Look at your card on page 94.

4 INTERPRETING
You and your brother are at a cafe. You meet an American girl. Your brother wants to invite her to a party, but he's too shy to speak English. Help him.

BROTHER Frag sie doch, ob sie zu unserer Party am Samstagabend kommen will.
YOU (to American girl) Do you want to ...?
GIRL That sounds great, thanks. Can I bring a friend?
YOU (to your brother) Sie kommt gern. Darf sie ...?
BROTHER Ja, klar. Sag ihr, dass die Party um 18 Uhr anfängt. Hier ist unsere Adresse.
YOU (to American girl) That's fine. The party starts ...

Remember:
on Monday, on Tuesday ...
at 9 o' clock, at night, ...

► W 8, 16–17 ► W

READING Party invitations

1 Read the invitations, Tyrell's letter and his e-mail.
- Why are these two birthdays special? (Tip: How old are Destiny and Diego?)
- What does "RSVP" mean, do you think? Pick the right answer.

a) Please come. **b)** Please tell me/us if you can come.

To everybody
From Diego Garcia <diegoG@hotwire.com>

PARTY!!

I'm having a party
'cause I'm going to be sixteen
So come on over –
my house is the scene!

October 7th is the date
The party starts at six – don't be late
There'll be lots of music, food and fun ...
The most awesome time for everyone!

RSVP by October 1st please!

Dear Mr and Mrs Moore,

Thank you for the invitation.
I'm afraid I can't come because
it's my grandma's 60th birthday
on the 3rd.

Best wishes,
Tyrell Stone

To Diego
From Tyrell

Hi Diego,
That's a terrible poem – but thanks for the invitation. See you there!
Tyrell

2 True, false or not in the text?
Read the texts again. Write *true* or *false*. If you can't find the information, write *not in the text*.

1 Destiny's party is on November 3rd, at 19.00.
2 Diego's party is on a Saturday.
3 The two parties are at home.
4 There's food at the two parties.
5 There's dancing at Destiny's party.
6 Destiny's party finishes at 11 p.m.
7 Diego's parents are sending the invitations to his party.
8 Tyrell can go to the two parties.

3 Parties in the USA and Germany

Ask and answer the questions with a partner.

YOU	YOUR PARTNER
Do your friends send invitations like Destiny's?	Yes, they do. / No, they don't.
Are 16th birthdays special in Germany?	Yes, they are. / No, they aren't.
Why is 16 a special age in the USA? Look at Destiny's card.	It's special because you can ...
What other special parties do people have?	For their ...th birthday. / For a wedding. / ...

WRITING Party invitations

1 AND YOU?

Imagine you can have a big party and money isn't important. Make notes about these things:

- When will it be?
- Where will it be?
- Who will you invite?
- What music will you play?
- What will you eat?
- How will it be special?

IDEAS
- at home / at a football club / at a hotel / at a club / at a shopping centre / on a beach / at a swimming pool / ...
- all my friends and family / all the class / my best friends / ...
- rap / house / techno / ...
- hamburgers / sandwiches / pizza / salad / fruit salad / cake / ...

2 Copy and write this invitation. OR make your own special invitation.

Use your notes from exercise 1.

Tip:
If you have computers in class, find a party invitation on the Internet. Write it. Then send it to your partner.

3 Your answer

a) Give your invitation to a partner. Read your partner's invitation.

b) Answer your partner's invitation. Give your answer to your partner.

Tyrell's letter and e-mail on page 20 can help you.

► W 9, 18–19 ► W ⊙

THE AMERICAN DREAM?

1 Read the article and answer the questions. What problems did Lanh and Maria have? Are they happy in the USA? Why or why not?

Did you know that about 3 million people in New York City were born in other countries? Lanh and Maria tell us about life in the USA.

My name is Lanh Nguyen and I was born in Vietnam. When I came to the USA I was only seven years old. The hardest thing was the language. But that became easier very quickly. The second problem was the different way of life. One example is the food – so much meat! In my family we eat healthier food with lots of vegetables. But I think New York is great – it's much more international than the cities in Vietnam. I love living here. Teenagers in the USA have more freedom than in Vietnam. My dream is to be a cook and have the coolest restaurant in New York.

My name is Maria Cortez. I moved here from Costa Rica when I was 14. My dad's biggest dream was to live in the USA. He wanted a better life for us. And one day he won a lottery so we could live in America. When you're young, it's OK to move to a new country. But it's harder when you're older. I don't like New York. It's too busy and there's too much traffic. But the worst thing is when people think you're stupid because your English isn't good. Mom and dad were happier in Costa Rica too. Now they miss our country.

2 AND YOU?

Would you like to live in the USA or another country? I'd like to live in ...
What would you like there? What would you miss? I'd like ... / I'd miss ...

3 WORD SEARCH

a) Find these words on this page.

1. That became ... very quickly. (Lanh)
2. In my family we eat ... food. (Lanh)
3. It's ... when you're older. (Maria)

b) Now find these.

1. The ... thing was the language. (Lanh)
2. My dream is to be a cook and have the ... restaurant in New York. (Lanh)
3. My dad's ... dream was to live in the USA. (Maria)

4 WORD SEARCH

a) Find these words on page 12.

1 Who has to be ... ... with the traffic? (ex. 2)
2 Who lives in Greenville and thinks New York is ... ...? (ex. 2)
3 Which is ... ... – white bread or brown bread? (ex. 3)

b) Now find these words on pages 14 and 15.

1 These were the ... ... years of Malcolm's life. (lines 7–8)
2 But he became one of the ... ... speakers in America. (line 31)
3 On that day America lost one of the ... ... men in its history. (lines 37–38)

5 OVER TO YOU! Finish the checkpoint.

CHECKPOINT

Vergleiche mit *-er/est* und *more/most*

- Bei einsilbigen Adjektiven (z. B. *hard*) und zweisilbigen Adjektiven auf *-y* (z. B. *happy*) hängst du ... bzw. ... an das Adjektiv.
- Bei dreisilbigen Adjektiven (z. B. *expensive*) und manchen zweisilbigen Adjektiven (z. B. *famous*) setzt du ... bzw. ... vor das Adjektiv.
- *good* und *bad* haben unregelmäßige Formen:
  good, ..., ...
  bad, ..., ...

Tip: Write the checkpoint in your exercise book.

Tip: Learn these three forms together.

► Eine Übersicht über diese Regeln findest du auf der *Summary*-Seite 136.
► Extra Practice, pp. 97 ff.
► W 10–11

NACH DIESER UNIT KANN ICH ...

über die Sehenswürdigkeiten von New York sprechen.	► *In Times Square there are lots of theatres. I'd like to go to Central Park.*
Vergleiche anstellen.	► *New York is more exciting than Greenville. It's my biggest dream.*
über Daten und Uhrzeiten sprechen.	► *Malcolm X died on February 21st 1965. The party starts at 7 p.m.*
ein Sandwich in einem „Deli" bestellen.	► *I'll have a roll with beef and tomato, please.*
jemanden den Weg mit der U-Bahn oder zu Fuß beschreiben.	► *Take line 2 or 3 to 125th Street. Walk three blocks to 128th Street.*
jemanden einladen.	► *Do you have any plans for Saturday evening? I'm having a party on Saturday. Do you want to come?*
eine Einladung annehmen oder ablehnen.	► *That sounds great, thanks. / I'm afraid I can't come.*

Unit 2

Life in LA

Surfers at the beach

The stalls in Venice

Busy LA roads

Shopping in Santa Monica

1 My Los Angeles video diary

1 17 **Listen to the video diary about LA. Which five pictures on pages 24 and 25 is the teenager talking about?**

2 About the pictures

1 18 **Listen. Look at the pictures. What's right: a), b) or c)?**

3 AND YOU? Tell the class.

E

The boardwalk

F

G

A homeless man

H

Smog

I

Disneyland

4 Talk about a photo

Partner A: Partner B has picked a photo. Find out which photo.
Ask some questions like these:

What can you see?
How many people are there?
What are the people doing?
What's happening?
How do the people look?
What's the weather like?

Partner B: Pick a photo. But don't tell Partner A which photo.
Answer Partner A's questions:

– I can see ...
– There are ...
– They're ...
– A man is/Some people are ...
– The man looks ...
– It's nice/terrible/ ...

► W 13, 1–3
► Wordbank 2, p. 127

FREE TIME IN LA

1 Look at A, B and C. What are they about?

TV • outdoor activities • dancing

A is about ... B is about ... C ...

A

TODAY'S HIGHLIGHTS

NEWS
Good Morning America 7 a.m. KABC

SPORTS
Baseball 5 p.m. NBC
Action from New York.

MOVIES
Best Man, Worst Friend 8 p.m. ABC FAMILY
A great family movie.

SERIES
Back Home 10:30 p.m. CBS
12 stars from Big Brother meet again!

B

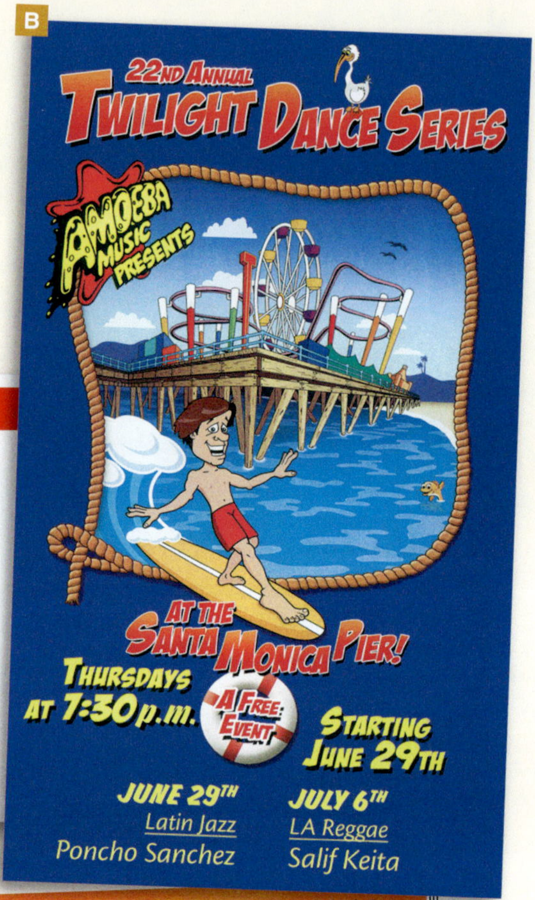

2 What do we learn in the texts?
Pick the right answers.

1 There's sports on TV ...
a) early in the morning.
b) in the afternoon.
c) late at night.

2 If you want to go to *Twilight Dance* ...
a) you have to pay.
b) you don't have to pay.
c) you only pay on Thursdays.

3 The magazine has information about ...
a) films and TV.
b) music in Santa Monica.
c) things to do in LA.

C

3 What is it in German?

highlights	**a)** Schlagzeilen	**b)** Höhepunkte	**c)** Lampen
twilight	**a)** Abenddämmerung	**b)** Tageslicht	**c)** Sonnenaufgang
Get out!	**a)** Steh auf!	**b)** Hau ab!	**c)** Geh raus!

Tip:
First find the words in the text. Check with a partner. Then check in a dictionary.

PROJECT A media survey

TV, films and computers are very important today. Which are most important for young people? Do boys and girls like the same things? Do this survey and find out.

a) Ask your partner these questions. Write the answers in your exercise book.

Are you – a boy/a girl?

TV	Films	Computers
1 How much TV do you watch every day? a Less than an hour b One or two hours c More than two hours	**4 How many films do you watch every week?** a No films b One or two films c More than two films	**7 Do you have your own computer?** a Yes b No
2 Do you have a TV in your room? a Yes b No	**5 How often do you go to the cinema?** a Every week b Sometimes c Never	**8 How often do you use a computer?** a Every day b Sometimes c Never
3 What kind of TV programmes do you prefer? a Sport b Chat shows c Series d ... ▸ Wordbank 3, p. 127	**6 What kind of films do you prefer?** a Action b Comedy c Romance d ... ▸ Wordbank 3, p. 127	**9 How often do you use the Internet?** a Every day b Sometimes c Never

b) Collect the results on the board.

Media Survey Class 8 B

		BOYS	GIRLS
1 TV time	< 1 hour	2	5
	1–2 hours	4	7
	> 2 hours	6	3
2 TV in room		6	4
3 Favourite TV programmes		Series	Series
4 Films every week	0	1	2
	1–2	5	8
	2+	6	5

c) Present the results in class.

In the survey, we found out that two boys and five girls watch less than one hour of TV every day. But four boys and seven girls watch one to ...
Ten pupils in our class have a TV in their room – six boys and ...

Most pupils prefer ...
Lots of pupils watch more than two films every week – six boys and ... But most pupils only watch between one and two ...

d) Look at the questions in the survey and write about you and the media.

I watch about 1 hour of TV every day. I don't have a TV in my room. I prefer series and ...

● **e) Write a report about the survey in your class (50–70 words). How many pupils did you ask? Are boys and girls different? You can use the ideas in c).**

▸ W 14, 4–6

1 Look at the pictures. Try to answer the questions.

a) Where do you think the story is happening?
b) Do you think that all the teenagers in the photos are friends?
c) Who would you like to be, the girl in the first picture or one of the teenagers in the second picture?

Lucky thing!

1◎19

Saturday 9.15 a.m., 3rd Street, Santa Monica
Richard Bailey was waiting for his daughter.
"Hurry up, Caitlin! We'll be late," he shouted.
Ten minutes later they were driving along the freeway towards Hollywood.
"Now remember Caitlin," Richard said. "You're the best. You can get this role. This is a day that you'll always remember. It could be the start of a great career in TV."
Caitlin was looking at the invitation to the audition that the studio had sent.
She was feeling nervous. But she didn't say anything.

KABC STUDIOS LA
invites: Caitlin Bailey
to an audition for: TEEN TALK
on: Saturday, October 3rd at 10 a.m.

10.15 a.m., Santa Monica Boardwalk
Two friends, Lee and Nina, were on the boardwalk. They had their surfboards. It was a nice morning. Lots of people were jogging, walking and cycling. After ten minutes the two friends arrived at Venice. This was always a busy place, with lots of stalls, food places and music. And there were homeless people who were sleeping on the grass. Lee and Nina sat on the grass too, watched the people and had their sandwiches.

12.30 p.m., KABC Studios, LA
Caitlin left KABC Studios. Her dad was sitting in the car. "How was it?" he asked.
"Terrible," she answered. "First, I was standing in line for a long time. Then, the man who asked the questions wasn't very nice. He was the director, so I won't get the role," she said.
"Well, we have to hurry up," her father answered. "Or we'll be late for your photo shoot."
"Appointments, auditions, photo shoots! I need a break, Dad!" Caitlin answered.
"Think of your future, Caitlin," Richard said and they went towards Santa Monica.

1.30 p.m., Santa Monica Beach

Lee and Nina were in the sea on their surfboards. The waves were great. The water was cold. But they were fine because they were wearing wetsuits.

1.40 p.m.

Caitlin was on Santa Monica Beach too. She was wearing nice, expensive surfing gear, but she wasn't surfing. A photographer and a make-up artist were with her. The photographer was taking photos. "Turn to the left ... no, not too much ... now turn to the right ... look at me ... smile ... look happy ...", the photographer was shouting. Caitlin looked at the sea. She saw something that made her jealous – surfers. "Lucky things!" she thought.

1.50 p.m.

Lee and Nina walked along the beach. Nina saw a girl who was standing on the beach in nice clothes.
"Look at that girl," she said to Lee. "She's a model."
"Yeah, it must be a photo shoot for a magazine," he answered.
"How do you get a job like that? Lucky thing!" Nina thought.

2 Who is it?

1. He does lots of things for his daughter. But is he really helping her?
2. She loves surfing. But she'd really like to be a photo model.
3. He loves Venice, the sea, free time ...
4. She has a busy life and no free time.

3 Finish these sentences.

1. In the morning Caitlin went ...
2. At the same time Lee and Nina were ...
3. After the audition Caitlin wasn't ...
4. Then she and her dad went to ...
5. At 1.30, Lee and Nina ...
6. Caitlin was doing a ...

4 On Saturday evening: Write the dialogue.

CAITLIN	today – terrible day
DAD	this – could – the start – great career
CAITLIN	tired – need – break
DAD	think of – future
CAITLIN	want – some – free time
DAD	OK – go to the beach – next weekend

5 Caitlin's e-mail

You're Caitlin. Write to your friend Alice. Tell her about Saturday.

Use words and phrases from the story.

To Alice From Caitlin

Hi Alice,
Saturday was a terrible day. First I went to KABC Studios for an audition. I was waiting ...

► W 15, 7–9

1 A Santa Monica scene

a) What can you see?
Work in teams of three or four pupils. Who can find the most things, activities, people?

The words are in the story on pages 28–29.

b) Finish these sentences with words from a).

1 The waves are great. Let's go ...
2 The water is cold. You need a ...
3 We can ride our bikes on the ...
4 Look. There's a cool T-shirt ...
5 That man has no home. He's ...

2 Networks: Finish these networks in your exercise book.

▸ Wordbank 3, p. 127

3 Definitions: What do you call ...

1 ... somebody who takes photos?
2 ... somebody who knows all about make-up?
3 ... somebody who surfs?
4 ... big roads that you find in the USA?
5 ... small shops that you find in Venice?
6 ... the track that goes along the beach?

4 Pick some of these words and ask your partner:

director • model • teenager • surfboard • wetsuit

What do you call somebody who is/makes/wears ...
What do you call something that you need when/you wear when ...

5 WORD SEARCH *Who* or *that*?

a) Find the right words on pages 28 and 29.

1 This is a day ... you'll remember. (ll. 7–8)
2 Caitlin was looking at the invitation to the audition ... the studio had sent. (ll. 9–10)
3 There were homeless people ... were sleeping on the grass. (ll. 21–23)
4 The man ... asked the questions wasn't very nice. (ll. 28–29)
5 She saw something ... made her jealous – surfers. (ll. 45–46)
6 Nina saw a girl ... was standing on the beach in nice clothes. (ll. 48–49)

b) When do you use *who* and *that*? Look at the answers to a). Make a rule.

You use ... for people.
You use ... for things.

▸ W 16, 10–12 ▸ W ⊙

DICTIONARY WORK

1 What's the text about?

Read the advert and find out what a SEGWAY is.

a) It's only a toy for kids.
b) You can travel to places on it.
c) You use it for sport.

Tip:
There are lots of new words in the text, but you don't have to understand everything.

SEGWAY

The SEGWAY can take you to places that cars and bikes can't go – like stores, offices, airports and streets. With a SEGWAY you can go shopping, go to work or just have fun. The SEGWAY is clean, quiet and good for the environment. You don't need gas – the SEGWAY uses batteries. You can charge the batteries anywhere – in the home or in the office. Using the SEGWAY is easy. To go forwards, you lean forwards. To go backwards, you lean backwards, to go left or right, you lean left or right. Maximum speed: 12.5 miles per hour (mph)
Price: $4000-$5500

2 Do you know the words?

a) What German words do these words sound like?

1 batteries **2** forwards
3 maximum

b) Now find the three words in the advert.
Do you think that you were right? Then check the words in a dictionary.

3 Find the words in the advert, look at the context and pick the right meaning.

gas	**a)** *Nomen* Gas, (AE) Benzin	**b)** *Verb* (mit Gas) vergiften	
charge	**a)** *Nomen* Gebühr	**b)** *Verb* berechnen	**c)** *Verb* aufladen
speed	**a)** *Verb* rasen	**b)** *Nomen* Geschwindigkeit	

4 Three dictionary entries

Read the three entries. Then find the words in the SEGWAY advert and look at the context. What's the right meaning in German?

environment /ɪnˈvaɪrənmənt/ *Nomen* **1** Umgebung, Umwelt **a bad environment** ein schlechtes häusliches Milieu
2 the environment die Umwelt **laws to protect the environment** Gesetze zum Umweltschutz

lean[1] /liːn/ *Adj (Fleisch)* mager; *(Person)* schlank
lean[2] /liːn/ *Verb* **(leaned, leaned** /liːnd/, *BE auch* **leant, leant** /lent/) **1** *ohne Obj* sich lehnen **lean backwards** sich zurücklehnen **lean over to one side** sich zur Seite lehnen **He leaned across the table to pick up the phone.** Er beugte sich über den Tisch, um den Telefonhörer abzunehmen. **lean forwards** sich vorbeugen
2 *ohne Obj* lean against/on sth sich an etw lehnen, sich auf etw stützen
3 + *Obj* lehnen **Please don't lean bicycles against the shop window.** Bitte keine Fahrräder an das Schaufenster lehnen.

office /ˈɒfɪs; *AE auch* ˈɔːfɪs/ *Nomen* **1** Büro **the firm's head office** der Hauptsitz der Firma **an office block** ein Bürohaus
2 *(AE) (Arzt-, Zahnarzt-)* Praxis
3 *(oft in Zusammensetzungen)* Amt **the Foreign Office** das Auswärtige Amt **the tax office** das Finanzamt
4 *kein Plural* Amt, Amtszeit **the chairman holds office for one year.** Der Vorsitzende ist ein Jahr lang im Amt. **the party that is in office** die Regierungspartei

From: *Das Oxford Schulwörterbuch, Oxford University Press, 2007*

► W 17, 13 ► W ⊙

LISTENING Phone messages

1 An important message

1 ⊙ 20 **a) Caitlin's mum wrote three phone messages. Listen to the phone call. Which message do you hear?**

b) Listen again and check.

A

PHONE MESSAGE

For: *Caitlin*

From: *KABC Studios*

Message: *Call Jack between 8 p.m. and 10 p.m.*

Tel.: *310-555-0719*

B

PHONE MESSAGE

For: *Richard*

From: *Brown's Books*

Message: *New movie book has come. Please pick it up tomorrow after 10 a.m.*

Tel.: *310-555-4570*

C

PHONE MESSAGE

For: *Caitlin*

From: *Bob Brown*

Message: *Call Bob after 8 p.m.*

Tel.: *310-555-0901*

2 Can I take a message?

1 ⊙ 21 **a) Listen. What's right – a), b) or c)?**

1 Caitlin is talking to ...
a) Bob Brown.
b) her dad.
c) a woman at KABC Studios.

2 Bob Brown ...
a) is at home.
b) can't come to the phone.
c) isn't at the studio.

3 Bob can call Caitlin ...
a) on her mobile.
b) at home.
c) at school.

Tip:
mobile (BE)
= cellphone (AE)

b) Write this message in your exercise book.

PHONE MESSAGE

For: *Bob ...*

From: ...

Message: *Call Caitlin on her ... after ...*

Tel.: *310-555-2279*

c) Finish the message. Then listen again and check.

3 Caitlin's news

1 ⊙ 22 **a) Listen and make notes.**

1 Who's calling?
2 Who's answering the phone?
3 What can Caitlin have?
4 How does Caitlin feel?
5 When can Caitlin come to the studio?
6 Who must come too?

Tip:
Before you listen, read the questions and write the question words in your exercise book.

b) SAY IT IN GERMAN
Tell a partner about the phone call – in German. Use your notes for a).

► W 18, 14 ► W ⊙

SPEAKING Phone calls

1 Two phone calls

1 23

a) Listen to or read the two dialogues.

CAITLIN Hi. Can I speak to Josh, please?
MAN Josh? (*Er*), I think you have the wrong number.
CAITLIN Oh, sorry.
MAN No problem. Bye.

CAITLIN Hi. Can I speak to Josh, please?
MRS STONE I'm afraid he isn't here. Can I take a message?
CAITLIN Yes, please. Can you tell him that Caitlin called? Can he call me back? My new number is 310-555-2279.
MRS STONE OK, Caitlin. No problem. Bye.
CAITLIN Thanks, Mrs Stone. Bye.

b) Answer these questions.

1 Who has a wrong number?
2 Who wants to speak to Josh?
3 Who isn't at home?
4 Who can take a message?
5 Who has a new number?

c) Practise the phone calls with a partner.

2 SAY IT IN ENGLISH

a) Make a phone call with a partner. Write the dialogue on the left or on the right.

A: Frage, ob du mit Alex sprechen darfst.

B: Sage, dass er gerade nicht da ist. Frage, ob du ihm etwas ausrichten kannst.	B: Sage, du glaubst dass er/sie falsch verbunden ist.
A: Sage ja. Er soll dich zu Hause anrufen. Die Nummer lautet 320-798-8305.	A: Sage, es tut dir leid.
B: Sage, dass das in Ordnung ist.	B: Sage, dass das nichts macht.

A: Bedanke dich und beende das Gespräch.

b) Act the dialogues with a partner.

3 ROLE PLAY

Partner A: Look at your card on page 94. Then phone Partner B.

Partner B: Look at your card on page 94. Answer Partner A and write the message.

► W 18, 15–16 ► W

READING A teen newspaper online

Tip:
You can read LA YOUTH online:
www.LAYOUTH.com

1 **Look at the six articles in LA YOUTH.**
Which article do you think looks the most interesting?

LA YOUTH
– the newspaper by and about teens

I won a ticket to see my favorite band!

Nattalie, 16, won a ticket to see *My Chemical Romance*. And she met her hero, Gerard Way, the lead singer.

A day that made a difference

Mel Shin and her class went to Mexico for a day. They took food and clothes to orphans there.

Is Disneyland uncool for teens?

Is it only for young kids?
Some people say yes. Some people say no. Write to us and tell us what you think.

Halloween tricks

Three teen writers tell funny stories about this "scary" day: Fred (16), Katherine (17) and Stephanie (16).

CD reviews

Our teens recommend *The Pixies*, *Within Temptation* and the movie soundtrack for *The Chorus*.

TV or not TV?

Could you give up TV for two weeks? No TV at home! No TV at friends' houses!
Sue Li (16), Connie (16) and Nicole (15) try.

2 **Correct these sentences.**

1 Nattalie met a famous film star.
2 Mel Shin bought clothes in Mexico.
3 All teenagers love Disneyland.
4 Three teenagers tell Christmas stories.
5 The teenagers hate the *Pixies* CD.
6 Three teens watched TV for two weeks.

● **3** **Find words in the text that mean:**

1 somebody who you find great
2 kids who have no parents
3 not fun or interesting
4 something makes you frightened
5 tell somebody that something is good
6 film music

► W 19, 17

WRITING An article for a teen newspaper

1 TV or not TV?

Look at these sentences. Are they FOR TV or AGAINST TV? Write two lists.

1 You can learn lots of things on TV.
2 People watch too much TV – they don't read books or newspapers.
3 TV is like a drug. When you start, you can't stop.
4 You can relax when you watch TV. That's great.
5 If you watch too much TV, you won't do outdoor activities.
6 If you don't watch TV, you can't talk to your friends about your favourite shows.
7 It's nice to sit with your friends or family and watch TV together.
8 In our family everybody wants to watch something different. So we often fight.
9 TV helps you to forget your problems.
10 TV programmes can help teens with their problems.

2 For and against TV

Read this article and pick the right words. Write the article in your exercise book.

Tip:
This article has four paragraphs. Every paragraph has a different main point.

Useful phrases:
- This is what I think.
- On the one hand, ...
- On the other hand, ...
- All in all I think ...

Is TV good (**1**) bad? Could I live (**2**) TV? This is what I think.

On the one hand, I think that TV is great. When I'm tired (**3**) school, I watch some TV. When I'm sad, it makes me (**4**). When I'm bored, TV is (**5**).

On the other (**6**), you shouldn't watch too much TV. Some teens watch TV for 3 or 4 (**7**) every day. They don't (**8**) their homework or sport. That (**9**) good!

All in all, I think TV is OK. But you mustn't (**10**) TV too much.

1 and / or / if
2 without / with / for
3 at / between / after
4 happy / bored / hungry
5 boring / stupid / fun
6 foot / hand / head
7 minutes / days / hours
8 do / like / find
9 is / isn't / wasn't
10 play / see / watch

3 For and against computer games

Write an article for a teen newspaper.

You can use ideas from exercise 1.

You can write a text like exercise 2.

Look at the tip and useful phrases in exercise 2.

● 4 TV and you

Write 50–70 words. Do you watch TV? When? How much? Could you live without TV? Is TV good? What's good? What isn't so good? Why?

►W 19, 18 ►W ⊙

A LETTER TO *LA YOUTH*

1 **Is Disneyland uncool? Is it only for young kids? What do you think?**

2 **What is the letter about?**
Pick a main point for every paragraph.

→ Disneyland is for everybody • Long lines • The rides

Dear LA Youth,

Last summer I went to Disneyland with my younger brother. It was a Saturday. When we arrived, lots of people were waiting at the gates. They were standing in long lines, so we had to wait too. Kids were running everywhere. After an hour we went in. (Tip number 1 – don't go to Disneyland on the weekend!)

First we went on *The Pirates of the Caribbean* ride. We were in a boat and pirates were shouting, singing and fighting! It was OK. One pirate looked like Johnny Depp. But I didn't have my camera! (Tip number 2 – bring your camera!) Then we went on the *Splash Mountain* ride. That was a roller coaster ride in a mountain. It was fun. But there was lots of water and we were very wet. (Tip number 3 – bring a jacket!) Then we went on another ride – *Space Mountain*. It was great. Our train was going very fast. Everybody was screaming. But my brother was crying. (Tip number 4 – don't bring young kids on the *Space Mountain* ride!) In the night I was feeling tired, so we watched the fireworks.

Is Disneyland only for young kids? No, Disneyland is cool for teenagers too. But you should remember my tips.

Sophie (16)

3 **WORD SEARCH** ***was/were***

a) First guess the missing words in these sentences.

1. When we arrived, lots of people ... waiting at the gates. (ll. 2–3)
2. They ... standing in long lines. (l. 3)
3. Kids ... running everywhere. (l. 4)
4. Pirates ... shouting. (l. 8)
5. Our train ... going very fast. (l. 13)
6. Everybody ... screaming. (l. 13)
7. My brother ... crying. (ll. 13–14)
8. In the night I ... feeling tired. (l. 15)

b) Now check your answers in the letter on this page.

4 WORD SEARCH

Look at the pictures. Guess the missing words. Check on pages 28–29.

1 Richard Bailey ... ... for his daughter. (l. 2)

2 Caitlin ... ... at the invitation. (l. 9)

3 I ... ... in line for a long time. (l. 26)

4 Lots of people ... . (l. 15 – 16)

5 Homeless people ... ... on the grass. (ll. 20 – 21)

6 They ... ... wetsuits. (l. 33)

5 OVER TO YOU!

Finish the sentences in the checkpoint and make the rule.

Tip:
Write the checkpoint in your exercise book.

CHECKPOINT

Past progressive: was/were + -ing

Wenn du sagen willst, was in der Vergangenheit gerade im Gange war:
Nach *I, he, she, it* benutzt du ...
Nach *we, you, they* benutzt du ...
Das Verb endet auf ...

► Eine Übersicht über diese Regeln findest du auf der *Summary*-Seite 133.

► Extra Practice, pp. 100 ff.

► W 20–21

NACH DIESER UNIT KANN ICH ...

über eine Umfrage berichten.	► *In the survey we found out that boys watch more TV than girls.*
Telefonnachrichten notieren.	► *Message for Anna: Call your dad after 8 p.m.*
Anrufe machen/beantworten.	► *Can I speak to Josh, please? / I'm afraid he isn't there. / Can I take a message?*
meine Meinung über Fernsehen sagen.	► *On the one hand, I think TV is great. On the other hand, too much TV isn't good.*
erzählen, was in der Vergangenheit gerade im Gange war.	► *Caitlin was looking at the invitation.*
genauere Informationen über Personen oder Sachen geben.	► *The man who asked the questions wasn't nice. She saw something that made her jealous.*

Weitere Übungen: www.new-highlight.de

► W 22, Test yourself ► W 23–24, Portfolio ► W ◉

► Extra Reading, p. 120–121

Unit 3

At Sullivan High

Sullivan High School

SULLIVAN HIGH SCHOOL

TIGERS

- About 1,100 students
- Grades 9–12
- Special lessons in English as a Second Language
- Extra classes after school and in summer for students who need more help
- Two gyms, swimming pool

6631 North Bosworth Avenue, Chicago, IL 60626
www.sullivanhs.org

1 **Read the school brochure.**
- Where is Sullivan High?
- Find AE words for *pupils* and *years*.

2 **Listen to the tour of the school. Put the photos A–E in the right order.** 1 24

Photo ..., photo ..., photo ...

3 **Match the photos with the phrases from the box. Then listen again and check.** 1 24

medical classroom • flag • locker • cheerleaders • security check

● **4** **Write sentences for the photos. Use the words in exercise 3. Example:**
Students put their books in lockers.

▸W 25, 1

C

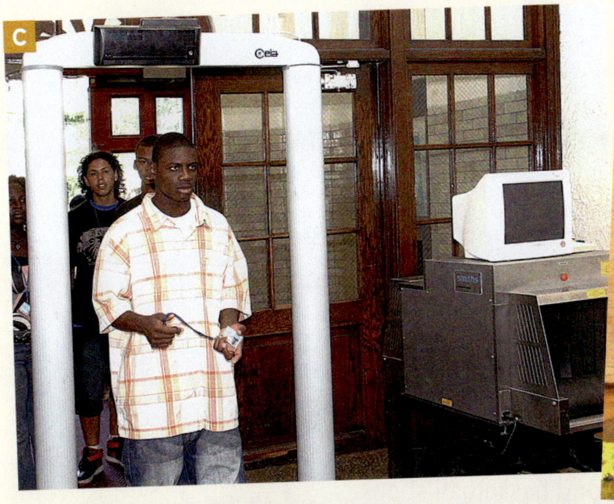

D

E

Tip:
You can find more pictures of Sullivan High School on their website.

5 **Compare your school with Sullivan High School. What's the same? What's different? Make lists with a partner.**

→ a swimming pool • flags • cheerleaders • extra classes after school • lockers • a homework club • summer classes

At Sullivan High School and at our school there is/there are	*At our school we don't have*	*But at our school we have*
– lots of pupils	*– a medical classroom*	*– first aid lessons*
– ...	*– ...*	*– ...*

▸W 25, 2–3

BASKETBALL DREAMS

1 **Is basketball popular at your school? Do you watch it on TV?**

2 **Work with a partner. Look at the pictures and finish the file.**

BASKETBALL FILE

Teams:	There must be ... teams of ... players.
Place and equipment:	You need a basketball ... and two ...
Gear:	You should have a T-shirt, shorts and basketball shoes.
What you must do:	Players must get the ball in the ... to get points.
Points:	Free throw = 1 point, shot = 2 points, long shot = 3 points.
Rules:	Players mustn't touch other players and they mustn't kick the ... (these things are fouls).

3 **SONG** ***YMCA***

1 25 **a) Listen to the song. Do you know it? Do you like it? Tell the class.**

I think it's great / cool / OK / bad / terrible.

b) Listen again and read the words. Does the song have a happy ending? Find the lines in the song that tell you.

c) Finish the summary of the song.

The singer had a problem. He wanted to ..., but he didn't have ... . Then ... helped him. The singer played at ... . One day there was a ... . The singer made ... . Now he's a ...

I spent many long days with nothing to do
Which way should I go? I have no clue
A basketball in my hand, but I got no hoop
Gotta find me a place so I can shoot
I got dreams of being like Michael J.
But a ball's no good with no place to play
Till this old man came, showed me the way
Now I play at the YMCA

Five years later, the old man came
So happened to be the day of the big game
The score was tied, 3 on the clock
It's up to me to make the last shot
So I got the ball, jumped sky-high
Released the ball, then closed my eyes
Now I'm a star and it's OK
Thank you for the YMCA

It's fun to stay at the YMCA
It's fun to stay at the YMCA
They have everything for young men to enjoy
You can hang out with all the boys
It's fun to stay at the YMCA
It's fun to stay at the YMCA
You can get yourself clean
You can have a good meal
You can do whatever you feel

► W 26, 4

4 Candice from Sullivan High

1 26 **Listen. What's Candice's problem?**

Her basketball shoes are … . But good shoes are really … and cheap shoes are …

5 Read the website advert.

1 How much are the shoes?
2 What's special about the shoes?
3 Where can you buy the shoes?
4 What's the AE word for *trainers*?

The Starbury One:
STEPH'S NEW SNEAKERS

Colors available in: white/white, white/orange/royal, white/pink, black/black

Exactly the same as the most expensive shoes on the market, but available at the lowest price ever for NBA quality sneakers.

Visit your local Steve and Barry's store to see the full line of gear.

Not available online.

PRICE: $14.98

6 AND YOU? Tell the class: How important are brands for you?

Brands are important. They show that you're cool.

I agree. People laugh if you have cheap gear.

I think the … brand is cool.

Brands like … are too expensive.

I don't agree. You shouldn't pay lots of money for a name.

…

Clothes should look good. You shouldn't wear them because they have a special label.

PROJECT Team sports

- **Work in five groups. Each group picks one of these team sports: baseball, American football, soccer, softball, volleyball.**
- **Go to www.new-highlight.de. Find the window for the webcode and put in NHL-4-41.**
- **Make notes about your sport. Print out photos or find other pictures.**
- **Make a file like the basketball file in ex. 2.**
- **Make new groups. Now you're the expert for your sport. Present your file:**
  For … there must be … / you need …

Tip: The *Presentation Phrases* at the start of the book can help you.

► W 26, 5–6

1 **Can you remember these words? If you can't remember, check them in the *Dictionary* (pages 160–179).**

court • hoop • shot • score • on the clock

1 27

2 **Read the story. Who won the game?**

Fair play

It was the day of the basketball game between Sullivan High School and North High School. Candice from Sullivan High loved basketball. She wasn't very good at other school subjects, but she was great at sport. Her dream was to become a famous basketball player when she finished school. Her family lived in a small apartment in a neighbourhood with lots of drugs and violence. Candice wanted a better life for her family – she needed a good job.

The cheerleaders left the court and the two teams came on. Candice felt confident. "It'll be a good game," she said to her friend April from the Sullivan team. Lana Hill from the North team said, "New shoes, Candice? They look good, but they won't make you faster, you know. North is going to win today." "Not with you on the team!" Candice said.

The game started and soon Candice got the ball. She moved down the court and threw the ball at the hoop – two points. The Sullivan students cheered.

The game was fast. At half-time Candice had scored 12 points but it was 24–18 to North.
"Too bad!" said Lana to Candice and smiled.
"We're going to win!"
"Don't be so sure," said Candice.
"Well done, girls! You played well – but you must move faster!" said Ms Harris, Sullivan's coach. She looked at Candice. "Do your best, Candice! ... OK, let's go. Good luck!"

The game started again. The Sullivan team played faster. Now there was a minute on the clock: 44–42 to North! Candice ran. She got the ball and she was ready to shoot. But suddenly somebody's arm hit her in the face and she felt a terrible pain in her right eye.
"Foul!" April shouted.
"Lana," Candice thought. Candice was really angry, she wanted to hit Lana. She started to walk across the court. Then she stopped. "Wait a minute," she thought. "Don't do anything stupid."

Candice looked at the referee. He was talking to Lana. Then he gave Candice a sign – she had two free throws. "I mustn't miss," Candice thought. First throw: Candice's eye hurt and she couldn't see the hoop. The shot missed. Second throw: The shot missed again. The game was over. 44–42 to North.

Candice walked off the court. She felt bad. And she felt stupid. "Basketball star," she thought. "Forget it!"
Then Ms Harris stopped her.
"Hey, Candice," she said. "Don't be sad. You're the best player that I've trained. You play by the rules and you have self-control, that's very important. You have a good future – you shouldn't give up your dream."

3 Who's who? Match the names with the people in the story.

1 Candice	**a)** Sullivan's coach
2 Lana	**b)** a Sullivan team player
3 April	**c)** a North team player
4 Ms Harris	**d)** Candice's friend and Sullivan team player

Tip:
Find the first place in the text where you can read the names.

4 A report about the game

a) Finish the sentences.

1 Sullivan High School played against ... High School. (ll. 1–2)
2 The game was ... . (l. 18)
3 At half-time the score was ... . (l. 19)
4 When the game started again, the Sullivan team played ... . (l. 27)
5 Lana's arm hit Candice ... . (l. 29)
6 Candice had two free throws. Her shots ... . (l. 36)
7 In the end, the score was ... to ... . (l. 37)
8 The coach said Candice shouldn't ... her dream. (l. 46)

● **b) Write a report about the game for the Sullivan School website.**
Yesterday Sullivan High School played ...
The game ... . It was a ... game.

Tip:
Pick sentences from exercise 4a).
Put in words like *suddenly*, *then*, *so*.
Then say what the game was like.

5 What is fair play?

Put the sentences together.

1 You play	other players.
2 You help	with the referee.
3 You don't fight	by the rules.

6 AND YOU? What do you think?

I think ... | I agree. | I don't agree.

– Fair play is the most important thing in sport.
– Fair play is important, but you don't always have to play by the rules.
– The most important thing is to win.

▶W 27, 7–9

WORDPOWER

1 Match the phrases with the pictures.

These phrases are in the story on pages 42–43.

→ Too bad! • Good luck! • Well done!

1

2

3

2 Sport words

a) Match the words with the pictures.

These words are on pages 40–43.

→ kick • score • miss • cheer • hit • throw

b) Write sentences for the pictures.

1 The football player has scored! 2 The people are …

3 A sport network

Work with a partner. Put in words from pages 38–43, then find more words.

▸ Wordbank 4, p.128

4 WORD SEARCH Imperative

a) Find these sentences on pages 42 and 43.

1 … your best, Candice! (ll. 25–26)
2 … a minute. (l. 32)
3 … it! (l. 40)
4 … … so sure! (l. 22)
5 … … anything stupid. (ll. 32–33)
6 … … sad. (l. 42)

b) Write what the coach says.

1 ☺ drink – lots of water
2 ☺ wear – good shoes
3 ☺ use – the right equipment
4 ☹ hurt – other players
5 ☹ do – dangerous things
6 ☹ lose – your self-control

▸ W 28, 10–13 ▸ W ⊙

1 School subjects and activities

a) Work with a partner. Make a list of school subjects and activities.

English, maths, homework club, ...

▸ Wordbank 5, p.129

b) Talk to your partner about your school subjects and activities. Use the phrases in the box.

I (really) like ... • I love ... •
I'm not keen on ... • I can't stand ... (because) ...

2 At school

a) Look at Sullivan's timetable and finish the sentences.

1 School starts at ...
2 School finishes at ...
3 Lessons are ... minutes long.
4 There are ... minutes between lessons.
5 Lunch is at ... or at ...

Lesson	Time
Class meeting	7:45 – 8:00
1	8:04 – 8:50
2	8:54 – 9:40
3	9:44 – 10:30
4	10:34 – 11:20 (lunch)
5	11:24 – 12:10 (lunch)
6	12:14 – 1:00
7	1:04 – 1:50
8	1:54 – 2:40
9	2:44 – 3:30

b) Write about your school.

3 About school and me

a) Put in the words in the box.

about • at • by • in • near • on

I'm Mack. Let me tell you ... me. I live ... my school. I usually walk there, but sometimes I go ... bus. My favorite sport at school is baseball. I'm not ... the school team. At school I'm good ... art and computers. ... the future, I'd like to be a detective.

b) Make notes about you. Then tell a partner. Talk about:

live near school? walk to school? favourite sport? school team? good at? future?

4 In the classroom

a) WORD LINK Work with a partner. Find words or phrases that come after each of these verbs.

look at • play • sit • talk to • wear

Look at the board / the teacher / ...

b) Look at the photo for one minute. What are the people in the photo doing? What are they wearing? Then close your book and write sentences about the photo.

Some students are ... . One boy / girl is ...

c) Compare your sentences with a partner.

▸ W 29, 14–16 ▸ W ⊙

LISTENING Giving orders

Tip:
First read the questions. Then listen. You don't have to understand every word. Only the answers to the questions are important.

1 American school scenes

1 28 **Listen to six conversations. Pick the right answer. Then listen again and check.**

1 Who's speaking?
a) a student
b) a parent
c) a teacher
d) a coach

2 What are the girls talking about?
a) shopping
b) the cinema
c) a basketball game
d) a party

3 What's the boy wearing?
a) sneakers
b) a jacket
c) walking shoes
d) a cap

4 What are the students going to do?
a) write a report
b) watch a DVD
c) listen to a CD
d) do a test

5 Where are they?
a) in the classroom
b) in the school car park
c) at the bus stop
d) in the playground

6 What are they going to do?
a) go to school
b) go to the hospital
c) leave school early
d) phone Nick's dad

2 Match the phrases from the listening texts in exercise 1 with the right pictures.

1 Put your tray back.
2 Don't leave anything in the car.
3 Put your shoes over there.
4 Don't forget the popcorn!

3 INTERPRETING An American exchange student at a German school has a problem.

1 29 **Listen. Then practise the conversation.** The phrases in exercise 2 can help you.

WOMAN Stell dein Tablett zurück. Lass deine Sachen nicht auf dem Tisch liegen!
GIRL Why is she shouting? What's she saying?
YOU She says put ... . And don't ...
GIRL Oh, er sorry. Tell her I didn't know.
YOU Sie ... . Sie ...
WOMAN In Ordnung, aber sage ihr, sie soll ihr Glas da drüben hinstellen. Und sie soll ihre Tüte nicht vergessen.
YOU She says OK, but ...

► W 30, 17–18 ► W

SPEAKING What you must do and mustn't do

1 An exchange student

1 30

Read the dialogue or listen to it. Which of these things (1–5) can you wear or bring to Sullivan High?

CANDICE What do you want to know about school?
ADRIENNE What about clothes? What must you wear?
CANDICE Well, you don't have to wear anything special. But you mustn't wear T-shirts with bad messages or bad pictures on them.
ADRIENNE OK. Can I bring my cellphone to school?
CANDICE Yes, but you must turn it off and leave it in your locker.
ADRIENNE What about my MP3 player?
CANDICE That's OK. You can use it in class. But you must turn it off if the teacher asks you.

1

2

3

5

4

2 A new student

Finish the dialogue.
Then read it with a partner.

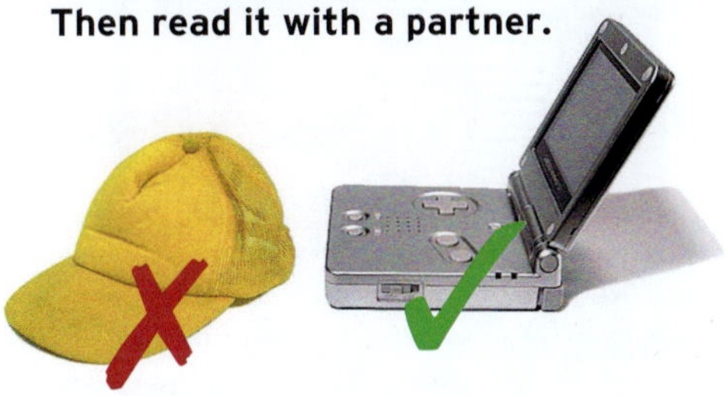

MIGUEL What do you want ...?
DAN What about ...? What ...?
MIGUEL Well, you ... anything special. But you ... baseball caps.
DAN OK. ... my video game player to school?
MIGUEL Yes, but you ... and leave it in your locker.

3 ROLE PLAY

You're going to talk about what you must do and mustn't do at your school.
First make two lists with your partner.

You mustn't wear ... (dirty clothes, short T-shirts, ...)
You mustn't bring ... (alcohol, drugs, skateboards, ...)

Partner A: You're a pupil. Look at your card on page 95.

Partner B: You're an English exchange student. Look at your card on page 95.

4 SAY IT IN GERMAN What do these signs at Sullivan High mean?

In the classroom

BE RESPECTFUL.
Don't be late.

In the computer room

NO E-MAIL
INTERNET ONLY FOR SCHOOL PROJECTS

On a door

DRUG-FREE ZONE
HATE-FREE ZONE

► W 30, 19 ► W

READING Messages

1 Match the messages (1–4) with the photos (A–D).

1 To: Candice From: Troy

Hi, Candice!
I must see you! Can we meet at the fountain in Millennium Park at 4 p.m.?
Troy

2

A

B

C

D

2 Pick the right answer a) or b).

1 Troy wants to meet Candice
a) in the morning.
b) in the afternoon.

2 Damon
a) has tickets for a baseball game.
b) has to get tickets for a baseball game.

3 April wants to
a) buy a new watch.
b) find her watch.

4 April's watch
a) is expensive.
b) is special.

5 Adrienne is
a) a student from another country.
b) an American student.

6 Adrienne would like to
a) learn French.
b) practise her English.

►W 31, 20

3 What is it in German?

Find these words on page 48. Pick the right German word. Then check in the *Dictionary* (pages 160–179).

Remember:
Read the sentences. The context can help you.

1 fountain	**a)** Quelle	**b)** Rathaus	**c)** Brunnen
2 silver	**a)** silbern	**b)** albern	**c)** sinnvoll
3 valuable	**a)** nützlich	**b)** hygienisch	**c)** wertvoll
4 fix	**a)** stehlen	**b)** reparieren	**c)** benutzen

4 SAY IT IN ENGLISH

Find these phrases in English in messages 1–4 on p. 48.

1 Können wir uns treffen?
2 Bitte nicht vergessen.
3 Hast du sie gefunden?
4 Kannst du mir helfen?

WRITING Messages

1 You're an exchange student at Sullivan High. Pick a) or b).

a) You want to find somebody who can speak English with you. Write a message for the school noticeboard.
Message 4 on p. 48 can help you.

- **Say who you are and ask for help.**
  I'm ... and I ...
- **Say what you're interested in.**
  I'm interested in sport/music/computer games/...
- **Say what you can offer.**
  I can offer German/... conversation.
  I can fix your .../...

b) You've lost your bag. Write a message for the noticeboard.
Message 3 on p. 48 can help you.

- **Say what your bag is like.**
  It's big/blue/new/...
- **Say what's in it.**
  My books/pencil case/lunch ... is/are in it.
- **Ask if somebody has found it.**
  Have you ...?
- **Write your e-mail address.**
  Send an e-mail to ...

2 Put your message on the board in your classroom. Read the other messages.

● 3 Pick one message from exercise 2 and write an e-mail.

Hi ...,
My name's .... I saw your message on the noticeboard.
I would like to .... I'm interested in ... /
I've found .... It was in ...
You can ...
(your name)

►W 31, 21 ►W ⊙

LOOK AT LANGUAGE

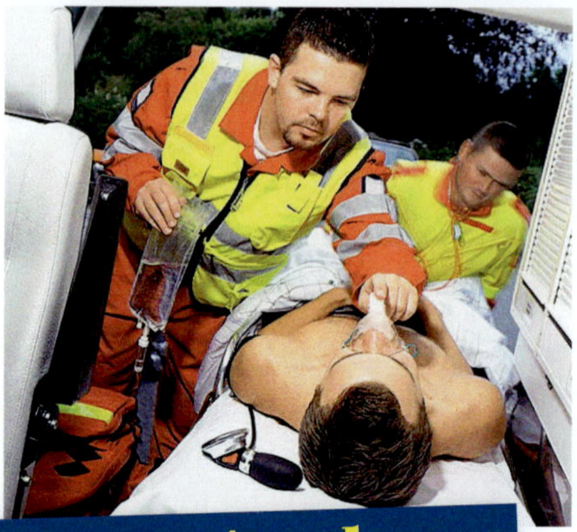

1 Read the information about paramedics. Say if the sentences are true or false.

1. Paramedics help people in accidents.
2. Paramedics have easy jobs.
3. Paramedics only work Monday to Friday.
4. It's important to be healthy when you're a paramedic.
5. The training is very short.
6. You get lots of money as a paramedic.

Sullivan High School Medical Career Academy
Career information: Paramedic

Do you know the people who bring people in the hospital on TV shows like *ER*? They're paramedics. They give people first aid when they have an accident or become sick. Then they take them to hospital.

Paramedics have hard jobs. As a paramedic, you must work in the evening and on the weekend and the work can be dangerous. You must be very fit and you mustn't be nervous. You mustn't panic when things are difficult and you mustn't be too emotional when somebody dies. The training is hard too – you must do 1000–2000 hours of training.

You shouldn't become a paramedic if you want to earn lots of money. But you should become a paramedic if you want an exciting job where you can really help people.

If you would like more information, then you should talk to the teachers in the Medical Career Academy.

2 WORD SEARCH *Must* or *mustn't*? Put in the words. Then check on this page.

1 You ... work in the evening.

2 You ... be very fit.

3 You ... be nervous.

4 You ... panic when things are difficult.

5 You ... be too emotional when somebody dies.

6 You ... do 1000–2000 hours of training.

3 WORD SEARCH

***Should* or *shouldn't*? Guess, then check on pages 40–41.**

1 You ... have a T-shirt, shorts and basketball shoes. (p. 40, ex. 2)
2 What ... I do? (p. 41, ex. 4)
3 You ... worry, Candice. (p. 41, ex. 4)
4 You ... pay lots of money for a name. (p. 41, ex. 6)
5 Clothes ... look good. (p. 41, ex. 6)
6 You ... wear them because they have a special label. (p. 41, ex. 6)

4 OVER TO YOU!

Finish the checkpoint.

Tip:
Write the checkpoint in your exercise book.

CHECKPOINT

Die Hilfsverben *should/shouldn't* und *must/mustn't*

- Mit ... rätst du jemandem, etwas zu tun.
- Mit ... rätst du jemandem, etwas nicht zu tun.
- Mit ... sagst du, was jemand tun muss.
- Mit ... verbietest du jemandem, etwas zu tun.

► Eine Übersicht über diese Regeln findest du auf der *Summary*-Seite 135.
► Extra Practice, pp. 104 ff.
► W 32–33

NACH DIESER UNIT KANN ICH ...

Schulen in den USA und Deutschland vergleichen.	► *At Sullivan High there are extra classes in summer, but at our school there aren't any lessons in summer.*
über Sport und Sportregeln sprechen.	► *There must be two teams of five players. A free throw is one point.*
jemandem raten, etwas zu tun oder nicht zu tun.	► *You should play to win. You shouldn't worry.*
jemandem sagen, was er/sie tun muss.	► *You must turn off your MP3 player.*
jemandem verbieten, etwas zu tun.	► *You mustn't bring skateboards.*
jemanden anweisen, etwas zu tun oder nicht zu tun.	► *Put your tray back! Don't forget, please!*
eine kurze Nachricht schreiben.	► *Have you found my schoolbag? It's black and green. I think I left it in the gym.*

Weitere Übungen: www.new-highlight.de

► W 34, Test yourself ► W ⊙

The Evergreen State

Welcome to Washington State, in the north-west of the USA.

Visit Olympic National Park – with its mountains and forests.

Washington is famous for wild animals.

Visit the Makah Reservation in Neah Bay. There's a big festival every August.

1 A holiday trip

2 1

a) Read the two questions. Then listen and look at the brochure.

1 Which places in Washington did Emma visit?
2 What animals did she see?

b) Listen again. Are these sentences true or false?

1 The trip started in Seattle.
2 There are lots of trees in the national park.
3 They didn't go to the sea.
4 They visited a reservation.
5 Emma liked Anacortes.
6 She took a photo of a whale.
7 She didn't buy presents for her friends.

▶ W 35, 1

Anacortes – you can go whale watching here.

Washington's islands – great for fishing and boat trips.

Seattle is Washington's biggest city.

Park Rangers – always ready to help.

Cape Flattery – popular for hiking.

2 Brochure game

a) First write all the things that you can see in the brochure.

mountains, trees, animals, ...

b) Then play this game with your partner.

A I see something that starts with b.
B Is it a bear?
A Yes, it is. / No, it isn't. Try again!

3 Your Washington holiday

a) Work with a partner. Plan your holiday. Pick three places. Think about what you want to see and do there.

b) Tell the class.

– First we want to go to ...
– We want to see / meet / ...
– Then we want to ...

Tip:
Make notes about your plans.
Use your notes when you're talking to the class.

▸W 35, 2–3

IN A NATIONAL PARK

1 Pick the right sign or brochure:

a) You want to go camping in a national park.
b) You want to find out about trees and animals.
c) You're worried about fires in national parks.
d) You want to go hiking in a national park.

1

2

3

4

2 National park words

a) Find words in the texts that mean:

1 A fire in a forest
2 A place where you can go camping
3 A club for young people
4 A wild animal in Olympic National Park
5 People who work in national parks

b) Find nouns for these verbs:

1 drive a ...
2 find out about ...
3 feed ...
4 learn about the ...
5 make lots of ...

● 3 Look at the texts and finish these sentences. Find as many examples as you can.

1 In a national park you shouldn't smoke, ...
2 In a national park you can ...
3 In a national park you should ...

►W 36, 4

PROJECT A wall newspaper about national parks

a) Look at this wall newspaper about Olympic National Park.

1 Which activity would you pick? 2 What animals would you like to see?

OLYMPIC NATIONAL PARK

WHERE?
In Washington State, in the north-west of the USA

NEAR?
Port Angeles

ENVIRONMENT?
Mountains, forests, rivers and lakes

ANIMALS?
Bears, cougars, deer and beavers

deer

beaver

ACTIVITIES?
Hiking, boat trips and camping

ENTRANCE FEE?
$5 for a person or $15 for a car

INFORMATION?
At visitor centers or on the Internet: www.nps.gov/olym

b) Make groups of three or four.

1 Pick another national park on the map of the USA.

2 Find out about the national park. Go to www.new-highlight.de and put in the webcode NHL-4-55.

Tip:
Use the questions in the Olympic National Park wall newspaper.

3 Make a wall newspaper about your national park.

4 Ask and answer questions about the parks.

Tip:
An "expert" from each group should stand near the wall newspaper and answer questions.

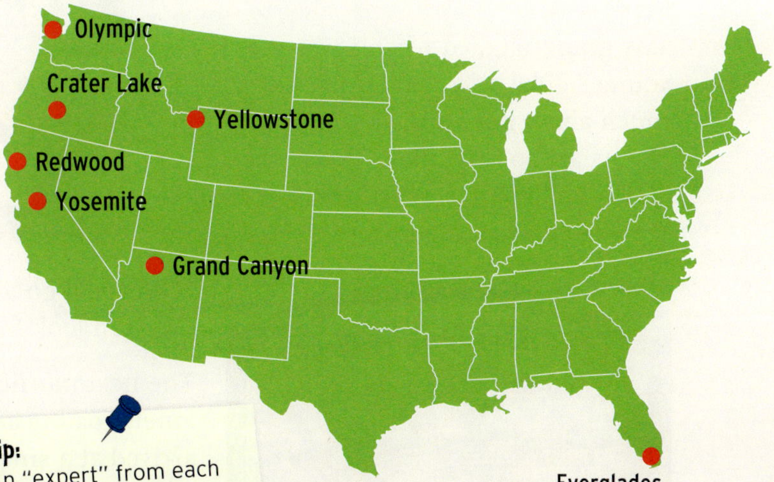

▸W 36, 5

1 Look at the pictures. What do you think happens in the story?
This story is about two ... . They live in ... . First they go camping in ...
Then they drive to ... . They hear stories about whale ...

Roots

2⊙2

Toby and Mark from Anacortes

Toby Brown sat in his big, old car. Mark, his friend, sat next to him. The two boys had their camping gear – tents, food and clothes. It was early when they left Anacortes and the town was quiet. The teenagers were looking forward to getting out of town for the weekend.

After leaving Port Townsend, the boys drove to Port Angeles. Then they turned left and drove into Olympic National Park, to the Heart O' the Hills Campground. They put up their tent and ate some food.

Toby loved outdoor activities like camping and hiking. So that afternoon the two boys hiked to Hurricane Ridge. It was great up there. The boys could see the beautiful, blue sea in the north and the Olympic mountains in the south. In the evening they sat at the campfire and planned the next days.
"What about going to Neah Bay?" Mark said.
"Neah Bay?" Toby answered. "My grandma came from that town. But I've never been there!"
"Really? It's on a reservation," Mark said.
"Was your grandma Native American?"
"Yeah, sure!" Toby answered.
"But that means that you're Native American too! That's interesting!" Mark said.
"My grandma died when I was very young," Toby said. "So I don't know much about her family."
"Roots are so important," Mark said.
"My grandparents came from Germany. We went there last summer. It was great."

A campground in Olympic National Park

"OK. We'll go to Neah Bay tomorrow," Toby said.
"We can look for my grandma's family, the Parkers."

The next morning the boys drove along a narrow, lonely road near the sea. In the afternoon they arrived at a small, quiet town – Neah Bay. The teenagers stopped at the visitor center. The man there told Toby where the Parker family lived.

The Parker family was very happy to meet Toby and his friend. Their house was small, so the two boys put up their tent in the garden. That evening there was a big party. All the family came – and neighbours too. There was lots of great Makah singing and dancing. A nice, old woman was there – Halma Parker. She remembered Toby's grandma. She was her cousin.

Whale hunting in the past

Later, everybody sat at the fire and Halma told stories. She talked about the days before white people came to Neah Bay.
"The Makah people didn't live in tepees, but in longhouses. All the family lived together – grandparents, parents, children, uncles, aunts and cousins. Fishing was very important. But whale hunting was the most important thing. The men used small canoes. It was very dangerous, but they were good at whale hunting. Life wasn't always easy, but our people were happy. Then the white people came. They brought illnesses and lots of Makah people died. They prohibited our language. They fished in our ocean. And they prohibited whale hunting. So in the end lots of our young people had to leave Neah Bay and go to work in the white people's towns and cities. Your grandma too, Toby! Some people never came back. They forgot their roots. Roots are important, Toby!"

Tip:
You can find out more about the Makah people at www.makah.com

2 True, false or not in the text?

1 The two boys went to Olympic National Park in Toby's car.
2 They saw animals on Hurricane Ridge.
3 They made a campfire.
4 Going to Neah Bay was Toby's idea.
5 Mark's family visited Germany last year.
6 The boys stayed in the Parkers' house.
7 Fishing was important in Neah Bay.
8 Toby's grandma left Neah Bay in 1900.

3 Neah Bay today

a) Listen to the end of the story. 2⊙3
- Do people live in longhouses now?
- Is there lots of work in Neah Bay today?
- Do people fish with canoes?
- Do they hunt whales?
- Who comes to Neah Bay every summer?
- Will Toby go back to Neah Bay?

b) Listen to Little Steven's song about Native Americans. Is it happy or sad? 2⊙4

● 4 Back in Anacortes: Finish the dialogue between Toby and his mom.

MOM Hi, Toby. How was your trip?
TOBY Hi, Mom. It was ...
MOM What places did you visit?
TOBY First we ... . Then we ...
MOM Did you meet the Parkers?
TOBY ...
MOM Where did you stay in Neah Bay?
TOBY ...
MOM What's Neah Bay like?
TOBY ...
MOM Do you think that you'll go back?
TOBY ...

▸W 37, 6–9

WORDPOWER

1 Hobbies: What are they saying?

These words are in the story on pages 56–57.

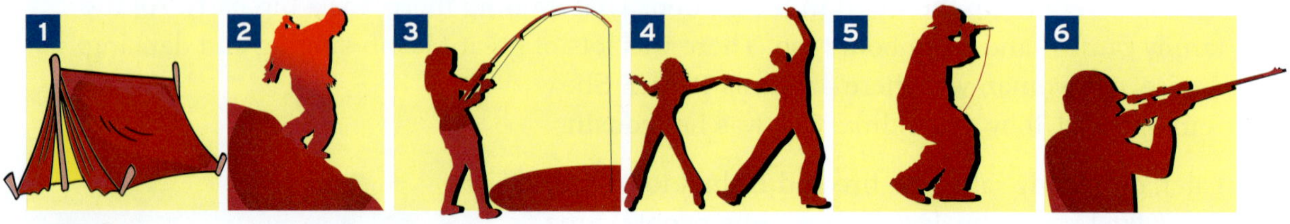

Let's go ... | I love ... | My hobby is ... | They like ... | He's good at ... | I don't like ...

2 Signs

a) What do these signs mean in German? Tell a partner.

CAMPING IS COUGAR COUNTRY

Campfires only on the campground

Welcome to Anacortes in beautiful Washington.

Join the Junior Rangers now!

NO HUNTING!

b) What do these signs mean in English? Tell a partner.

BOOTFAHREN nicht gestattet

ZELTLAGER GESCHLOSSEN

EINTRITT €10

ANGELN VERBOTEN

3 WORD SEARCH Find the missing adjectives.

Tip:
Adjectives tell you about people, places and things. Adjectives make a text more interesting.

1. Do you like watching ... animals? (p. 54)
2. Keep ... children near you. (p. 54)
3. Toby sat in his ..., ... car. (p. 56, l. 1).
4. The boys could see the ..., ... sea. (p. 56, l. 12).
5. The boys drove along a ..., ... road. (p. 56, ll. 31–32)
6. They arrived at a ..., ... town. (p. 56, l. 33)
7. A ..., ... woman was there. (p. 57, l. 39)
8. The men used ... canoes. (p. 57, l. 48)

4 Make it interesting.

a) Put the adjectives in the right place.

It was a night in March (**cold**). Toby and Mark were at a campground (**lonely**). They were in their tent (**small**). Toby was reading a book (**good**). Mark was listening to his MP3 player (**new**). Then Toby heard a noise (**terrible**). The boys looked out and saw a bear (**big/black**).

● **b) Put in: *old, tired, nervous, black, lonely, funny, quiet.***

Toby and Mark shouted and the ... bear ran into the forest. The ... boys didn't sleep that night. There was no noise in the forest. It was very ... . They talked and told ... stories all night. In the morning the ... boys put their things in the ... car and they left the ... campground – quickly!

► W 38, 10–13 ► W ⊙

USING MIND MAPS

1 A good job?
Would you like to be a park ranger? Read the text and find out.

2 Main points
a) What's this text saying? Pick two main points.

- A ranger's life is terrible.
- A ranger's job is easy.
- A ranger does many jobs.
- A ranger has a boring job.
- A ranger has to be fit and sporty.
- A ranger's work is dangerous.
- A ranger has a great job.

b) Does your partner agree?

NATIONAL PARK RANGERS

Rangers have to do lots of different jobs. They look after the national parks (the animals, forests, rivers and lakes). They give information to visitors. Rangers work on the park campgrounds too and they often lead tours in the parks. When hikers get lost in the parks, the rangers have to look for them. And they help visitors who have accidents.

Rangers have to be good at doing lots of things. They go hiking with groups of visitors in the forests and they go skiing in the mountains in winter. Rangers go camping in the parks and they often go on boat trips on the lakes and rivers. They watch the wild animals and take photos of America's most beautiful places.

IF YOU WANT TO BECOME A RANGER, VISIT OUR WEBSITE.

3 A park ranger's mind map
First draw this mind map in your exercise book. Then read the text again and finish the mind map.

4 Remembering
Close your book and look at your mind map. What can you remember from the text? Write it down. Then tell a partner.

Tip:
Mind maps help you to remember main points. Pictures and colours make your mind map more interesting and make it easier to remember.

► W 39, 14 ► W ◉

LISTENING Talking about a town

1 Anacortes adverts

2/5 **Look at the pictures. Listen to the CD. You'll hear three adverts for each picture. Pick the right advert – a), b) or c).**

1

2
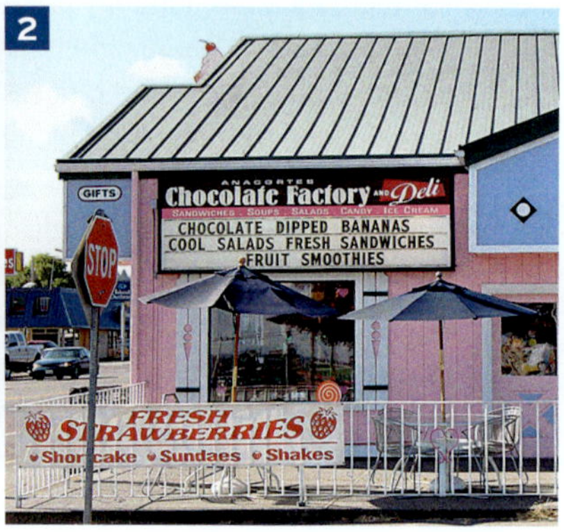

3

2 A survey about Anacortes

2/6 **Toby Brown has done a survey for the school radio.**

a) Listen to the five people. Pick a), b) or c).

1 This boy thinks that Anacortes is ...
  a) OK **b)** terrible **c)** cool
2 This girl likes the ...
  a) weather **b)** people **c)** food
3 This boy says that Anacortes is busy in ...
  a) spring **b)** summer **c)** winter
4 This girl comes to Anacortes for ...
  a) work **b)** school **c)** whale watching
5 The teenagers think that Anacortes is ...
  a) boring **b)** exciting **c)** beautiful

b) Listen to the survey again. Pick the right words in the box.

good • uncool • nice • great • quiet

1 **Boy** It's ... for water sports.
2 **Girl** The people here are ...
3 **Boy** In winter it's ...
4 **Girl** It's a ... place to make money!
5 **Teens** Anacortes is ...

3 The story of Fidalgo Island and Anacortes

2/7 **First copy this table in your exercise book. Then listen to the CD and put in the years.**

... years ago	Native Americans lived here.
17...	The first Europeans came.
1790 – ...	Hunters came.
187...	The town got a post office and a name.
18...	200 people lived in Anacortes.
19...	4000 people lived here.
1950 – ...	Lots of businesses came to the town.
...	About 15,000 people live here.

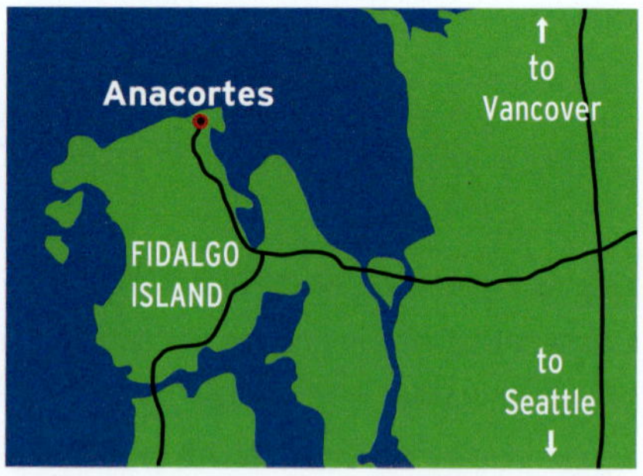

► W 40, 15 ► W

SPEAKING At the visitor center

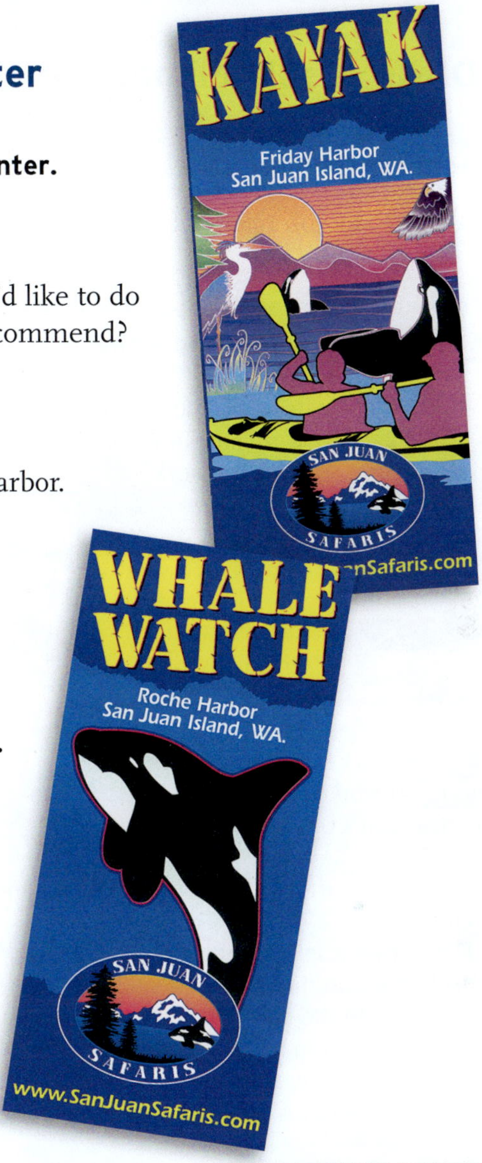

1 Rita works at the Anacortes visitor center.

2 ◉ 8

a) What are these visitors going to do?

RITA Hi. Can I help you?
GIRL Hi. We're in Anacortes for a day and we'd like to do something interesting. What can you recommend?
RITA Oh, there are lots of things to do. What about kayaking? It's fun!
BOY That sounds good. Where can you do it?
RITA At San Juan Safaris. They're in Friday Harbor. Here's a brochure.
GIRL Great. Thank you.

b) Practise the dialogue with two partners.

2 More tourists need help.

2 ◉ 9

a) Look at the brochure and finish the dialogue.

RITA Hi. Can I ...?
BOY Hi. We'd like to do something ... What can you ...?
RITA What about ...?
GIRL That ... good. Where can you ...?
RITA At ... . They're in ... . Here's ...
BOY Great. ...

b) Act the dialogue with a partner.

3 INTERPRETING

You're at the visitor center with your grandma. Help her.

GRANDMA Wir wollen gern etwas Interessantes unternehmen. Was kann die Frau uns empfehlen?
YOU Hi. We'd like to ... . What ...?
RITA Are you interested in learning about Native Americans? There's a great museum.
YOU Willst du ...? Es gibt ...
GRANDMA Ja, das klingt sehr interessant. Wo ist das Museum?
YOU That ... . Where ...?
RITA It's at Neah Bay. There's a bus every day at 10 a.m.
YOU Es ist ...
GRANDMA Vielen Dank für die Hilfe. Auf Wiedersehen.
YOU ...

4 ROLE PLAY

PARTNER A: You work at the visitor center. Look at your card on p. 95.
PARTNER B: You're a tourist. Look at your card on p. 95.

►W 40, 16–17 ►W ◉

READING A school magazine article

1 Read the article and pick a title.

a) Job adverts **b)** Job tips for teens **c)** My dream job

Tip:
Don't worry about new words.
First try to guess them.
Then check in a dictionary.

Lots of students at our school have part-time jobs. This is what some people say:

Hassan (15): "My uncle is a baker and I work part-time for him. It's hard work."

Britany (15): "I work as a sales clerk in a clothes shop for teens. The job is cool because I like meeting people. I work there every Saturday.

Ashley (15): "I work as a cleaner in a movie theater. It's OK. But you have to work fast."

Brad (16): "I'm a part-time babysitter. It's easy and I like children."

Calina (16): "I work in a library. I'm an assistant. I put books back on the shelves. It's boring, but I only work on Saturdays. And the pay is OK."

Sancha (16): "I work in a coffee shop – I'm a cashier. I have to work every Saturday and Sunday, so I don't have much free time. But the pay is good and there are lots of tips.

Are you thinking of looking for a part-time job? Do you want work experience? Here are some ideas to help you.

1 Pick a job that you like. Maybe you'll find your dream job!
2 You must write a good résumé and cover letter.
3 Before you go to your interview, find out about the business, store or restaurant. And think about why you want that job. The interview is important, so practise it with a friend.
4 If you go to an interview, wear nice clothes. And don't forget to ask the interviewer for information about the job.
5 Don't work too many hours. Remember, your school work is the most important thing, so you shouldn't be too tired for school.

2 Read the first part of the article. Who could say these things?

1 "I love nice clothes, so my job is cool."
2 "Now I know everything about bread!"
3 "I watch TV when the kids are in bed."
4 "I often go early and watch a movie."
5 "When it's quiet I can read."

3 Now read the second part of the article and correct these sentences.

1 There are six job tips.
2 Your résumé isn't so important.
3 Don't worry about the interview.
4 Only the interviewer can ask questions.
5 You should work as much as you can.

4 What do you think? Finish these sentences.

1 I'd like a job as a ... because ...
2 I wouldn't like a job as a ... because ...

▸ Wordbank 6, p.130

Tip:
Look at the jobs in the magazine article. Think of other jobs too.

▸ W 41, 18

WRITING Applying for a job in the USA

1 A job advert

Read the advert. Would you like this job?

ANACORTES ADVENTURES
933 Commercial Avenue

Anacortes' best outdoor store!

We are looking for a

part-time sales clerk

Saturdays 9 a.m. – 6 p.m.
$8 per hour.
Apply today
to Angela King.

2 A résumé

Read Toby Brown's résumé. Do you think he'll get the job?

FAMILY NAME	Brown
FIRST NAME	Toby
ADDRESS	1241 14th Street Anacortes, WA 98221
PHONE	360-555-8441
CELLPHONE	360-555-7712
AGE	16
SCHOOL	Anacortes High School
GRADE	10
HOBBIES	Hiking, camping, music
EXPERIENCE	Junior Rangers (3 years) Part-time cashier (1 year)

3 A cover letter

Read Toby's letter. Find the missing words. Exercises 1 and 2 can help you.

1241 14th Street
Anacortes, WA 98221
April 4th, 20…

Ms Angela King
Anacortes Adventures
933 Commercial Avenue
Anacortes, WA

Dear Ms (1),

I saw your (2) in the newspaper last week and I would like to apply for the job of (3). I am (4) years old and I am in grade (5) at Anacortes High School. I am interested in outdoor activities like (6) and (7). I have some work (8) – I was a (9) in a shoe store for one year. And I was a Junior (10) for three years. I'm looking forward to hearing from you.

Yours truly,
Toby Brown

4 More job adverts

Which job would you prefer?

I'd prefer the job at … because …

ODEON CINEMA
We are looking for
cleaners
Tuesdays–Sundays, 5–7 p.m.
$8 per hour.
Apply to: Rick Mason

DADDIO'S PIZZA
Part-time cashier
Mondays–Saturdays from 5 to 10 p.m.
$5 per hour.
Apply to: Janet Seaman

WHALETOURS
ASSISTANT
$7.50 per hour.
Saturdays 9 a.m.–5 p.m.
Apply to: Harold Hughes

5 AND YOU?

Apply for a job in exercise 4.

a) Write your own résumé.

● **b) Then write a cover letter.**

Look at Toby's résumé and cover letter.

► W 41, 19 ► W ⊙

WHALE HUNTING

1 Which of these texts comes from ...
- a newspaper article?
- an animal rights brochure?
- a book about the Makah people?

A Whale hunting is a very important tradition here. In the past our people hunted in small canoes. After killing a whale, we took it to the beach in Neah Bay. We ate the meat. We used the oil for cooking and for lamps.

B **Stop whale hunting today!**
Whale hunting is wrong.
Some whales are nearly extinct.
We're against whale hunting.
We should stop whale hunting now!

C **Trouble at Neah Bay**
There was lots of activity at Neah Bay, WA last weekend. Whale hunters met at Neah Bay early on Saturday morning. Animal rights people were there too. They protested against whale hunting. They say that whale hunting is wrong. But for the Makah people it's an old tradition. There was some trouble and the police came. The Makah people can go whale hunting again. They can kill four whales every year.

2 For or against whale hunting?
a) Put these sentences in two lists: for whale hunting / against whale hunting.

I don't like whale hunting. • Four animals per year is OK. • We don't need whale oil. • It's OK for the Makah people. • People have always hunted, so hunting is OK. • There aren't many whales in the world – we have to save them. • All hunting is bad. • There are lots of grey whales again. • I have no problem with whale hunting. • It's an old tradition and traditions are important. • Whales are beautiful animals.

b) What do you think about whale hunting? Talk about this question in your class. Use the phrases in a).

3 SENTENCE SEARCH Find sentences in the texts on this page for the pictures.

1) The Makah people can go ...

2) After killing ...

3) Stop ...

4 WORD SEARCH

Look at the pictures. Can you guess the missing words? Check on pages 56–57.

1 The teenagers were looking forward to ... out of town. (ll. 5–6)

2 After ... Port Townsend, the boys drove to Port Angeles. (l. 8)

3 Toby loved outdoor activities like ... and ... (l. 11)

4 "What about ... to Neah Bay?" (l. 15)

5 There was lots of great Makah ... and ... . (l. 38)

6 ... was very important. (ll. 46–47)

5 OVER TO YOU!

Look in the unit and find more examples for the rules.

Tip:
Write the checkpoint in your exercise book.

CHECKPOINT

Die *ing*-Form

- kann Subjekt eines Satzes sein und steht oft am Anfang.
  Smoking is dangerous.
- folgt oft auf bestimmte Verben.
  Do you like learning about horses?
- wird häufig nach Wendungen mit Präpositionen gebraucht.
  It's a great place for fishing.

► Eine Übersicht über diese Regeln findest du auf der *Summary*-Seite 134.
► Extra Practice, pp. 108 ff.
► W 42-43

NACH DIESER UNIT KANN ICH ...

über Urlaubspläne sprechen.	► *First we want to go to Seattle. Then we ...*
Orte beschreiben.	*Anacortes is busy in summer. It's great for water sports. It's a good place to ...*
über Walfang diskutieren.	► *All hunting is bad. / It's OK for the Makah people.*
um Informationen in einem Fremdenverkehrsamt bitten.	► *We'd like to do something interesting. What can you recommend?*
über Berufe sprechen.	► *I'd like a job as a cashier. I wouldn't like ...*
mich um eine Arbeitsstelle bewerben.	► *I'd like to apply for the job as ...*
meinen Lebenslauf schreiben.	
mind maps erstellen.	

Weitere Übungen: www.new-highlight.de ► W 44, Test yourself ► W 45-46, Portfolio ► W ⊙

Music in Miami

1 Match the sentences in the box with the photos.

Spanish signs in Little Havana	– photo E
Old men playing games	– photo ...
Crime in Miami	
A Miami rapper on stage	
MTV music awards in Miami	
Miami's famous South Beach	
A picture on a wall in Little Havana	
The Calle Ocho festival	

2 10 **2 Listen to the radio programme. Match the speakers and the photos.**

Mariela: photo ..., ..., ... and ...
Ramon: photo ..., ..., ... and ...

►W 47, 1

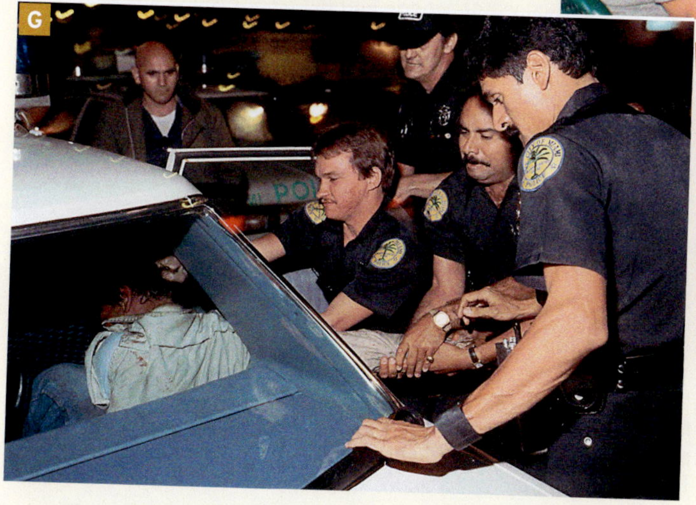

3 Work with a partner and pick a), b) or c). Then listen again and check.

1 10

1 In Miami **a)** lots of people **b)** some people **c)** not many people speak Spanish.
2 The Hispanic population in Miami is **a)** 6% **b)** 16% **c)** 66%.
3 In Little Havana crime is **a)** no problem **b)** a small problem **c)** a big problem.
4 Miami has a great **a)** music **b)** theatre **c)** film scene.
5 The Calle Ocho festival is a big **a)** art festival **b)** street party **c)** food festival.
6 The MTV awards brought lots of **a)** film fans **b)** musicians **c)** problems to Miami.

Tip:
% = per cent

4 GAME Pick a photo. Write a description. Write one wrong thing. Your partner reads it and says what's wrong.

There are lots of people. I can see two musicians. They're playing instruments. There's a table behind one musician. Five people are sitting under an umbrella. It's nice weather.

Three people are sitting under the umbrella.

Tip:
Use the present progressive to write about activities in pictures:
A boy and a girl are dancing.
The boy is wearing ...

▸W 47, 2–3

MY MUSIC

1 Look at Ramon's page on a website for friends. Do you have a page like this or use websites for friends?

2 Read about Ramon. What would he like to be when he leaves school?

mypage

HOME | NEWS | BLOGS | GUIDE | LOGOUT

Male
15 years old
Miami, USA

Ramon's interests

General	Music, dancing, friends, blogging
Music	Pop, rap, R & B. I like most music really, but I'm not a big fan of punk or metal. I play the guitar and the piano, and I sing too.

Hips don't lie
Shakira and Wyclef Jean

About me
I'm from Colombia, my family moved to Miami when I was 11. I spend lots of my time in front of my computer. I look at music websites, watch videos and download songs. I listen to music on my MP3 player too. I like listening to music when I do my homework. I can work better like that. And I often watch music TV – concerts and the music awards.

Who I'd like to meet
I'd like to meet Shakira. She's from my country and she sings in Spanish and English. She's a fantastic dancer! I like Justin Timberlake too. He lives in Miami, so maybe I'll meet him!

Ramon's blog
Yesterday I went to an audition for a new boy band. They said I sang really well and I have to go back next week.
I hope I'll be in the band. I'd like to be a singer when I finish school. But my parents say most singers have a hard life. They think I should get a good, safe job.

3 What you know about Ramon: Finish the sentences.

1 Ramon's general interests: ..., ..., ... and ...
2 Ramon's favourite music: ..., ... and ...
3 Ramon plays the ... and the ...
4 He uses his computer to ..., ... and ...
5 He listens to music on his ...
6 He listens to music when he does ...
7 He'd like to meet ... because ...
8 He'd like to meet ... too.
9 Yesterday he went to an ...

4 What you know about your partner: Write the answers to the questions. Then check your answers with your partner.

1 What are your partner's interests?
2 What music does he/she like?
3 Does he/she play an instrument or sing?
4 How does he/she listen to music? (MP3 player, videos, ...)
5 Does he/she download music from websites?
6 Does your partner listen to music when he/she does homework?
7 Which musician would he/she like to meet? (Why?)
8 Has your partner been to a concert? (What concert?)

▸ Wordbank 7, p.130
▸ W 48, 4
▸ Wordbank 8, p.131

5 SONG *Hips don't lie*

2◉11

a) Listen to the song.

b) What's the song about? It's about ...

1 Spain **2** love **3** dancing **4** violence

c) How do they sing? I think he/she sings ...

sadly • happily • confidently • angrily • quickly • slowly • wildly

d) Do you like the song? Why?/Why not?

I like / don't like the singer / the singer's voice / the rhythm / the words / ...
The music sounds sad / happy / ...
The music is good for dancing / singing / relaxing.

▸ Wordbank 7, p. 130

6 Pick a song that you like. Tell the class about it.

The title of the song is ...
It's by ...
It's about ...
I like this song because ...

Tip:
- Talk about:
  - the title
  - the singer
  - what it's about
  - what you like about the song
  - how the music sounds
  - how the singer sings
- Use the phrases in exercise 5.

PROJECT My page

- **First find a good picture of yourself. Write about yourself:**
  - **male / female**
  - **age**
  - **where you live**
- **Write about your interests:**
  General: friends / football / TV / computers / ...
  Music: pop, rap, R & B, metal, ...
- **Put in your song from exercise 6.**
  Write two or three sentences about it.
- **Write more about yourself: interesting things, what languages you speak, what you do in your free time:**
  I'm from / My parents are from ...
  I speak ...
  I listen to music / send texts to my friends / ...
- **Write who you'd like to meet:**
  I'd like to meet ... because ...
- **Write your blog for yesterday.**
  Yesterday I went to ... / I met ... / I watched ... / I played ...

Tip:
Look at Ramon's page again.
- Make a page that looks like *mypage*. Use the same headings.
- Use Ramon's sentences to help you.
Exercises 4 and 6 can help you too.

Tip:
Write your page and put it on the classroom wall.
OR
Write your page on the computer and put it on a website for friends, or on your school/class website.

▸ W 48, 5–7

1 What are the most important things and activities in your life?

My MP3 player / swimming / ...

2 Read the story. Why is there no music in the girl's life?

A life without music

2 12

by Elizabeth Urban

Elizabeth Urban is 16 years old and lives near Cleveland, Ohio. She likes writing stories in her free time.

I wake up suddenly. The moon is high above the trees next to my bedroom window. I get up. Everything is quiet. I don't hear the door when I go to the bathroom. I don't hear the light switch when I turn on the lights. I look in the mirror. I see a tired fifteen-year-old girl. You can't see why I never hear anything: why I can't hear my little sister laugh, why I can't hear my brother read every night, or why I can't hear my own voice.

I wasn't always deaf. I was twelve years old, and I lost my hearing on my birthday. My parents had come into my bedroom to sing happy birthday. They sang loudly, but I didn't wake up. My mother shook me and then I woke up, but I only saw her mouth moving. The most frightening thing was when I tried to talk and heard nothing. I haven't heard my own voice now for three years.

I go back to my bed, but before I sleep, I get up again, open my closet and close its doors. I hear nothing. I sigh. *Maybe I'll have my hearing back tomorrow.* I've been thinking that for three years; I try to hope.

I wake up in the morning to the sound of nothing ... again. My 11-year-old brother, Kyle, is shaking me. I walk down to my little sister's room. She is two years old with blonde hair. When Sophie sees me, she opens her arms and I pick her up. She kisses me and we go to the kitchen. Mom is looking for her keys in the kitchen and Kyle is playing a video game. Mom finds her keys and shouts something at Kyle. He turns off his game and they leave.

Sophie is trying to say something to me. I shake my head, but she doesn't understand. Her mouth is open, her hands are on her ears. I say, "What's wrong?" She doesn't take her hands off her ears. There's a car in the street opposite our house. A woman comes out of her house and pushes a button on something in her hand. *Of course*! I think. *Car alarm. Stupid!* We eat breakfast.

Five minutes later Mom is home and we go out. In the car Mom turns on the radio. I look out the window. I can't listen to music. I can't listen to the talk shows that Mom listens to. In the street I see people talking on their cellphones. *Can't do that.* I see a

woman running with an MP3 player on her arm. *Can't do that.* I see a man between two young children. They're all talking. I sigh sadly. I close my eyes. Everything is so quiet. I read that in a famous horror movie, a director didn't use any music because people feel nervous when everything is quiet. My life is like that movie.

3 Find the information about the girl in the story.

Age: ...
She can't hear, she's ...
She lost her hearing when she was ... years old.
Her brother's name and age: ...
Her sister's name and age: ...

4 Put the sentences in the right order. 1 d), 2 ..., ...

a) Her little sister isn't happy and the girl doesn't know what's wrong.
b) In the morning her brother shakes her and she wakes up.
c) She sees people in the street: they can all do things that she can't do.
d) At night the girl wakes up and thinks about how she became deaf.
e) The girl's mum and her brother leave. She looks after her little sister.
f) The girl goes out with her mum and sister.

5 Feelings: Pick a word from the box.

→ confident • bored • frightened • angry • sad • stupid • uncool

1. When the girl can't hear her voice on her birthday, she feels ...
2. When the girl doesn't know what Sophie wants, she feels ...
3. In the car the girl feels ...

6 Deaf

a) What things can't the girl in the story do? Make a list with a partner.

She can't hear ...
She can't listen to ...
She can't talk on a ...
She can't use ...

● **b) Imagine you are deaf like the girl in the story. Write about your day.**

- **What can you do? (with friends, alone)**
- **What can't you do?**
- **How do you feel?**

▸W 49, 9–11

WORDPOWER

1 ODD WORD OUT Which word is wrong?

These words are in the story on pages 70–71.

1 hand, arm, key, ear
2 happy, deaf, frightened, sad
3 feel, sleep, wake up, get up
4 voice, mouth, talk, shake
5 next to, opposite, loud, above
6 mirror, closet, car alarm, light switch

2 A music fan blog

a) Put in the words in the box.

These words are on pages 66–69.

> stage • rhythm • awards • musicians • piano • male

Justin Timberlake comes from Tennessee, but he lives in Florida. He's one of the best **(1)** ... singers today and he has won many **(2)** ... He plays the guitar and the **(3)** ... too. Justin has worked with lots of other famous singers and **(4)** ... . I love his songs because they always have a good **(5)** ... . And Justin is fantastic on **(6)** ...

● **b) Write a fan blog about another singer or musician.** Use the text in a) to help you.

3 WORD SEARCH Prepositions

a) Look at the pictures and finish the sentences. Then check on pages 67–71.

1 There's a table ... one musician. (p. 67)
2 Three people are sitting ... an umbrella. (p. 67)
3 I spend lots of time ... my computer. (p. 68)
4 The moon is high ... the trees. (p. 70, l. 1)
5 There's a car ... our house. (p. 70, ll. 30–31)
6 I see a man ... two young children. (p. 71, ll. 39–40)

b) You're talking about a holiday picture. Use the words in a).

There's a cafe **(1)** ... two trees. The name *Amy's Place* is **(2)** ... the door. There's a big hotel **(3)**... the cafe. There are some tables **(4)**... the cafe. That's me in the pink T-shirt. I'm sitting **(5)** ... my dad. There's a dog **(6)**... one of the tables.

►W 50, 12–15 ►W ⊙

1 Jobs

a) Write the music jobs.

1 A ... sings songs.
2 A ... dances on stage.
3 A ... plays music at clubs.
4 A ... puts make-up on people.
5 A ... plays an instrument.
6 A ... makes films or music videos.

b) What other jobs do you know? Make a list with the class.

● **c) Pick three of the jobs in b). Write short definitions like in a).**

2 Your job

a) What job would you like to do?

- I'd like to be a ...
- I'd like to work at an airport / a hospital / restaurant / hotel / ...
- I'd like to work for *Greenpeace* / ...

Tip: Use a dictionary or ask your teacher for help.

b) Say why:

- I'd like to work alone / with people / with animals / with my hands / outdoors / indoors / at night / ...
- I'd like to have an interesting job / help people / get lots of money / have lots of free time / ...

3 The music business

a) Put the verbs in the article.

→ deal • take • sleep • dream • relax • follow

Do you **(1)** ... of a career as a singer or in a band? The music business is hard. Musicians often have to travel and **(2)**... in hotels. For many famous singers and musicians it's hard to **(3)** ...: Photographers often **(4)** ... them, so they can **(5)** ... their photos. And some musicians have to **(6)** ... with drug and alcohol problems.

● **b) AND YOU? Would you like to be famous? Why / Why not?**

Yes, because your life is ... / you meet lots of ... / ...
No, because you are never alone / you always have to look ... / ...

4 Music websites

a) You're online on your favourite singer's website. You see these links:

Home | News | Photos | Tour | Media | Mobile | Fan Club | Store

Which link do you use if you want to ...

1 find out dates for concerts?
2 get a new ringtone for your phone?
3 send the singer a message?
4 look at pictures?
5 go to the first page of the website?
6 buy CDs and other things?
7 find out new information?
8 watch videos and listen to songs?

b) SAY IT IN GERMAN **Tell a partner what the links mean.**

►W 51, 16–18 ►W ◉

LISTENING Useful phrases

2⊙13 **1 Salina is going to Florida. Listen and pick the three topics that Salina talks about.**

cold winters • warm winters • hurricanes • beaches • theme parks • TV shows

2⊙13 **2 Listen again. Pick the right answers.**

1 In winter in Florida it's about ...
a) 12° C
b) 20° C
c) 21° C

Tip:
° = degrees

2 There are hurricanes ...
a) all year
b) from June to November
c) from July to December

3 At Sea World there are ...
a) shows with pirates
b) shows with whales
c) lots of boats

4 At Epcot you can learn about ...
a) our environment
b) sports
c) food

5 At the Kennedy Space Center you can ...
a) go into space
b) find out about planes
c) be an astronaut for a day

Tip:
Don't worry if you can't remember a word or you said something wrong. Use these phrases!

2⊙13 **3 Listen again and put in the missing phrases from Salina's talk.**

1 So I'm going to tell you something about Florida. *(Er)*, just ...
2 But there is a problem with *(er)* – what's ... – yes, hurricanes.
3 Hurricanes have hit lots of houses in Florida and killed lots of people. What I'm trying ... that Florida has warm weather, but it can be dangerous too.
4 A theme park is *(er)* something ... a "Freizeitpark", but much bigger.
5 Epcot is a theme park where you can learn about our environment and "Technologie", sorry, I ... technology.

● 2⊙14 **4 Put the phrases from exercise 3 in the sentences. Then listen and check.**

1 Theme parks are great but they're – ... – expensive, very expensive.
2 You can see a shuttle at the Space Center. A shuttle is *(er)*, ... a plane that goes into space.
3 Many people in Florida not speak English, ... they don't speak English at home.
4 Now I'm going to talk about, *(er)*, ..., I'm going to talk about crime in Miami.
5 I didn't explain that very well! ... that Miami has a big problem with crime, but it's a fantastic city.

▸W 52, 19 ▸W ⊙

SPEAKING Polite phrases

1 Salina is staying with an exchange family in Miami.

2 15

a) Listen and match the conversations and the pictures. Picture A is conversation ...

A

B

b) What was the problem in conversation 1?

2 Be polite!

a) Match the sentences (1–6) and the answers (a–f).

1 Hello, I'm Barbara.
2 Do you mind if I sit here?
3 Could you give me the salad, please?
4 I'm afraid I don't eat meat.
5 Could you tell me where the bathroom is, please?
6 Thank you.

a) Go ahead.
b) It's on the right, opposite the kitchen.
c) I'm Salina. Nice to meet you.
d) Yes, of course. Here you are.
e) You're welcome.
f) Oh, I'm sorry.

2 15

b) Listen to conversation 2 again and check your answers in a).

c) Practise the sentences and answers with a partner.

3 Find the right phrases in 2a).

What do you say when ...

1 somebody tells you his/her name?
2 you want to do something?
3 you ask for something?
4 you say politely that there's a problem?
5 somebody says thank you?

Tip:
Be polite! Always say *please* and *thank you* and use these phrases.

4 ROLE PLAY

Partner A: You're at a party. You sit down at a table and meet Partner B. Look at your card on page 96.

Partner B: You're an exchange student in Miami. You meet Partner A at a party. Look at your card on page 96.

▸W 52, 20–21 ▸W

READING Winners!

1 **Read the article. What do the winners get?**

This week in Greatest Hits we're looking at our favorite music awards and TV shows.

MTV Video Music Awards

The MTV Awards for the top artists and music videos of the year started in 1984. Famous Hollywood stars present the nominees and the winners. There are eleven categories (like *Male Artist of the Year*, *Female Artist of the Year*, *Best Group*) and there are usually five nominees in each category. A jury votes for the winners. In one category – *Best New Artist* – MTV viewers can vote. The winners get a statue of a moon man – like the statue in the photo. Madonna has won the most moon men: she has twenty MTV awards!

American Idol

American Idol is the most popular talent contest on American TV. The show tries to find the best young singer (between 16 and 28 years old) in the USA. First there are auditions with thousands of singers in lots of different states. In the finals, the twelve best singers sing on stage. Viewers vote for the winner who gets a million dollar recording contract. Kelly Clarkson was the winner of the first *American Idol*. The show was the start of her career. After *American Idol* Kelly had lots of number 1 hits and won many important awards. She's a big star now.

2 **Read the article again. Are the sentences true or false or not in the text?**

1 There are five categories of MTV awards.
2 Viewers pick the winner of the *Best New Artist* award.
3 The people who present the awards should look good.
4 There are twelve singers in the finals of *American Idol*.
5 Before *American Idol* Kelly Clarkson worked at a club.
6 Kelly Clarkson has had a terrible career as a singer.

3 **Find words in the article that mean …**

1 a prize
2 a singer or musician
3 a person who could win
4 people who watch TV
5 to pick somebody for a prize
6 a competition for singing and dancing

4 **AND YOU? Tell the class.**

a) **Do you watch music TV? What do you watch?** I watch concerts, music videos, news, …
b) **Do you watch the music awards? What do you like most?**
I like finding out the winners / the music / the clothes that the stars wear / …
c) **Would you like to be in a talent contest?** Yes, I would. / No, I wouldn't (because) …

► W 53, 22

WRITING A letter

AWARD COMPETITION

Win concert tickets! Write to *Greatest Hits* magazine.
Tell us which singer or band should win our "Nicest Star" award and why. Pick one of our musicians or pick your own.

Courtney Long
- gives money to homeless young people
- never says no to a fan who wants an autograph

Ricky West
- helps young singers to start their careers
- took drugs but now tells young people about the problems of drugs

1 Read about the competition and then read Ramon's letter. Answer the questions.

- What's the award for?
- Who does Ramon think should get the award? Why? Find three reasons.

1942 SW 8th St.
Miami, FL 33135
April 28th

Tip: Write your address and the date here.

Tip: Start your letter with *Dear ...*

Dear Greatest Hits,

In my opinion, Shakira should get your award. She's a big star, but she doesn't take drugs or go to wild parties every night like lots of other singers. She's very nice to her fans too and she always answers messages on her website. I believe that she's one of the nicest people in the music business.

Shakira helps children and teenagers in Colombia. She gives money to poor families and children who have had problems with violence. I think this is fantastic.

I'm sure that she would like to win your award.

Best wishes,
Ramon Ramirez

Tip: Finish your letter with *Best wishes* and your name.

2 Look at the letter again. Find four phrases that Ramon uses to say what he thinks. (They're all at the start of a sentence.)

3 Your letter for the competition

a) Write to *Greatest Hits* (60–80 words).

- Write your address and the date.
- Start your letter with the right phrase.
- Say who you think should get the magazine's award and why.
- Finish the letter and write your name.

Tip: Remember to use the phrases in exercise 2. Look at Ramon's letter for help.

b) Your teacher reads the letters and picks three musicians. The class votes for the winner.

▸W 53, 23 ▸W ⊙

1 **Read the website information. How many Hispanics are there in the USA?**

Facts

The number of Hispanics in the USA is growing fast. There are now about **44** million Hispanics in a population of about **300** million Americans. Experts think there will be about **100** million Hispanics in the USA in 2050.

Hispanics and the economy

About 12 million people in America came to the USA illegally – they have no papers. Most of these illegal immigrants are Hispanic and many come across the border from Mexico. They pay lots of money to get into the USA safely. American employers often pay them badly – but they get more money than in Mexico. Other illegal immigrants come to the USA as tourists and then stay longer. They can easily buy papers on the street.

Some Americans say that all illegal immigrants should go home. Others think differently and say that they should stay because the American economy needs them. Illegal immigrants work hard and they do the worst jobs.

HISPANIC POWER!

Hispanic stars

Some people think that all Hispanics are illegal immigrants, poor and only speak Spanish. Of course that isn't true!
Many Hispanics are born in the USA, have good jobs and speak English very well. And some are big stars – like the singers Jennifer Lopez and Marc Anthony (their parents come from Puerto Rico).

2 **WORD SEARCH**

a) Find these words on this page.

1 About 12 million people in America came to the USA ...
2 They pay lots of money to get into the USA ...
3 American employers often pay them ...
4 They can ... buy papers on the street.
5 Others think ... and say that they should stay.

b) Now find these words on this page.

1 The number of Hispanics is growing ...
2 Illegal immigrants work ...
3 Many Hispanics are born in the USA and speak English very ...

3 Adjectives and adverbs

a) Look at exercise 2a) again and find the adverbs.

Adjectives	Adverbs
illegal	*illegally*
safe	...
bad	...
easy	...
...	...

Tip:
Be careful with the spelling!
See *Summary*, page 137.

b) Now look at exercise 2b) and find these adverbs.

Adjectives	Adverbs
fast	...
hard	...
good	...

4 OVER TO YOU!

Finish the checkpoint.

Tip:
Write the checkpoint in your exercise book.

CHECKPOINT

Adverbien

- Mit Adverbien kannst du beschreiben, wie man etwas macht.
- Die meisten Adverbien bildest du, indem du ... an das Adjektiv anhängst.
- Achtung! Bei den folgenden Adjektiven gibt es besondere Adverbformen: *good* - ... , *fast* - ... , *hard* - ...

► Eine Übersicht über diese Regeln findest du auf der *Summary*-Seite 137.
► Extra Practice, pp. 112 ff.
► W 54–55

NACH DIESER UNIT KANN ICH ...

über meinen Musikgeschmack und meine Musikgewohnheiten sprechen.	► *I like R & B and pop music.* *I play the piano. / I don't play an instrument.* *I often download songs from websites.*
über Songs sprechen.	► *I like the rhythm. I don't like the singer's voice.* *The music is good for dancing.*
sagen, wo sich etwas oder jemand befindet.	► *There's a sign above the door.* *Our school is opposite the park.*
Gesprächsstrategien anwenden: – um eine Redepause bitten, – mich selbst verbessern, – etwas umschreiben.	► *Just a minute. / What's the word?* *What I'm trying to say is ... / Sorry, I mean ...* *It's something like ...*
eine höfliche Konversation führen.	*Nice to meet you.* *Do you mind if I sit here?*
höflich auf ein Problem hinweisen.	*I'm afraid ...*
meine persönliche Meinung äußern.	► *In my opinion, ... / I believe ...* *I think ... / I don't think ...*

Weitere Übungen: www.new-highlight.de
► W 56, Test yourself ► W 57–58, Portfolio ► W ⊙
► Extra Reading, pp.122–125

Unit 6*

Going west

Before 1840 most people lived in the east of the USA. But between 1841 and 1868 more than 300,000 people went west to Oregon. It was a long and difficult trip. It was called the Oregon Trail. And the people were called pioneers.

People sat at the campfires, ate, talked and sang songs.

The pioneers wanted a better life.

1 On the Oregon Trail

Look at the pictures, texts and map.

What do you think – why was the Oregon Trail difficult?

2 The diary of Abi Russell

2 16

Listen to the radio programme.
Look at the map.
Which places can you hear?

3 Listen to the first part of Abi's diary.

2 17

Are these sentences true or false?

1 Abi Russell lived in Richmond, Missouri.
2 Abi's brothers and sisters wanted to leave.
3 Abi said goodbye to her parents.
4 First Abi's family went to Independence.
5 On the trail most people were on horses.
6 The pioneers had lots of animals with them.
7 Fort Laramie was a small town.

*Unit 6 ist nur Pflichtstoff für den E-Kurs in Nordrhein-Westfalen.

The wagon trains were often long, with lots of people and animals.

At night the pioneers camped together. It was safer. They were frightened of Indians and wild animals like cougars and buffaloes.

These wagons were very important for the pioneers. They put lots of things in them, like food, clothes and furniture.

2 18

4 Listen to the second part of Abi's diary. Pick the right answer.

1 Independence Day is on **a)** May 10th **b)** June 20th **c)** July 4th **d)** August 20th.
2 Abi liked Joseph **a)** Dunn **b)** Brown **c)** Russell **d)** Jones.
3 In the mountains things were more **a)** expensive **b)** exciting **c)** different **d)** difficult.
4 Abi didn't like **a)** fish **b)** bread **c)** buffalo meat **d)** vegetables.
5 The Indians were very **a)** friendly **b)** angry **c)** young **d)** frightened.
6 On October 1st, the Russells got to **a)** California **b)** Oregon City **c)** Washington **d)** Chicago.
7 The Russells' new farm was **a)** at Snake River **b)** at Deschutes River **c)** in Oregon City **d)** near Richmond.

▸W 59, 1–3

A SUMMER IN OREGON

1 Summer plans

Scan these e-mails. What can you find out about Laura and Martin?

a) Where are they from?
b) Are they friends?
c) Who's going to travel next summer?

Tip:
When you're looking for information in a text, you "scan" it.

Laura Russell

Martin Maier

From: martin.maier29@wannabe.de
To: laurarussell@xyz.com

Dear Laura,
Thanks for your invitation. If I had enough money, I'd visit you in the USA.
But you know that I have four brothers and sisters. If we all went to the USA, it would be very expensive. So I think that we'll stay here in Bielefeld this summer.
What are your summer plans? Would you like to come to Germany?
Best wishes from your e-pal.
Martin

From: laurarussell@xyz.com
To: martin.maier29@wannabe.de

Hi Martin,
Thanks for your e-mail and for your invitation. If I had time, I'd love to go to Germany. But summer is busy here on the ranch. I have to help with the horses. And I have to practice for the rodeo at the County Fair. If you came to Bend in August, we'd take you to the fair. It's awesome! And we'd go to the coast. And if you wanted, I'd teach you to ride. So you really should come to the USA. If you came alone, it wouldn't be so expensive. And if you came to Portland, we'd pick you up at the airport. It's only three hours from here.
Bye,
Laura

From: martin.maier29@wannabe.de
To: laurarussell@xyz.com

Hi again, Laura!
Great news! My grandma is going to give me some money for my birthday. And I have a weekend job. So I can come to the USA in August – alone. I'm really excited. Can you send me some information about Bend and Oregon – or some links?
Martin

2 What are these words in German? Guess first. Then check in a dictionary.

1 enough **2** e-pal **3** fair
4 coast **5** teach **6** excited

3 Who writes about these things: Martin, Laura or nobody?

1 a big family
2 a busy summer
3 riding horses
4 a part-time job
5 Christmas in Bend
6 a trip to the coast
7 a great present
8 hiking in Germany

4 AND YOU? Finish these sentences.

1. If I went to the USA, I'd visit / try / eat / ...
2. If an American friend came to Germany, we'd go to / meet / ...
3. If I had lots of money, I'd buy / give / ...

● 5 An American e-pal

Imagine that you have an American e-pal. Write an e-mail. Invite him/her to visit you. Say what you'd do.

▶ W 60, 4

6 The history of Bend

Laura sent this brochure to Martin. Read it and finish the "Short history of Bend".

Deschutes County Historical Society
Bend, Oregon

The first pioneers came to the Bend area in 1813. But they didn't stay. They were going to California. Then in 1874 the first houses were built near the Deschutes River. More people came and in 1881 the first school was built. It had 5 students. A post office was established in 1886. In 1900 the little town was named Farewell Bend. That was because lots of people said farewell (goodbye) here, before they went to California. But in 1905 the name was changed to Bend.

A SHORT HISTORY OF BEND

1813	The first ... came to the area.
1874	The first ... were built.
1881	The first ... was built.
1886	A ... was established.
1900	Name: ...
1905	New name: ...

PROJECT More about Oregon

a) Work in groups. Each pupil in the group picks one of these topics, looks for information and makes notes.

Tip:
- Use online encyclopedias like *wikipedia.org* or *infoplease.com*
- When you use a search engine, put in two or more words. Examples: *Oregon Bend* or *Oregon activities coast*

1 Bend, Oregon

- What's the population?
- What can you do there?
- What should tourists see?

2 Oregon's geography

- Towns and cities?
- Mountains, lakes and rivers?
- The weather?

Tip:
Scan the texts on the websites. Look only for the information that you need.

3 Oregon's animals

- Oregon's nickname?
- What's a Jackalope?
- What's a skunk?

4 Activities in Oregon

- Activities on the coast?
- Activities in Oregon's schools?
- What's *disc golf*?

Tip:
- Don't worry about new words.
- Pictures and titles can help you to find what you need.

Tip:
The *Presentation Phrases* at the start of the book can help you.

b) Write a paragraph about your topic. **c) Present your topic to your group.**

▸W 60, 5–7

1 Martin's holiday: Look at the pictures and answer these questions.

1 How did Martin travel? **2** What did he see? **3** Do you think he had a good holiday?

An Oregon diary

2◎19

When Martin was planning his trip to the USA, his English teacher in Bielefeld asked him to write a diary in English. Martin agreed. Here are parts of his Oregon diary.

Monday, August 4th

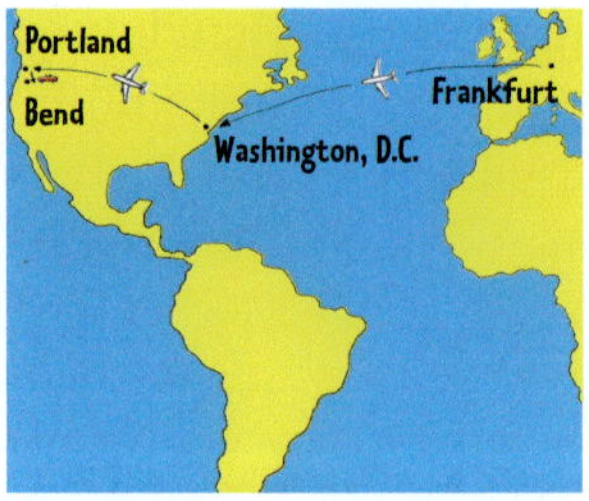

I'm at Dulles Airport in Washington now. I left Frankfurt today at 9 a.m. The flight to Washington was nine and a half hours. But it's only 12.30 p.m. now! I'm so tired! If I had time, I'd find a quiet place and sleep. But my flight to Portland is soon. Laura's family is picking me up there. I don't know them, so I'm feeling nervous. Everybody here speaks so fast. I can't understand much! And writing my diary in English is difficult.

Tuesday, August 5th

Yesterday was a long, long day! I got to Portland and the Russells were waiting. Laura is very nice. Her mum and dad are friendly too. And her little brother, Dylan is really funny. He's only seven. First we drove on the highway. That was a big road, but the cars weren't going very fast. The speed limit here is only 65 miles per hour (that's about 100 kilometres per hour). We got to Bend at 11 p.m. and I fell into bed. I was very tired. This morning Laura and Dylan showed me the ranch. It's nice. There are lots of big, old barns. The house is big and modern. The tractors are big too. In fact, everything is big here – bigger than in Germany!

Thursday, August 7th

Yesterday I tried riding Laura's horse. I almost fell off and Laura laughed. But it wasn't funny! Today we're in Bend. It's a very nice town – typical American like in the films! I met some of Laura's friends. They're nice, but I don't understand a word when they talk together. So I stay quiet. We had hot dogs for lunch. But I didn't like them – they're different from German sausages. Laura and her friends are shopping now. But it's too hot for me, so I'm sitting at a diner writing my diary and drinking a soda. You can get refills and they're free! That's great. I think I'll have another soda!

Friday, August 8th

I stayed in my room for a long time today. Laura wanted to go riding again, but I said no. And she wanted to meet friends, but I was too tired. I played some games with Dylan. That was fun – and I can understand Dylan!

The food here is different from home. The bread isn't very nice. People here eat lots of white bread! I miss the food from home. I miss my family too. In fact, I'm feeling homesick! If I had a plane ticket, I'd go home now.

Sunday, August 10th

I'm feeling much better now. Today was a great day. It was very hot – hotter than in Bielefeld! So Laura, Dylan and I went to the Deschutes River, near Bend. We met some of Laura's friends there. We went *tubing*. We sat in big tubes and went slowly down the river. We laughed all the time. It was great. Then we made a campfire near the river and had *s'mores*. That's an American tradition – marshmallows are grilled on the fire. You can eat them with chocolate and crackers. They're great!

My English is better now and I can understand Laura's friends. I told them about life in Germany. They were very interested. They told me about the pioneers and the Oregon Trail.

Friday, August 15th

This week has been awesome! (Laura says "awesome" all the time.) We did so much. We went to the County Fair. Laura was in the rodeo competition. She didn't win, but she was very good. And the best news is that I learned to ride. But no rodeo for me! Now I'm in Portland with all the family. My holiday is almost over. On Sunday I'm going to go home.

So what do I think of Oregon? It's a great place. People are so friendly and the area is very beautiful. I'm not surprised that the pioneers wanted to come here. But I'm looking forward to going home. And I'm really looking forward to eating German food again!

2 Something is wrong in every sentence. Correct the sentences.

1 Martin's flight to Washington was 12 hours.
2 The speed limit on highways is the same in the USA and in Germany.
3 Martin learned to ride on his third day.
4 Martin's first week in Bend was boring.
5 You need boats for tubing.
6 Martin's second week was terrible.

3 In Oregon: Finish the sentences.

1 Martin liked lots of things, for example ...
2 He didn't like some food, for example ...
3 Some things were very different: ...
4 It was a good holiday because ...

● 4 Home again

Imagine that you're Martin. Write an e-mail to Laura. Say thanks for the holiday. Say what you learned about Oregon.

The e-mails on page 82 help you to start and finish.

► W 61, 8–10

WORDPOWER

1 ODD WORD OUT All the words are on pages 84–85.

1 river, highway, speed limit, miles per hour
2 white bread, s'mores, rodeo, hot dogs
3 awesome, typical, great, beautiful
4 marshmallow, ranch, barn, tractor
5 airport, plane ticket, flight, refill
6 nervous, homesick, tube, tired

2 Find the missing words in these sentences.

1 In Germany you say "kilometres per hour", but in America you say "..."
2 In Germany people eat lots of brown bread, but in America people often eat "..."
3 Americans often say "awesome", but British people say "..."
4 In Britain drinks like lemonade are called "fizzy drinks". In America they're called "..."
5 In Germany a big road is called an "Autobahn". In America it's called a "..."
6 In America a small restaurant is often called a "..."

3 Finish these networks in your exercise book.

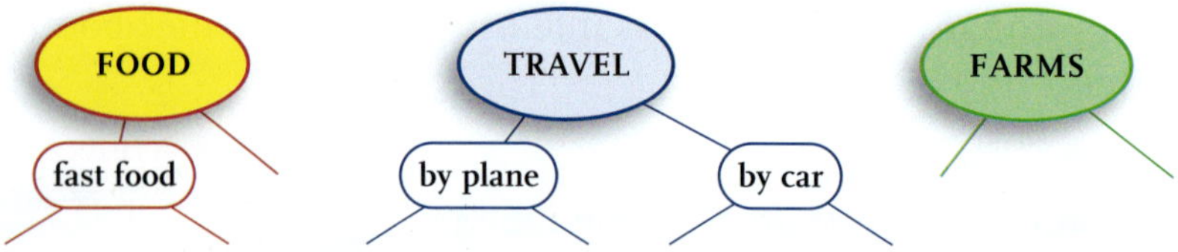

Tip:
Put in words from this unit. Then find more words for the networks.

▸ Wordbank 9, p. 131

4 Useful phrases

a) First try to remember what these phrases are in English.

1 Möchtest du nach Deutschland kommen? (p. 82)
2 Du solltest wirklich in die USA kommen. (p. 82)
3 Ich bin echt begeistert. (p. 82)
4 Ich kann nicht viel verstehen. (p. 84, ll. 7–8)
5 Dylan ist wirklich lustig. (p. 84, l. 14)
6 Typisch amerikanisch! (p. 84, l. 25)
7 Ich freue mich darauf, nach Hause zu fahren. (p. 85, ll. 62–63)

b) Now check your answers to a) on pages 82, 84 and 85.

5 WORD SEARCH The passive

a) Put in *was* or *were*. Then check your answers in exercise 6 on page 83.

1 In 1874 the first houses ... built.
2 In 1881 the first school ... built.
3 In 1886 a post office ... established.
4 In 1900 the town ... named Farewell Bend.
5 In 1905 the name ... changed to Bend.

b) When do you use the passive? Make the rule.

The passive
You use the passive when
- it is/isn't important who did it
- you know/don't know who did it.

▸ W 62, 11–14 ▸ W ◉

Reading logs

STEP 1 Start a reading log.

When you read a story or a book, you can write a reading log. It's like a diary. It can help you to understand and remember the story. Start a reading log for the story *An Oregon Diary* on pages 84/85.

STEP 2 Write notes on the story.

Title: An Oregon Diary		
PAGE	WHAT HAPPENS	WHAT DO THE CHARACTERS FEEL/THINK
84	Martin leaves Frankfurt. He goes to Portland. He meets the Russells. They drive to Bend. Martin sees the ranch.	Martin is nervous. He thinks that the Russells are nice. He says Dylan is funny. He's tired. Martin likes Laura's friends.

Tip:
- Write the title of the story.
- Write the page numbers.
- Say what happens.
- Say what the characters feel and think.
- You can use the simple present.

Finish these notes about *An Oregon diary*.

STEP 3 Write what YOU think and feel.

What I think/feel about:		
THE CHARACTERS I like ... I don't like ... I think that the Russells are ...	THE PLACE I think that the ranch is ... Bend sounds ... I think that Oregon is ...	THE STORY I think that the story is ... Tubing sounds ... I like/ don't like it when ...

Tip:
Use:
☺ 😐 ☹

Finish these notes and write what you think about *An Oregon diary*.

STEP 4 Pick one of these activities. Write ...

A SHORT SUMMARY This story is about a German boy who goes to Oregon. He visits the Russells in Bend ...	A REVIEW I think that this is a good story because ... But I don't like it when ...	MRS RUSSELL'S E-MAIL Dear Mr and Mrs Maier, Martin is having a nice time here. But he's ...
LAURA'S DIARY FOR ONE DAY Monday, August 4th We drove to Portland. We met Martin at the airport. He ...	AN ADVERT FOR OREGON Come to Oregon. Visit Bend. It's a beautiful city. Go tubing on the ...	MARTIN'S LAST DAY Sunday, August 17th We got up early and went to the airport. I was sad ...

STEP 5 Read the story *The Road to Freedom* on pages 122–25. Write a reading log for that story. Then read other pupils' logs.

▸W 63, 15–18 ▸W ⊙

LISTENING A family trip

1 Booking a room in a motel

2 20 **a) Listen and find out:**

1 How many rooms do they need?
2 Does the motel have free rooms?
3 How much is a double room?
4 How many nights do the people want to stay?

b) Imagine that you work at the Sunset Motel. Copy this form. Listen again and fill it in.

SUNSET MOTEL, BANDON, OREGON
Name: Amanda
Arrive: Friday,
Leave: ______
Number of rooms: ______
Double rooms: ______ Single rooms: ______

2 On the road

2 21 **a) Listen to *Radio Cascades*. Are these sentences true or false?**

1 All the roads are quiet today.
2 Highway 101 is busy.
3 There's a wildfire.
4 Highway 5 is closed.
5 Bend is going to be warm and dry.
6 It's going to be hot on the coast.

b) Listen again and check.

3 On the coast

2 22 **Listen. Pick the right answer.**

1	Now the Russells are	**a)** in the mountains.	**b)** at home.	**c)** in Bandon.
2	Laura and Martin are	**a)** on the beach.	**b)** in a hotel.	**c)** in the car.
3	Martin thinks this place is	**a)** busy.	**b)** nice.	**c)** boring.
4	The weather here is	**a)** hot.	**b)** terrible.	**c)** cool.

5 Are Martin and Laura talking about sign **a)**, **b)** or **c)**?

a

b

c

4 SAY IT IN GERMAN Pick one sign in exercise 3 and explain it to a partner.

► W 64, 19

SPEAKING At a motel

1 The Russells at Sunset Motel, Bandon

2 23 **a) How much must Mrs Russell pay for two nights?**

MRS RUSSELL Hi. I've booked three rooms for two nights. My name is Amanda Russell.
RECEPTIONIST Hello Mrs Russell. You've booked two double rooms and a single room. Is that right?
MRS RUSSELL Yes, that's right.
RECEPTIONIST We have a special offer this week. I can give you a family room for four and a single room.
MRS RUSSELL How much is that?
RECEPTIONIST It's $120 per night for the family room and $45 for the single room.
MRS RUSSELL That's fine.
RECEPTIONIST You have rooms 187 and 188. Enjoy your stay, Mrs Russell.
MRS RUSSELL Thanks.

b) Practise the dialogue with a partner.

2 Mr and Mrs Brown at Sunset Motel

2 24 **a) Finish the dialogue.**

MRS BROWN Hello. I'd like a ... for one night, please.
RECEPTIONIST Hello. Do you want a ... room or a ... room?
MRS BROWN A double room, please. How ... is it?
RECEPTIONIST It's $85 ... night.
MRS BROWN That's ...
RECEPTIONIST You have room 359. Enjoy your ...
MRS BROWN ...

b) Act the dialogue with a partner.

3 Tom Wilson at Sunset Motel

a) Make the dialogue with a partner.

MR WILSON Sage hallo. Sage wie du heißt. Sage, dass du ein Zimmer reserviert hast.
RECEPTIONIST Begrüße den Gast. Frage, ob er ein Einzel- oder Doppelzimmer möchte.
MR WILSON Sage, dass du ein Einzelzimmer möchtest. Frage, wie viel das kostet.
RECEPTIONIST Sage, dass es $90 pro Nacht kostet.
MR WILSON Sage zu. Frage, wo das Zimmer ist.
RECEPTIONIST Sage, es ist auf der rechten Seite, neben dem Restaurant. Wünsche dem Gast einen angenehmen Aufenthalt.

b) Write your dialogue and practise it.

4 SAY IT IN ENGLISH

You work at a hotel in Germany. Explain the most important information on this sign to an English tourist.

▸W 64, 20–21 ▸W ⊙

READING Heroes of the Wild West

1 Scan texts A and B and find out:

- **Who are the two texts about?**
- **Which text is a song?**

A

THE STORY OF AN OUTLAW

Jesse James was born in Missouri in 1847. He had an older brother, Frank. The two boys joined a gang in 1866, when Jesse was only 19, they robbed a bank. A young man in the bank was killed.
After that the James brothers robbed banks and trains. Lots of people were killed. Jesse and Frank were often in the newspapers. They were famous.
Jesse changed his name to Thomas Howard. There was a reward of $10,000 for the person who helped to catch Frank or Jesse James. Then in 1882 Jesse was shot by a friend – Robbert Ford. Jesse James died and Ford got the reward.
Some people thought that the James boys robbed the rich and gave to the poor – like Robin Hood. But this wasn't true. They weren't heroes. They were just outlaws who robbed and killed people.

B

Jesse James

Jesse James was a lad
That killed many a man
He robbed the Glendale train
He stole from the rich
And he gave to the poor
He had a hand and a heart and a brain.

Well it was Robert Ford
That dirty little coward
I wonder now how he feels
For he ate of Jesse's bread
And he slept in Jesse's bed
And he laid poor Jesse in his grave.

Well Jesse had a wife
To mourn for his life
Three children
Now they were brave
Well that dirty little coward
That shot Mr Howard
He laid poor Jesse in his grave.

2 Work with a partner.

a) Partner A reads text A, Partner B reads text B.

b) Now try to answer all the questions together.

1 When was Jesse James born?
2 Who robbed the Glendale train?
3 Who was Frank James?
4 Was Jesse James married?
5 Did he have children?
6 Who was Mr Howard?
7 When did Jesse James die?
8 Who shot Jesse James?

3 Words in the text

a) Pick one of the texts. Find the words in the text and guess what they are in German.

Text A	Text B
1 outlaw (*noun*)	1 lad (*noun*)
2 robbed (*verb*)	2 robbed (*verb*)
3 reward (*noun*)	3 rich (*noun*)
4 catch (*verb*)	4 coward (*noun*)
5 rich (*noun*)	5 slept (*verb*)
6 hero (*noun*)	6 wife (*noun*)

b) Check your words in a dictionary.

4 Listen to the song. Then talk about these questions in your class.

2 25 **Do you like the song? Do you think that Jesse James was a hero? Why?**

► W 65, 22

WRITING A Wild West story

Imagine that you're writing a Wild West story for TV.
Look at the pictures and write the story (about 100 words). Think of an interesting ending.

1866 – cowboys – come to small town – Oregon

gang – bank – leave – horses in front of – go in

Tip:
Use phrases like:
- The year was ...
- It was 12 o'clock.
- At five past twelve
- After ten minutes
- Then
- Later
- Suddenly

cashier – give – money put in bags – people stand – next to wall

gang – leave – bank run into street

Tip:
Describe the scene with phrases like:
- It was hot.
- The town was quiet.
- People were frightened/ nervous/surprised.

no horses – in street cowboys – surprised

horses – shop – eat vegetables sheriff – surprised

Tip:
Use words like:
- because
- and
- but
- so
- when

►W 65, 23 ►W ⊙

DREAMING ABOUT AMERICA

1 **If you won a trip to the USA where would you go? Why?**
Look at the pictures and tell a partner.

New York

Los Angeles

Chicago

Washington

Miami

Oregon

Tip:
Look in Units 1–6 for more ideas.

2 **More dreams!**
If you went to New York, Oregon or the other places, what would you do there?

If I went to New York, LA, Oregon, Chicago, Washington, Miami, ...	I'd ...	visit see go play try eat ride meet	Ground Zero • Disneyland • Hollywood • Bend surfing • a Segway • basketball • bears tubing • whale watching • Neah Bay • a rodeo shopping • rangers • a horse • famous people kayaking • hot dogs • s'mores • a rodeo

3 WORD SEARCH

a) Look at the pictures. Guess what the missing words are. Check the e-mails on page 82.

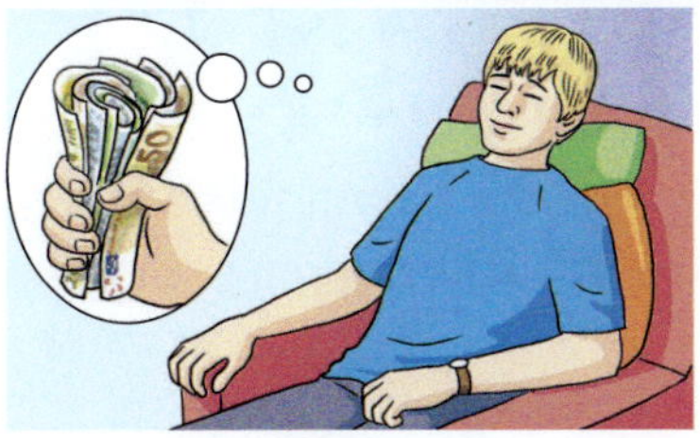

If I ... enough money,
I'd visit you in the USA.

If we all ... to the USA,
it would be very expensive.

If I ... time,
I'd love to go to Germany.

b) Now guess these missing words. You can check them on page 82.

If you came to Bend,
we'... ... you to the fair.

If you wanted,
I'... ... you to ride.

If you came to Portland,
we'... ... you up.

4 OVER TO YOU!

Write the checkpoint in your exercise book and put in:

- *would* / *'d*
- the simple past

CHECKPOINT

***If*-Sätze (Typ II)** verwendest du, wenn du sagen willst, was wäre wenn ...

	if-Satz	Hauptsatz
Die Situation ist eher unwahrscheinlich.	*if* + ...	... + verb

► Eine Übersicht über diese Regeln findest du auf der *Summary*-Seite 138.
► Extra Practice, pp. 116 ff.
► W 66–67

NACH DIESER UNIT KANN ICH ...

sagen, was gemacht wurde oder passiert ist.	► *The first houses were built in 1874. A post office was established.*
ein Lesetagebuch führen.	► *The title of the story is ... . Martin goes by plane from ...* ► *I think that the story is ... . I like ... . I don't like ...*
ein Zimmer im Hotel reservieren.	► *I'd like to book a room for one night, please.*
in einem Hotel einchecken.	► *Hello. My name is ... . I've booked a room for one night.*
eine Geschichte schreiben.	► *The year was 1866. Six cowboys were in a small town ...*
sagen, was wäre wenn ...	► *If I won a trip to the USA, I'd go to New York.*

Weitere Übungen: www.new-highlight.de

► W 68, Test yourself ► W ⊙

ROLE-PLAY CARDS

Unit 1 (page 19)

Card A
You invite a friend.

A Do you have any plans for Sunday afternoon?
B ...
A I'm having a party. Do you want to come?
B ...
A About 4 o'clock. There'll be some sausages and bread.
B ...
A Yeah, can you bring some fruit or cake?
B ...

Card B
A friend invites you.

A ...
B No, not really.
A ...
B That sounds great, thanks. When should I be there?
A ...
B That sounds good. Can I bring anything?
A ...
B OK. Thanks for the invitation. See you then.

Unit 2 (page 33)

Card A
You phone a friend.

B ...
A Hello. Can I speak to ..., please?
B ...
A When will he/she be back?
B ...
A Can he/she phone me back? I'm ... . And my number is ...
B ...
A Yes, that's right. Thanks. Bye.

Card B
You answer the phone.

B Hello.
A ...
B Oh, he/she isn't here. He/She's in ...
A ...
B After ... p.m. Can I take a message?
A ...
B No problem. I'll write your name and message. So you're ... . And your number is ...
A ...
B Bye.

Unit 3 (page 47)

Card A

You know about school.

A What do you want to know about school?
B …
A You must / mustn't wear shorts …
B …
A You can bring … / but you mustn't bring …
B …
A No, you mustn't bring … / That's OK. You can bring …

Card B

You ask about school.

A …
B What about clothes?
What / must / wear?
A …
B Can / bring / mobile / MP3 player / beer / …?
A …
B What about my …?

Unit 4 (page 61)

Card A

You're a tourist.

- We'd like to do **something interesting. What** can you **recommend?**
- That sounds **interesting/nice/… Where** is it?
- **What** can you **buy** there?
- **What day** is it open?
- **What time** is it open?
- Is there a **market every month?**

Card B

You work at the visitor center.

Anacortes Farmers Market
7th Street in Old Town

Fruit & vegetables
Cakes • Cheese • Bread
Saturdays 9–2
May–October
Remember … come hungry!

Unit 5 (page 75)

Card A

You say "hello" to Partner B.

A Hello, I'm ...
B ...
A mind / sit here?
B ...
A give / bread / please
B ...
A Thank you.
B ...

Card B

You meet Partner A at a party.

A ...
B pleased / meet / you
A ...
B Go ahead.
A ...
B yes / here / are
A ...
B You're welcome.

REVISION Simple present → Summary, p. 132

1 Famous New Yorkers

Put in the verbs.

→ designs • makes • plays • sings and writes • works

1 
Scarlett Johansson

She ... in Hollywood.

2 
Eddie Murphy

He ... funny films.

3 
Calvin Klein

He ... cool clothes.

4 
Alicia Keys

She ... songs.

5 
Carmelo Anthony

He ... basketball.

2 Jazmin's day

a) Write Tyrell's mum's questions for Jazmin.

1 When (**you / go**) to school? *When do you ...?*
2 When (**your parents / start**) work?
3 (**you / have**) lunch at school?
4 When (**your mom / come**) home?
5 What (**you / do**) after school?
6 (**your dad / work**) late?

Tip:
Sometimes you can have two **do**s in a question. Example: What **do** you **do** at the weekend?

b) Tyrell is telling a friend about Jazmin. Finish his sentences.

My cousin Jazmin (**live**) in Greenville in South Carolina. She has three brothers and they (**play**) lots of sports together. They (**not have**) a TV, but they (**listen to**) music all the time. Jazmin (**not like**) pop, but she (**love**) rap. She always (**know**) the best songs. She (**want**) to be a DJ when she's older.

Remember:
Use **-s** with *he, she, it*.

3 Your day

a) Write five sentences about your day.

I	always usually sometimes never	get up go to school have lunch do sport watch TV meet friends go to bed	at ... early. late. in the morning. in the afternoon. in the evening.

b) Now use your own ideas. Write 5–10 more sentences about your day.

Comparisons

→ Summary, p. 136

4 Match the sentences.

Spiderman helps people in New York! He's great!

1. He's faster than other people.
2. He has better eyes than most people.
3. He's braver than other people.
4. He's more dangerous than other people.
5. He's funnier than other people.

a. He's never frightened.
b. But not everybody likes his jokes.
c. Be careful!
d. He can see at night.
e. He can climb very quickly.

5 Travel

a) Travel in New York: Compare the New York subway and taxis. Pick words from the box.

→ cheap • clean • dangerous • easy • expensive • fast • nice • popular • safe

Tip: Check your spelling!

1. The subway is ... than taxis.
2. It's ... than taxis.
3. It's ...

4. Taxis are ... than the subway.
5. They're ... than the subway.
6. They're ...

b) Travel in your area: Write three sentences in your exercise book.

In my area you can go by ... . Bikes/Buses/Trams/Cars/... are ... than ...

6 Finish the text about the World Trade Center.

The two towers of the World Trade Center were (high) the highest skyscrapers in New York. But on September 11th, 2001, one of (terrible) ... and (sad) ... things in New York's history happened: two planes flew into the towers in (busy) ... part of New York. One of (famous) ... skyscrapers in the world fell to the ground. It made (big) ... hole in New York: Ground Zero. Soon there will be new skyscrapers there. The Freedom Tower will be (exciting) ... tower in New York. It's one of the city's (expensive) ... projects.

7 **Work with a partner. What's wrong with these sentences? Write new sentences.**

Eat at Sam's.

It's the dirtiest deli in the city!

Our sandwiches are worse than the sandwiches in other delis!
We have the highest prices in NYC!
We have the most terrible cooks in the neighborhood!

8 **An advert for your school deli**

a) Work with a partner. Look at exercise 7 again and write an advert for your deli. Write about:

- The place
- The food
- The prices
- The cooks

→ cheap • clean • cool • early • exciting • friendly • good • great • healthy • hungry • late • new • nice • polite • romantic

b) Compare your adverts with other pupils. Who has the best advert?

TEST PRACTICE

9 **A New York postcard**

a) Talk about the picture with a partner. What can you see? What's the place like?

Tip:
- Use *There is ... / There are ...* to talk about things and people.
- Say what the place is like: *It's big/small/...*, *It's bigger/busier/more ... than ...*
- Use these phrases to say where they are: *in the background, in the foreground, on the right / on the left.*

b) AND YOU? Compare your town or village with New York. Which is busier/nicer/...?

10 **You want to send a postcard from New York to an English friend. Write the postcard (40–50 words). Write:**

– where you are and why you are there
– what the weather is like
– what you did yesterday
– what you are doing today

Tip:
- Start your postcard with *Dear ...,* or *Hi ...,* Finish with *Love, ...* or *Best wishes, ...*
- Check your postcard.

EXTRA PRACTICE

REVISION Present progressive

→ Summary, p. 132

1 What's happening?

a) Describe the picture in eight sentences.

A girl	is	working	in the park.
A boy	are	playing	bikes.
A man		riding	a chat.
A woman		walking	on a mobile.
Some girls		having	baseball.
Some boys		reading	with his dog.
Some men		sitting	a book.
Some women		talking	on the grass.

b) Look at the picture again.
Write five more sentences.

2 What's happening?

Pick a picture on pages 24–36 of this book. Write five things. Tell your partner.
Can your partner guess which photo you picked?

Who/That

→ Summary, p. 138

3 Who's who and what's what? Put the parts together and make the sentences.

1 Richard Bailey is a man ...	that has lots of smog.
2 Caitlin is a student ...	who often surf.
3 Nina and Lee are teens ...	that's very popular in Los Angeles.
4 Surfing is a sport ...	who goes to Santa Monica High School.
5 Los Angeles is a city ...	that makes famous films.
6 Warner Brothers is a studio ...	who wants the best for his daughter.

4 A man in Hollywood

Put in *who* or *that*.

Tip:
WHO for people and
THAT for things

1 I watched a DVD ... I thought was very funny.
2 It's about an English man ... goes to Hollywood.
3 He stays with some people ... have a nice house.
4 He visits a museum ... has lots of famous pictures.
5 This man does some things ... are very stupid.
6 What's the name of the man ... is the star of this film? – It's Mr Bean!

5 AND YOU? Finish these sentences with more information.

1 I know a girl who likes ...
2 I know a boy who hates ...
3 I go to a school that ...
4 I have friends ...
5 Maths is a subject ...
6 I have a mobile ...

Past progressive → Summary, p. 133

6 The Herrmann family in Los Angeles: Pick the right word.

When the Herrmanns from Berlin (1) was/were visiting LA last summer, they did lots of interesting things. They (2) was/were staying in a hotel in Santa Monica and every day they went to different places. When they visited Hollywood, they saw lots of people who (3) was/were walking along Hollywood Boulevard. Nora (4) was/were looking for famous stars, but she didn't see any. Andi (5) was/were reading the names of famous people on the pavement – and he saw the Simpsons!
The next day the Herrmanns went to Warner Brothers Studios. When they (6) was/were visiting the studios, the tour guide told them lots of interesting stories. They (7) was/were going past a film scene, when Andi and Nora saw Sean Penn. He was with other actors and they (8) was/were wearing cowboy gear. They (9) was/were making a new cowboy film. Nora (10) was/were feeling very happy now – she loves Sean Penn!

7 At a TV show: Put the verbs in the past progressive form.

That evening the Herrmanns were at *Teen Talk*, the new chat show. Nora was happy again.
1 "When we got to the KABC Studios, lots of people (**wait**).
2 A young woman (**check**) the tickets.
3 When I looked behind the scene, the camera people (**talk**) to the director.
4 The director (**shout**) all evening.
5 Nobody (**listen**) to the director.
6 The star of *Teen Talk* (**look**) very nervous.
7 I couldn't see everything because I (**sit**) at the back.
8 When everybody (**leave**), I looked into another studio."

8 In another studio

When Nora looked into another studio, lots of things were happening. Look at the picture and write some sentences.

Some actors were ... One cowboy was ...
Another cowboy ... The director ...

9 An accident in Santa Monica

Officer Kennedy has lots of questions. Put in the verbs.

buying • talking • jogging • driving • walking • riding

Who was ... the car?

Who was ... the bike?

Were you ... on your cellphone?

Was the boy ... across the street?

Were the joggers ... in the street?

Were the shoppers ... vegetables?

10 We weren't doing anything! What are the teenagers saying to Officer Kennedy?

1 I wasn't driving ...!

5 We ...!

2 We weren't using ...!

3 I wasn't ...!

4 We ..!

11 INTERPRETING A German tourist saw something on the beach.

He's talking to Officer Kennedy. Can you help?

OFFICER Where were you sitting?
YOU Wo saßen Sie ...?
TOURIST Ich saß gerade am Strand.
YOU He was sitting on ...
OFFICER What happened then?
YOU Was ...?
TOURIST Ich sah zwei Männer. Sie waren gerade dabei, Taschen zu stehlen.
YOU He saw two men. They were ...
OFFICER What were they wearing?
YOU Was ...?
TOURIST Sie hatten schwarze Kleidung an.
YOU They ...
OFFICER Thank you for your help.
YOU Danke ...

TEST PRACTICE

12 At Disneyland with Peter Pan: What can you see in the picture?

1. What does the picture show?
   The picture shows ...
2. What are the people doing?
   The children are ...
3. How do you think the people are feeling?
   I think that ...
4. What are the people wearing?
   One boy is wearing ...
   A girl ...
   A woman ...
   Peter Pan ...

13 Who can teach me?

a) Sarah Greene (15) can't surf. So she has put this advert in her school newspaper:

I can ride a bike and a quad!
I can drive a car and I can swim like a fish.
I have a surfboard and I live near the beach.
But I can't surf!
So who can teach me?
Phone number: 310-555-7383
Please call after 8 p.m.
Help!

b) Now write Brad's advert.

Brad Wilson (15) can't surf. But he has a new surfboard and surfing gear. He isn't a very good swimmer.
He doesn't live near the sea, but he has a car. He has a mobile (310-555-6534), but you can't call him between 8 a.m. and 4 p.m. on school days. He works on Saturday mornings – he's a photo model!

14 An e-mail to an American friend

You were in LA last month for a holiday. Your friend Mike has sent you an e-mail.

a) First read Mike's questions.

From Mike

Hi!
Welcome home. Did you have a good time in LA? How long were you there? What places did you visit? What were the people like? What was the weather like? Did anything happen? Did you see any stars? Was LA different from Germany?

b) Write an e-mail to Mike. Write 50–80 words.

To Mike

From: (Your e-mail address)
To: mikewilson999@tmail.com

Subject: My holiday in LA

Hi Mike,
Thanks for your e-mail. I had a great holiday.

REVISION *Can/Can't* → Summary, page 135

1 In Chicago: Match the sentences with the pictures.

1 You can go on a boat trip on the Chicago River.
2 You can go shopping at one of the biggest department stores in the world.
3 You can visit the funfair on Navy Pier.
4 You can relax by Lake Michigan.
5 You can look at the city from the top of Sears Tower.
6 You can go to a concert in Millennium Park.

2 Sightseeing

a) Read the advert. Finish the sentences with *can* or *can't*.

> Go on a tour of Chicago's greatest landmarks and neighborhoods on our double-decker buses. Buy tickets and get on the bus at all our bus stops. Tours start at 9 a.m. All day tickets mean that you can jump on and off any of our vehicles. It's the only tour in Chicago that goes to Chinatown, Greektown and Little Italy.

1 You ... go sightseeing in Chicago by bus.
2 You ... start the tour at different bus stops.
3 You ... travel without tickets.
4 You ... go on a tour at 8 a.m.
5 You ... use different buses.
6 You ... visit immigrant neighbourhoods.

b) What can or can't you do in your area? Compare it with Chicago. Write 5–8 sentences.

You can use words and phrases from exercise 1.

In my area you can ...
But you can't ...

see • visit • go • go on • go to • take • look at • ...

REVISION *Have to/Don't have to* → Summary, page 135

3 Put these sentences in two lists: basketball or American football.

1 You have to wear a helmet.
2 You have to play on a special field.
3 You don't have to play outdoors.
4 You have to get the ball in a hoop.
5 You don't have to wear protectors.
6 You don't have to jump.
7 You have to have five players in a team.
8 You have to play for sixty minutes.

4 The Chicago Bulls: Finish the sentences with *you have to / you don't have to.*

If you're in Chicago, ... see a Chicago Bulls game! But ... buy tickets early because they sell quickly. ... pay lots of money for tickets – the cheapest tickets are only $10. And ... go to the United Center for tickets, you can buy them online. The United Center is always busy, so ... get there early before the game starts. And remember: ... take your own food – you can buy hot dogs and potato chips there.

Ben Gordon

5 Write about Ben Gordon and the Chicago Bulls players. Use *have to / don't have to / doesn't have to.*

Ben Gordon doesn't have to ..., but he ... . The players ...

Ben:
- ✘ get up early
- ✔ go to the gym every day
- ✔ relax between games
- ✘ play in every game

The players:
- ✔ stay healthy
- ✘ eat special food
- ✔ play together as a team
- ✘ practise together every day

Imperative

→ Summary, page 134

6 What adults say to pupils at school

Match the sentences with the places.

→ music room • classroom • gym • playground • library • swimming pool

1 Don't forget to do your homework.
2 Go back to your classrooms! Break has finished.
3 Throw the ball to your partner.
4 Don't run or you'll fall! It's wet.
5 Practise that song again, please.
6 Please be quiet and don't write in that book.

7 Classroom phrases

a) What pupils say to other pupils: Make five sentences.

Please	(don't)	talk to me	in English • in German • now • ...
		give me	the dictionary • the book • that pen • ...
		look at	my answers • the exercise • the map • ...
		kick	my bag • my foot • the table • ...

b) Work with a partner. Write more classroom phrases. Collect the phrases on the board and write them in your exercise book.

→ be • help me • do • explain • take • write

EXTRA PRACTICE

Should / Shouldn't

→ Summary, page 135

8 Candice's advice

a) April has a problem. Read Candice's advice.

b) Pick the right answer.

April has a problem with ...

1 her homework
2 bullies
3 her parents

9 The school yearbook

Every year a team of students makes a yearbook. Candice is giving advice to a younger student. Put in the words in the box.

→ be (2x) • forget • have • help • look

You know the yearbook should ... students to remember their school days. So the yearbook should ... everybody's photos and names in it. And of course you shouldn't ... the teachers! There should ... something about sports, special school activities and parties. The book should ... good but it shouldn't ... expensive.

10 Advice for Candice

Pick one of Candice's problems. Give her advice.

I don't like the food at school.

I can't sleep.

I need new clothes.

My mom has lost her job.

You should ...
You shouldn't ...

Must / Mustn't

→ Summary, page 135

11 Match the school rules with the pictures.

1 You mustn't use cellphones.
2 You must have the right books and pens.
3 You mustn't eat or drink in class.
4 You must listen when others speak.
5 You mustn't be late.
6 You must turn off the lights when you leave.

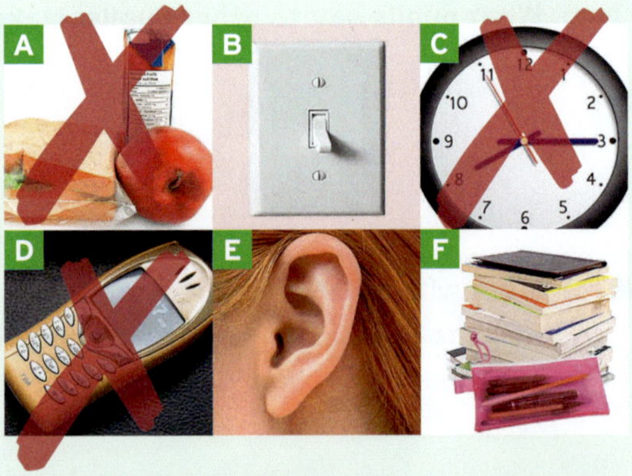

12 Homecoming

a) Read this report by an exchange student about homecoming. Put in *must* or *mustn't*.

In homecoming week, old students visit their school. Students at the school ... do lots of activities. At Sullivan High students wear different clothes: one day girls ... wear boys' clothes and boys ... wear girls' clothes. On another day students ... come to school in the school colours: blue and gold. This is the day of the big homecoming game. You ... miss it!

b) Finish the report about the homecoming dance. Use the notes.

- students decorate school in school colours
  Students must decorate the school in the school colours.
- students pick homecoming king or queen
- students wear nice clothes
- not wear jeans
- teachers and parents be there too
- students from other schools not come

TEST PRACTICE

13 Sport and me

a) Find an object for a sport that you do or that you like watching on TV: a football, a helmet, ...

b) Make notes:

- Say what your object is and what it's like.

Tip: Use colours and words like *new*, *expensive*, ...

- Talk about when/where you do this sport or when/where you watch it.

Tip: Use the simple present for activities that you often do.

- Say why you picked this sport.

Tip: Use *because*.

c) Show a partner your object and talk about it. Use your notes.

Tip: Talk in complete sentences.

- football shirt
- red, number 7
- play every Saturday
- school team
- watch matches on TV
- like football, fast and exciting

I'm going to talk about football. This is my football shirt. It's red with the number 7. I play football every Saturday with the school team. I watch matches on TV too. I like football because it's fast and exciting.

REVISION Simple past

→ Summary, page 133

1 Natalie's first trip to America

a) What two things did Natalie like?

NATALIE: My aunt moved to Seattle in America many years ago. Last June she wrote an e-mail and she invited me to visit her. Of course I said yes! On July 10th, I went by plane from Frankfurt to Seattle. The trip took 13 hours. That evening my aunt picked me up at the airport in Seattle and we drove to her house. It was only 7 p.m., but I was very tired and I fell into bed! The next day we visited the centre of Seattle. It was beautiful. I ate my first American hamburger and it was great!

b) Draw this table in your exercise book. Put in all the simple past forms in the text. Then put in the infinitives.

Simple past	Infinitive
moved	*move*
wrote	...

c) Now find the time words.

Many years ago, ...

2 Natalie's work experience: Put the infinitives in the simple past.

Last summer, when I (**be**) in Seattle, I (**work**) in my aunt's German restaurant. I (**get**) up very early every morning. I (**take**) the bus to the centre and then I (**walk**) ten minutes to the restaurant. First I (**go**) to the supermarket with my aunt and we (**buy**) lots of vegetables and fruit. Then I (**help**) in the kitchen. We (**eat**) lunch at 12 o'clock. The restaurant (**be**) very busy at lunchtime, so we only (**have**) ten minutes. In the afternoon we (**make**) the food for the evening. At 5 o'clock I (**finish**) work.

List of irregular verbs p. 197

3 NOW YOU Pick a) or b) and write a paragraph (60–80 words).

a) Think of a special trip. When was it? Where? How did you travel? Who went with you? What happened?

b) Have you had a part-time job? Where was it? What was the job? What did you have to do? Did you like the work?

REVISION Adjectives

→ Summary, page 136

4 All about Seattle

Pick the right adjectives and finish the paragraph about Seattle.

Seattle isn't the capital of Washington (that's Olympia), but it's the biggest/smallest city in the state. There are lots of new buildings, so the city looks very old/modern. There are lots of shops, people and traffic in the centre, so it's always very busy/quiet. And it's a very boring/interesting city because it has great museums, restaurants and clubs. The area near Seattle is beautiful/bad with its mountains, sea, islands and lake.

5 All about Anacortes

Put some of the adjectives into the text.

beautiful • busy • clean • cold • exciting • friendly • interesting • long • modern • new • nice • old • quiet • small

I live in Anacortes. It's a ... town in Washington State. It's on a ... island – Fidalgo Island. There are lots of ... buildings from the 1880s here. Only 15,000 people live in Anacortes, so it's very ... in winter. But in summer there are lots of visitors, so the town is very ... There's a ... supermarket here, where you can get everything. But there are lots of ..., ... shops too. Come to Anacortes – it's a ... town!

6 All about your town or village

Now write about a place that you know (60–80 words).

Tip:
Use lots of adjectives and make your text interesting. Exercise 5 can help you.

ing-form

→ Summary, page 134

7 Leavenworth, Washington

a) Write the text in your exercise book. Put the verbs in the *ing*-form.

(**Live**) in Leavenworth in the 1960s wasn't easy. (**Find**) a job was a problem then. So people started (**leave**) the town and (**look**) for work in other places. Then some people had an idea – they thought of (**make**) Leavenworth a German town! So they started (**change**) the shops, hotels, cafes and houses. Today Leavenworth looks like a town in Bavaria! So if you're interested in (**visit**) a German town in the USA, you should go to Leavenworth. If you like (**listen**) to the music of Bavaria – Leavenworth is the place for you! And if you like (**ski**), (**hike**) in the mountains, (**eat**) German food and (**sing**) German songs, visit Leavenworth.

b) Joel and Leanne have no plans for the weekend. Finish their dialogue.

LEANNE
Hey, Joel, do you want to go  ?
What about  to the ocean?
Well, are you interested in 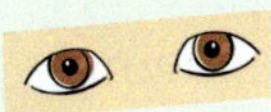 Leavenworth?

You can go !
It's a great place for  .

JOEL
– No thanks. 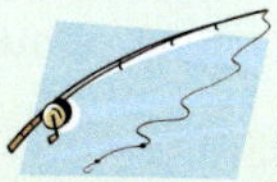 is boring!
– It's too far! And I hate  when it's hot!
– Leavenworth? What can you do there?
– No thanks!!!
– OK, let's go! I love  .

c) Make an advert for Leavenworth. Use phrases like:
Do you like ...? Are you interested in ...? Do you want to try ...? What about ...?

8 A Native American story

Telling stories is an important tradition for Native Americans. Their stories are often about animals. Here's a popular Native American story from Washington. It's about two birds – a raven and a crow.

a) Can you guess what kind of birds a *raven* and a *crow* are?

Tip:
Think of the names of birds in German. Then check in a dictionary.

"Looking for food isn't my favourite activity," Raven thought. "Working is stupid. I prefer sitting here in my tree, doing nothing. I love watching all the other animals when they collect food for the winter." But winter came and Raven had no food. He was hungry. So he went to his friend, Crow. Crow had lots of food for the winter. "Crow, you like singing! Right?" Raven asked. "Er, yes," Crow answered. "But I'm not very good at singing," he said. "Oh, that isn't true," Raven said. "You're famous for your great singing!" "Really?" Crow said. He was very happy. "Yes," Raven said. "So what about having a big winter party, with lots of nice food? And you can sing." "OK," said Crow and he started making the food. Raven went to all the other animals in the forest and he invited them to 'his' party. Lots of animals arrived and Crow started singing. Raven and the other animals started eating. "Another song!" Raven shouted. So Crow sang lots of songs. But when everybody had finished eating, poor Crow could only sing "caw, caw." And today crows can't sing. They can only say "caw, caw."

b) Read the story and put these pictures in the right order.

c) Answer these questions about the text.

1 What's an important tradition for Native Americans?
2 What activities didn't Raven like?
3 What did Crow like doing?
4 What did the other animals do when Crow started singing?

Tip:
We often use *ing*-forms when we talk about hobbies and activities.
Example: singing, reading, playing football, ...

9 What about your hobbies? Finish these sentences.

1 Playing ... is my favourite sport.
2 I think ... is stupid!
3 I like reading, ...
4 I love ...
5 I often go ...
6 I'm not very good at ...
7 I never go ...
8 I hate ...

TEST PRACTICE

10 SAY IT IN GERMAN

Pick one of the brochures and tell your partner about it – in German, of course.

A

Anacortes

A natural destination for your North-West vacation

Kayaking • Fishing • Boat trips • Whale watching
Hiking • Shopping • Walking on the beach

B

Hobuck Beach
Campground and Resort

Come see the beaches!

– Relax
– Watch wild animals
– Hike
– Fish
– Surf
– Swim

Visit us at the Hobuck Campground & Resort in Neah Bay, Washington, along the coast of the Pacific North-West.

Tip:
Only talk about the main points.
You can use a dictionary.

11 Port Townsend: Pick a) or b).

a) Write an advert for Port Townsend (30–40 words).
b) Write a short article about Port Townsend for a tourist magazine (60–80 words).

PORT TOWNSEND

State	Washington
Population	8800
Activities	Boat trips, fishing, shopping, swimming, hiking, whale watching, kayaking, cycling
Visitor Center	2437 E Sims Way, Port Townsend, WA 98368
Internet	ptguide.com

12 An e-mail to a visitor centre

You want to visit Port Townsend next summer. Write an e-mail to the visitor centre there (60–80 words).
Write about these points:

Are you travelling with your family or with friends?
How many people are going to travel to Port Townsend?
How long do you want to stay?
What activities do you want to do?

You have questions about:

the weather in June / Port Townsend /
a campground in Port Townsend

To: ptguide.com Date: May 1st
Subject: a holiday in Port Townsend

Dear Sir/Madam,

I'm planning a holiday in Port Townsend next month. I'm travelling with my ...

EXTRA PRACTICE

REVISION *Will*-future

→ Summary, p. 134

The Fourth of July is **Independence Day**, an important day in America. On July 4th, 1776, the USA became free from Britain. Most cities and towns have Fourth of July festivals.

1 Fourth of July hopes

a) Look at the weather for July 4th and read what Ramon and his mum say. Who will be right?

RAMON: I hope it'll be really hot and sunny on the Fourth of July. And I hope it won't rain later because of the fireworks.

RAMON'S MOM: I hope it won't be wet, of course. But I hope it won't be too hot, I like it best when it's cloudy.

b) Finish the advert for Miami's Fourth of July celebrations with *will*, *'ll* or *won't*.

MIAMI BEACH

At 7 p. m. on the Fourth of July, there will be a special celebration: children from other countries who live in Miami **(1)** ... become Americans. Later there **(2)** ... be a free concert by Carlos Oliva. Fireworks **(3)** ... start at 10 p.m. There **(4)** ... be a better place to be on the Fourth of July! The celebrations **(5)** ... be on the beach at 10th Street and Ocean Drive.

TROPICAL PARK

There **(6)** ... be lots of Fourth of July activities. But there **(7)** ... be food, so bring a picnic. And make other plans for the evening: there **(8)** ... be fireworks here in Tropical Park.

2 A Fourth of July picnic: Put in the right words.

→ cook • ask • look • take • buy • wear

1 Dad: I'll ... some drinks at the supermarket.
2 Ramon: I'll ... my guitar with me.
3 Mom: I'll ... some chicken.
4 Grandma: I'll ... my new shoes.
5 Ramon: I'll ... for the camera.
6 Ana: I'll ... my friend to come.

3 Future hopes

a) For a Fourth of July project, Ramon is writing about his hopes for his country and family for the next year. Look at Ramon's notes. Write his sentences.

I hope mom will ... . I hope dad won't ...

– mom find better job
– dad not have another accident
– mom and dad win some money
– not be any more problems with hurricanes
– the Miami Heat win all their games
– I learn to play the guitar better
– I not have any problems at school
– I get a girlfriend

b) Write 5–8 sentences about your hopes for the future.

REVISION Prepositions of place

→ Summary, p. 137

4 Look at the pictures. Pick the right word.

1 The guitar is between / opposite the chair and the bed.
2 The two women are behind / in front of the man.
3 The CDs are on / under the table.
4 The piano is above / opposite the door.
5 The photographer is in front of / between the band.
6 The club is next to / above the cafe.

5 Eight things are different. Write them in your exercise book.

In picture 1, KC is standing between BB and TJ. In picture 2, TJ is standing ...

6 An interesting picture

a) Find a picture from a magazine or the Internet with lots of things on it. Write about it. Say where things are and why the picture is interesting. Don't say people's names!

b) Put the pictures on the board. Read out your description. Can the class guess the picture?

Adverbs

→ Summary, p. 137

7 Match the pictures with the sentences.

A

B

C

D

E

F
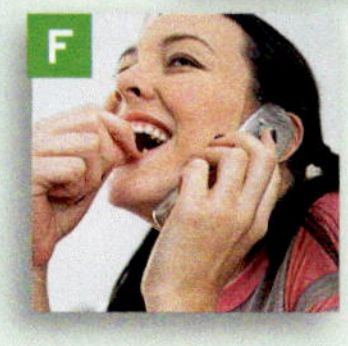

Tip:
It's not only important WHAT people say. HOW people say it will help you to understand.

1 She's speaking loudly.
2 She's speaking sadly.
3 She's speaking happily.
4 She's speaking nervously.
5 She's speaking angrily.
6 She's speaking politely.

8 Downloading music

a) Finish the text. Use adverbs.

Lots of people download music on the Internet. In my opinion, downloading music is great. You can get songs (**fast**) and very (**cheap**). Some musicians say they work (**hard**) and we take their songs (**illegal**). But some musicians think (**different**): they don't make CDs, they put their songs on the Internet.
I think things will change (**complete**) soon. Everybody will download music and not buy expensive CDs.

b) What do you think?

I think downloading music is ... because ... . In the future I think / don't think that ...

9 Rewrite the sentences for an article about a concert.

1 Bobbie sang his new song. He was confident.
Bobbie sang his new song confidently.
2 The fans sang. They were very loud.
3 Bobbie danced. His dancing was good.
4 The fans screamed. They were wild.
5 Bobbie smiled. He was happy.
6 He walked off the stage. He was tired.

10 AND YOU?

a) Say what you think your partner does ...

– well
– confidently
– carefully
– easily
– dangerously
– loudly
– nervously
– badly

b) If your partner agrees with your sentences, you can read them to the class.

Alex plays football well.
He plays his guitar loudly.

11 SAY IT IN ENGLISH **Your American friend Pauline has a letter in German, but she doesn't understand everything. Tell her in English what it means.**

Klara says thanks for your letter. The concert sounds ... . She'd like to ...

Liebe Pauline!

Danke für deinen Brief. Der Konzert klingt super, ich würde auch gern Gwen Stefani auf der Bühne sehen. Ich finde, sie singt wirklich gut auf ihrer letzten CD. Waren die Karten teuer? Letzte Woche habe ich Karten für "Tokio Hotel" gekauft – das ist eine deutsche Band, aber die Jungs singen auch auf Englisch. Und sie singen toll. Du kannst Lieder von ihrer Website billig herunterladen.

Ich schreibe dir bald wieder.

Viele Grüße von Klara

Tip:
Read the letter and pick the main points. Say these in English – you don't have to translate everything.

TEST PRACTICE

12 INTERPRETING You and your American friend have been to dinner with your grandma. Practise the dialogue with two partners.

FRIEND	Could you say thank you for dinner, please?
YOU	Er sagt, ...
GRANDMA	Keine Ursache.
YOU	She says ...
GRANDMA	Darf ich ein Bild von euch machen?
YOU	Do you mind if she ...
FRIEND	Go ahead.
YOU	...
GRANDMA	Ich kann leider nicht so gut fotografieren, aber ich werde dir das Bild schicken.
YOU	...

13 Partner A: Look at the information about Beyoncé's concert. Answer your partner's questions. Then ask Partner B about Gwen Stefani's concert.

Partner B: Ask Partner A about Beyoncé's concert. Then look at the information about Gwen Stefani's concert and answer your partner's questions.

A Beyoncé

Date:	May 22	Time:	8:00 p.m.
Venue:	Bank Center	Cost:	$69
Address:	One Panther Parkway, Fort Lauderdale, FL 33323		
Phone:	(954) 835-8000		
Event Details:	Beyoncé, with opening act Robin Thicke, will be live in concert at the Bank Center		

Ask your partner:
- where the concert is
- when it is
- when it starts
- how much tickets are

B Gwen Stefani

Date:	May 09	Time:	7:30 p.m.
Venue:	Sound Theater	Cost:	$10–$69.50
Address:	601-7 Sansbury's Way, West Palm Beach, FL 33411		
Phone:	(561) 793-0445		
Event Details:	Gwen Stefani is coming to town and she's bringing special guests Akon and Lady Sovereign with her!		

Ask your partner:
- where the concert is
- when it is
- when it starts
- how much tickets are

14 Write a letter to Ramon (about 100 words). Tell him about:

Tip:
Use phrases like *I believe, I think ...*

- **what kind of music you like and your favourite singers and bands**
- **how often you listen to music and how:** MP3 player / Internet / CDs or music TV / ...
- **what you think of downloading free music on the Internet:** great / not fair to musicians / ...
- **if you watch music awards and talent contests and what you think of them:** OK / boring / ...

EXTRA PRACTICE

REVISION Simple present / Simple past

→ Summary, pp. 132, 133

1 On the Oregon coast: Pick the right form – simple present or simple past.

Every summer lots of tourists (go/went) to the Oregon coast. It ('s/was) beautiful. There (are/were) beaches, rocks and forests. Last August Laura's family (take/took) Martin there for a weekend. The first day (is/was) sunny, so they (spend/spent) lots of time on the beach. But on Saturday morning the weather (changes/changed). "The weather often (changes/changed) suddenly here," the receptionist at the Sunset Motel (tells/told) them. "I (have/had) an idea," Laura (says/said). "I (want/wanted) to show Martin the Oregon dunes." "Where are they?" Martin (asks/asked). "You'll see," Laura (answers/answered).

REVISION Simple past / Past progressive

→ Summary, p. 133

2 Fun in the dunes

a) Put the verbs in the simple past.

The Russells (**leave**) the motel at 2 o'clock on Saturday afternoon. While they were driving along Highway 101, Laura (**see**) a sign: SPINREEL DUNES. They (**turn**) left. They were going along a small road when Martin (**shout**), "Wow!" The dunes (**look**) fantastic – they're more than 100 metres high! While they were walking in the dunes, they (**hear**) a noise. It was getting nearer when suddenly they (**see**) it. "It's a dune buggy," Dylan (**say**).

b) Now put these verbs in the past progressive.

It was a very big dune buggy and it (**go**) very fast. Six people (**sit**) in it and they (**have**) a great time. They (**shout**) and (**laugh**). While Martin (**take**) a photo, the Russels ran out of the dunes quickly. "Those people (**ride**) a dune buggy on the beach! Is that OK?" Martin asked. "Yes," Laura answered. "But only in special places."

3 Martin's e-mail

Martin is writing an e-mail to his family. He's telling Laura what's in the e-mail. Pick the main points and explain them in English.

I'm writing that I'm on the Oregon coast with you and ...
It's fantastic ...
We're staying ...
From my room ...

Hallo zu Hause,

ich bin gerade mit Laura und ihrer Familie an der Küste in Oregon. Es ist toll hier. Wir übernachten in einem kleinen Hotel. Von meinem Zimmer kann ich das Meer sehen. Und am Strand gibt es riesige Dünen! Als wir durch die Dünen liefen, haben wir "dune buggies" gesehen. Das sind so kleine Wagen, die durch die Dünen fahren. Die fuhren vielleicht schnell! Heute ist mein letzter Tag.

REVISION *Mustn't* → Summary, p. 135

4 Beach rules

a) Look at the sign. Find six things that you mustn't do:

You mustn't make ...
You mustn't bring ...
You mustn't use ...
You mustn't ...

b) SAY IT IN GERMAN
Pick three rules on the sign. Tell a partner what they mean.

Tip: Use a dictionary.

Passive → Summary, p. 138

5 Native American history

Put in *is*, *are*, *was*, *were*.

When Europeans first came to America, other people were living there. In the past they ... called *Indians* by the Europeans. Today these people ... called *Native Americans*. But sometimes the name *Indians* ... used today too. In the 1860s the east part of America ... taken by the Europeans. The Native Americans ... sent west. Then more Europeans came to America. So more land ... needed. In the end, reservations ... established. The Native Americans ... sent to these reservations.

Indian land 1492

Indian land 1890

6 A famous Native American

Put in *was/were* and these verbs:

→ killed (2x) • born • shown • called (2x) • changed

In 1829 a baby ... in Arizona. He ... Goyathlay. He was Native American. As a boy, he ... how to hunt, ride horses and swim. One day, when Goyathlay was away, white people came to his village and his family ... . On that day, Goyathlay's life ... . Later people gave him a new name – now he ... *Geronimo*. He was angry with the white people because they took Native American land. So the Indian Wars started and many people ... . Geronimo became very famous.

EXTRA PRACTICE

If-clauses (type II)

→ Summary, p. 138

7 City dreams: Laura Russell lives in the country. But she often dreams of living in the city. Finish her dreams.

1 If I could live anywhere, I'd live in the city.
2 If I lived in the city, I'd go …
3 But if I went out with friends every evening, I …
4 And if I was tired, …
5 If I wasn't good at school, …
6 If I didn't get a good job, …
7 If I didn't make enough money, …
8 If I didn't go out often, life in the city …
9 If life in the city wasn't interesting, I'd prefer …
So I think I'll stay in the country!!!

8 Country dreams: Martin Maier dreams of living in the country – in America. Look at the pictures and write about some of his dreams.

MARTIN: If I lived in America, I'd … / I wouldn't …

9 Your dreams: Pick a) or b) and write a paragraph.

a) Imagine that you could live where you wanted.

Where would you live? Would you live in a city or in the country? What would you do there? What kind of a house or flat would you live in? What hobbies would you have?

b) Imagine that you won a million euros.

What would you do with the money? What would you buy? Who would you give money to? Where would you live? What countries would you visit? Would you help people? Who?

TEST PRACTICE

10 Instructions in English

Your neighbour has bought a new photocopier and a laptop for his office.

a) Which instructions (A/B) are for the photocopier, which are for the laptop?

A

Xpect user's guide

1 Insert the battery pack.
2 Connect the cable to the telephone line.
3 Plug in the power cord.
4 Open.
5 Turn on by pressing the power button.

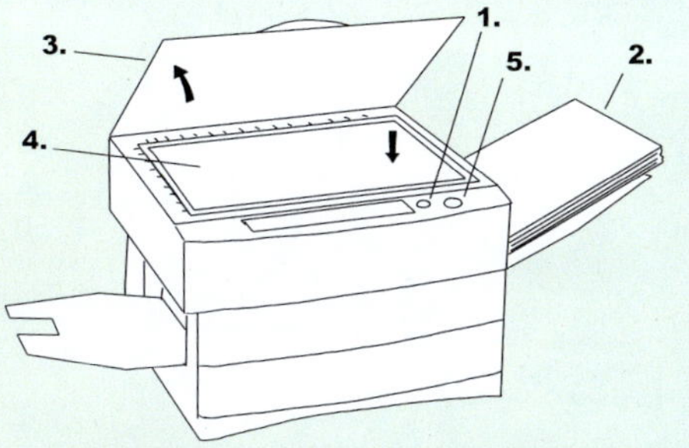

B

PIXON MT 500

Press button (1) to turn on.
Put paper in the auto feeder (2).
Lift the cover (3).
Put in your document (4).
Close the cover and press the "copy" button (5).

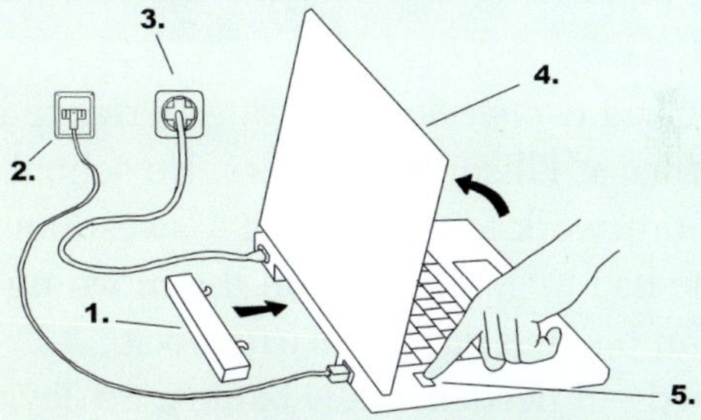

b) SAY IT IN GERMAN Help your neighbour and explain the instructions.

11 SPEAKING

a) Talk about the picture.
- **What can you see?**
- **What are the people doing?**

b) AND YOU?
- **Would you like to work here?**
- **Why?/Why not?**
- **Where would you like to work?**

12 WRITING Life in Germany

Your American penfriend wants to know all about your life in Germany. Write a letter (about 100 words) and tell him/her: where you live; what it's like there; the food you like; about your flat/house; your hobbies; your family; your school and if Germany is different from the USA.

Tip:
Don't forget
- your address,
- the date,
- how you start a letter,
- how you finish a letter.
Look at page 77 for help.

ISN'T TECHNOLOGY AWESOME?

2 26

Read the story. Then make a comic: ask your teacher for a copy of the story. Write what Taylor and Alexa say or think in the pictures.

Taylor had two weeks of work experience in the office at Ellison and Peters. No school and homework for two weeks – awesome! But he had to get up early in the morning. And on his first day his alarm clock stopped – it needed a new battery. So Taylor got to the office late.

Alexa showed Taylor the office. She was doing work experience too and she was really nice. She explained Taylor's jobs for the morning. First he had to make some copies and put them in the right files. It sounded very easy. "Yeah, no problem," Taylor said. Alexa smiled.

The photocopier in the office was bigger than the photocopier at school. Taylor tried different buttons for ten minutes: nothing happened. He read the instructions in the book near the photocopier and found the problem. But then the photocopier made 20 copies and Taylor only wanted one! "Dumb machine," he said.

Then Taylor had to find some information on the Internet. He loved the Internet. It was so easy to find information! Taylor found the website that he needed. But before he could print out the pages, the dumb computer crashed. "No problem," Taylor said to Alexa. He restarted the computer and found the information. The computer crashed again.

▸ You can find new words in the *Dictionary* (pages 160–179).

At lunch Taylor ate his sandwiches alone. The others read e-mails or played computer games. Nobody talked. After lunch Taylor went to the drinks machine to get a hot chocolate. But there was a big sign: "Out of order". "Why do these dumb machines never work?" thought Taylor. He got a glass of water from the kitchen.

In the afternoon Taylor had to scan in some pictures. Easy! His parents had a scanner at home, so he knew how to scan in things. But this machine used different software and Taylor didn't understand it. He looked at it for a long time and then saw Alexa. "Er, Alexa," he said. "I have a problem. Can you help me?"

After his first day, Taylor wasn't very happy. Alexa felt sorry for him. She asked if he wanted to meet her later. Of course Taylor wanted to see her! He really liked Alexa and he wanted to know her better. He felt happier now. Alexa put his number in her cellphone. "I'll send you a text message when I've been shopping," she said. "I need about an hour."

Taylor went to an Internet cafe and waited for Alexa's text message. He read the sports news and wrote an e-mail. After an hour he looked at his cellphone. It wasn't charged up! And he didn't have Alexa's number ... Another phone beeped. "A text from my daughter in England," a man at the next computer said to him. He smiled. "Isn't technology awesome?"

THE ROAD TO FREEDOM

2 27

The true story of Harriet Tubman

Harriet sat on the floor with a baby in her arms. The house was quiet. Her mother and brothers were working in the tobacco fields. Her father was working in the forest. And Harriet was looking after this little white baby.

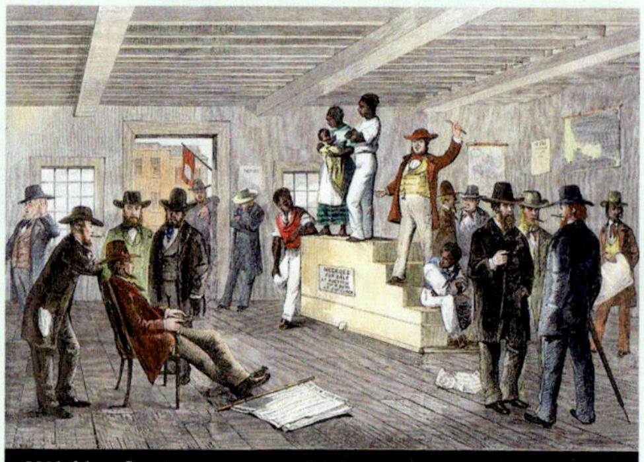
White farmers could buy and sell slaves.

The year was 1827 and the place was Maryland, on the east coast of America. It was a nice spring day – a day for running and playing in the fields. But Harriet was a black girl and a slave. She was the daughter of slaves and the granddaughter of slaves. A hundred years earlier, white people had taken her great-grandmother from her home in Africa. They had brought her to America and had sold her to a tobacco farmer. Harriet and her family "belonged" to a white farmer, Mr Brodess. They called him "Master". So Harriet never played in the fields. She was only a child – 8 years old – but she had to work.

People said that things were different in the northern states like Pennsylvania, New York and New Jersey. Some people said that there were no slaves there. They said that black people were free. They said that black children didn't have to work. All children went to school.

Harriet lived in a small cabin.

But Harriet didn't go to school. Her days were always the same. She got up before the sun. She had to make fires in the big house. She swept the floors. Then she helped in the kitchen. And sometimes she looked after Mr and Mrs Brodess's baby. She worked for 14 hours every day. At night she went back to the cabin where her family lived.

Tip:
Write what happens on each page.
Write the most important things.
You can use the *simple present*.

READING LOG 1 Write notes when you're reading the story.

Page 122: Harriet lives in a cabin with ...
She works in ...
She gets up ...
She makes ... / helps ... / looks after ...

Page 123: One day Harriet takes ...
Mrs Brodess ...
...

Page 124: Harriet leaves ...
She walks ...
...

Page 125: Harriet finds ...
She remembers ...
...

► You can find new words in the *Dictionary* (pages 160–179).

Harriet was often hungry. She saw the nice food that the Brodess family ate, but she couldn't eat it. One day she took some sugar. But Mrs Brodess saw her and was angry. She hit Harriet. Harriet lost her job in the big house. So she had to work in the fields. And that was very hard work. In the summer it was hot. In the winter it was cold and it often rained. But Harriet didn't complain – she was always a happy girl. She sang in the fields every day and the other workers liked listening to her. She made them feel happy too.

Slaves had to work hard in the fields.

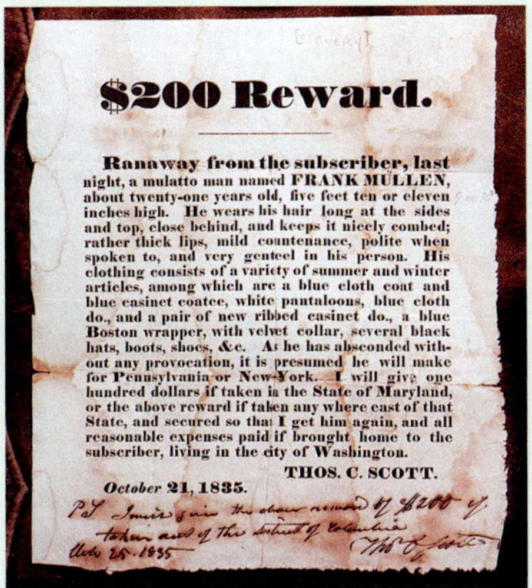
$200 Reward.

Ranaway from the subscriber, last night, a mulatto man named FRANK MULLEN, about twenty-one years old, five feet ten or eleven inches high. He wears his hair long at the sides and top, close behind, and keeps it nicely combed; rather thick lips, mild countenance, polite when spoken to, and very genteel in his person. His clothing consists of a variety of summer and winter articles, among which are a blue cloth coat and blue casinet coatee, white pantaloons, blue cloth do., and a pair of new ribbed casinet do., a blue Boston wrapper, with velvet collar, several black hats, boots, shoes, &c. As he has absconded without any provocation, it is presumed he will make for Pennsylvania or New-York. I will give one hundred dollars if taken in the State of Maryland, or the above reward if taken any where east of that State, and secured so that I get him again, and all reasonable expenses paid if brought home to the subscriber, living in the city of Washington.

THOS. C. SCOTT.

October 21, 1835.

Lots of slaves escaped to the north.

News came to the farm that the slaves in other states in the north of America were free now. But it was different in Maryland and in the states in the south. Slaves were important there on the tobacco and cotton farms. Harriet heard that slaves were escaping to the north. She heard that in some places they were fighting against their masters. Harriet listened to these stories and she dreamed of a better future.

Years passed. Harriet worked in the fields every day. She became very strong and fit. But she didn't want to be a slave. She dreamed of escaping to the north and living as a free woman. But how? She "belonged" to the master. He had lots of men who watched the slaves. He had dogs too!

One day a little boy came to Harriet in the fields. He was crying. He had some bad news. The Brodess family planned to sell their slaves to a cotton farm in the south. Harriet knew that she had to do something.

READING LOG 2 Say what you think about:

HARRIET	– I think she's ...
MR AND MRS BRODESS	– I think they're ...
BRODESS'S HOUSE	– I think ...
HARRIET'S CABIN	– ...
THE STORY OF HARRIET'S GREAT-GRANDMOTHER	– ...
HARRIET'S LIFE AS A SLAVE	– ...

Tip:
Use words like:
small - poor - nice - terrible - big - happy - sad - confident - difficult - good - bad
Write more notes like this about Harriet after page 125.

2 29

That night Harriet got a bag and some food. She waited till everybody was in bed. Then she left her parents' cabin quietly. She didn't say goodbye to her mother and father because she knew that they would be too sad. But she knew that she'd come back for them one day.

Work on the cotton farms was very hard.

Harriet waited, watched and listened. The farm was quiet. Then she walked across the fields. She went into the forest. She followed the North Star. She was excited because she was on the *Road to Freedom*. But she was frightened too. She knew that if the Master's men found her, they'd beat her. So she was very careful. Before the morning she stopped near a small river and slept for two or three hours.

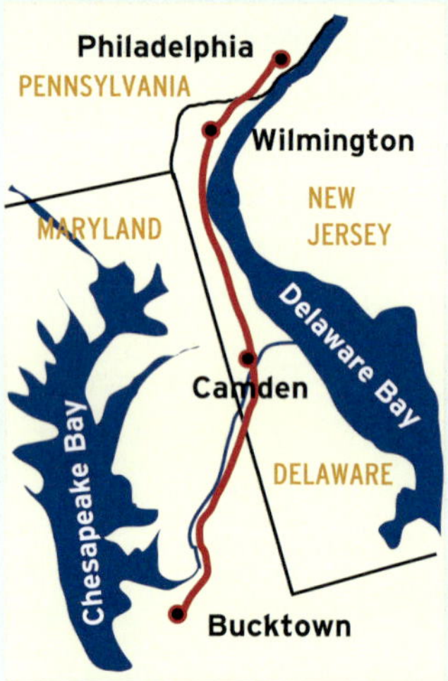

Harriet's *Road to Freedom*

In the morning she looked at the trees. She knew that the side with moss was the north side. She didn't walk on roads because that was dangerous. On the third day, at night, she heard dogs. The Master's men were looking for her. Then she remembered something that her father had told her. If you go across a river, dogs can't find you. She came to a big river and she jumped into the cold, black water. She waited behind some rocks. She could see the men and their dogs, but they couldn't see her.

For six days and nights Harriet walked across the country. When she saw a farm or a town, she went around them. Sometimes she heard men on horses, so she stayed in the forest. At last she came to the city of Philadelphia in Pennsylvania. This was a state with no slaves. Harriet was now a free woman.

READING LOG 3 Harriet's diary

Imagine you're Harriet. Pick one day and write your diary for a part of the trip to the north.

DAY 1 It was very late. Mom and pop were in bed. My brothers were in bed too. I got my bag and ...
DAY 2 It was early in the morning. I was tired. I looked at the trees. The moss ...
DAY 3 It was night. I was in a forest. It was quiet. Suddenly I heard ...
DAY 6 At last I was in ...

Tip:
Say how you felt. Use words like:
frightened - happy - sad - terrible - nervous - cold - hungry - lonely - tired - excited - safe.
Use your own ideas for the diary:
- I saw some slaves in a field. They ...
- The weather was ...
- I found some apples and I ...
- The city was ...

2◉30 Harriet found a job and an apartment in Philadelphia. Now she got $2 per week for her work. This was new for her. It was exciting too. But she didn't forget the people at home in Maryland. She wanted to help them to escape too, so she started to make plans. After a year in Philadelphia she had some money and lots of friends. So she went back to Maryland and started to help other slaves to escape – on the *Road to Freedom*. She guided them through the fields and forests at night. She knew that this was dangerous for her. But Harriet was very brave. She helped hundreds of black men, women and children – her own family too. There were posters with her picture everywhere: "$10,000 reward for Harriet Tubman!" Harriet was famous.

She helped other slaves to escape.

In 1861 a terrible war started between the states of the north and the states of the south.
When the war was over, all slaves were free.

Now things were better for black people. But there were lots of other problems. Black people were very poor. Many didn't have good jobs or houses. Many were hungry. Harriet Tubman helped these poor black people. She got money from the government. She built hospitals, schools and homes. She helped people all her life.

READING LOG 4 Pick one of these activities:

You can use ideas from reading log 1.

- **Write a short summary of Harriet's story.**
  This story is about a girl. She lives in Maryland in ...
  Her family ... . She works ...
- **Write a review of the story.**
  I think that this is a good/interesting/sad/ ... story because ... . I like it when ... . I don't like it when ...
- **Design a cover for a book about Harriet Tubman.**
  Think of a title. Find some photos on the Internet. Write a short text for the back of the book.
- **Imagine you can do an interview with Harriet for an American newspaper.**
  What questions would you ask? What do you think she'd answer?

Tip:
You can get more information and pictures on the Internet. Use a search engine and put in *"Harriet Tubman"*.

Wordbank 1

Unit 1

Meat and fish

beef, chicken, ham, salmon, sausage

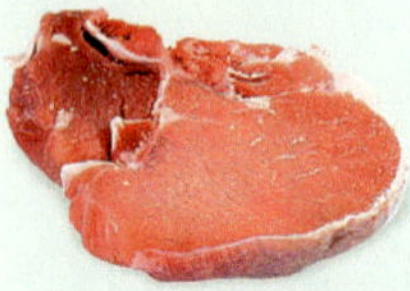
pork

lamb

squid

bacon

tuna

Fruit

apples, bananas, oranges

plums

strawberries

pears

cherries

melon

Vegetables

leeks, lettuce, potatoes, tomatoes

cauliflower

beans

pepper

mushrooms

broccoli

Other food

bread/roll, cheese, chips, eggs, hamburger, pizza

rice

pasta

soup

stew

biscuits

Wordbank 2

Unit 2

Photo A
surfers, walk along the beach, carry surfboards, wear wetsuits, blue sky, sunny

Photo B
stalls, bags, T-shirts, buy clothes, sit on a chair, look at the stall, nice weather

Photo C
drive on the highway, lots of cars and buses, traffic jam, road signs, busy, hot

Photo D
walk along the street, busy, carry shopping bags, wear sunglasses, no cars

Photo E
ride a bike, go in-line skating, mountains, blue sky, sunny weather, palm trees along the boardwalk

Photo F
famous Hollywood sign, cars, drive along street, trees, mountain, nice day

Photo G
ask for money, hold a sign and a cup, long grey beard, blanket round his shoulders, look cold

Photo H
city with skyscrapers, grey sky, lots of trees, smog, pollution

Photo I
lots of people, busy, nice day, blue sky, castle, bridge, flags

beard *Bart*; blanket round his shoulders *Decke um die Schultern*; carry *tragen*; grey *grau*; highway (AE) *Fernstraße*; palm tree *Palme*; pollution *Umweltverschmutzung*; sunglasses *Sonnenbrille*; sky *Himmel*; skyscraper *Wolkenkratzer, Hochhaus*; tree *Baum*; traffic jam *(Verkehrs-)Stau*; wetsuit *Surf-/Tauch(schutz)anzug*

Wordbank 3

Unit 2

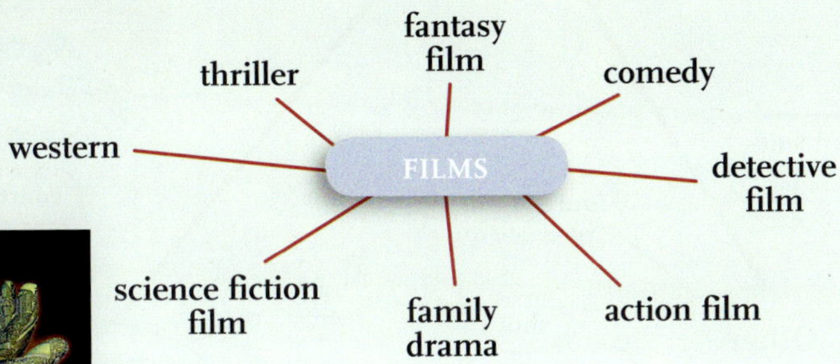

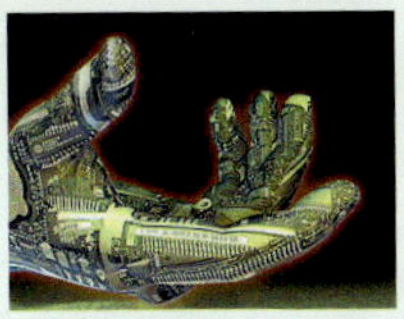

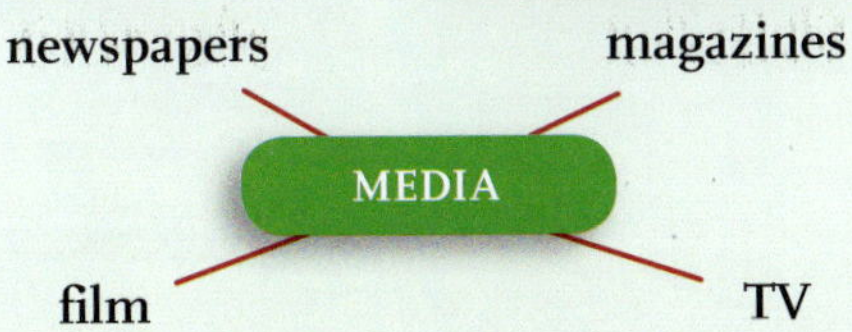

family drama *Familienfilm*; soap *Seifenoper, Unterhaltungsserie*; courtroom drama *Gerichtsshow, -sendung*; documentary *Dokumentarfilm*; sitcom *„Situationskomödie", Comedy-Serie*; talent contest *Talentwettbewerb*

Wordbank 4

Unit 3

SPORT

Sports gear

- shorts
- jogging trousers
- glove
- T-shirt
- trainers
- helmet
- boots

People in sport

- referee
- cheerleader
- player
- trainer
- team
- goalkeeper
- captain

Other sports words

- athletics
- foul
- match
- shot
- game
- fair play
- free throw
- kick the ball
- throw the ball

Places and equipment

- court
- gym
- track
- hoop
- clock
- swimming pool
- racket
- net

Wordbank 5

Unit 3

School subjects

English (Englisch)
maths (Mathematik)
German (Deutsch)
history (Geschichte)
PE = physical education (Sport)

biology (Biologie)
geography (Geografie)
art (Kunst)

music (Musik)
science (Naturwissenschaften)
RE = religious education (Religionslehre)
social studies (Gesellschaftslehre)
textile technology (Textilgestaltung)

ICT = information and communication technology (Informatik)
home economics (Hauswirtschaftslehre)
environmental studies (Umweltlehre)

Clubs and activities

school band (Schulorchester)
choir (Chor)
school garden (Schulgarten)
school magazine (Schülerzeitung)
school cafe (Schülercafe)
computer club (Computer-AG)
chess club (Schach-AG)
drama club (Theater-AG)
arts and crafts club (Bastel-AG)

in-line skating club (Inlineskating-AG)
volleyball club (Volleyball-AG)
table tennis club (Tischtennis-AG)
judo club (Judo-AG)

Special classes and activities

homework club (Hausaufgabenbetreuung)
extra classes (Förderunterricht)
school council (Schülermitverwaltung)
peer mediation (Streitschlichtung)

WORDBANKS

Wordbank 6

Unit 4

Part-time job?

babysitter, cashier, cleaner, courier
assistant (Assistent/-in)
builder's helper (Baugehilfe/-gehilfin)
kitchen help (Küchenhilfe)
porter (Gepäckträger/in)
shop assistant (Verkäufer/in)
waiter/waitress (Kellner/in)

Where?

cafe, garden, hotel, hospital, office, restaurant, shop, supermarket
building site (Baustelle)
garage (Autowerkstatt)
petrol station (Tankstelle)
retirement home (Seniorenheim)

Do what?

clear tables (Tische abräumen)
deliver newspapers (Zeitungen austragen)
hand out flyers (Handzettel verteilen)
make beds (Betten machen)
mow lawns (Rasen mähen)
run errands (Besorgungen machen)
serve food and drinks (Essen und Getränke servieren)
stack shelves (Regale auffüllen)
walk dogs (Hunde ausführen)

Wordbank 7

Unit 5

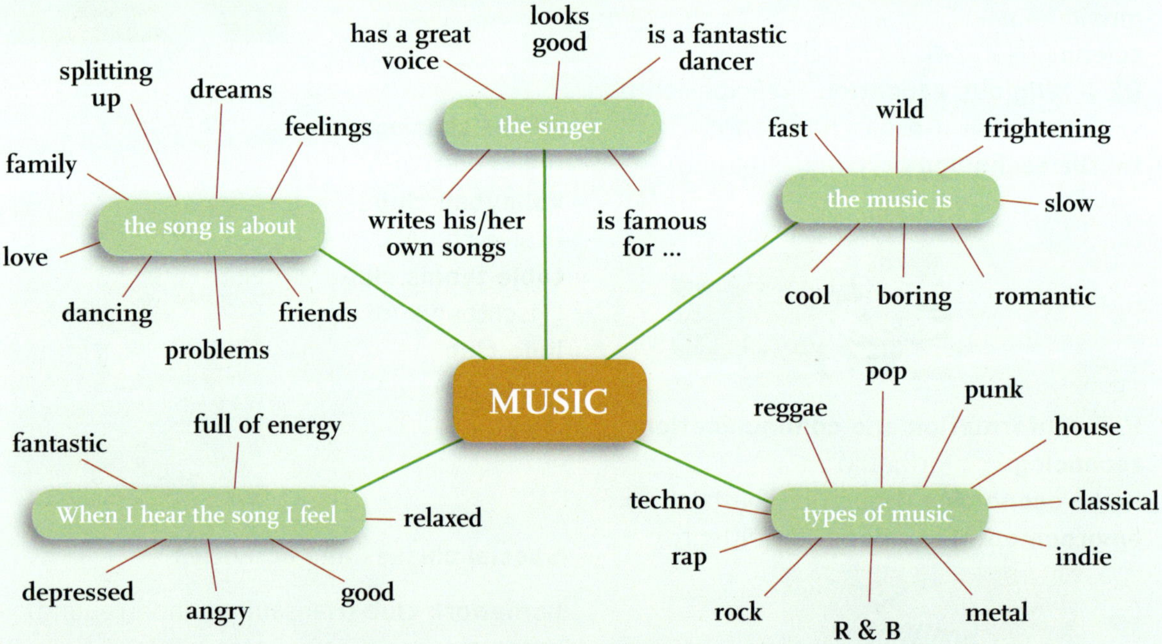

splitting up *Trennung*; feelings *Gefühle*; frightening *beängstigend, Furcht erregend*; slow *langsam*; full of energy *energiegeladen*; relaxed *entspannt*; depressed *deprimiert*; types of music *Musikrichtungen*; classical *klassisch*

Wordbank 8

Unit 5

Musical instruments

accordion

bass guitar

clarinet

drums

electric guitar

keyboard

piano

recorder

saxophone

trumpet

Wordbank 9

Unit 6

FARMS

- ANIMALS
  - sheep
  - chicken
  - goose
  - cow
  - pig
  - horse
  - cat
  - dog
- BUILDINGS
  - barn
  - farmhouse
  - stable
- MACHINES
  - milking machine
  - tractor
  - combine harvester
- THINGS TO DO
  - sow
  - harvest
  - feed

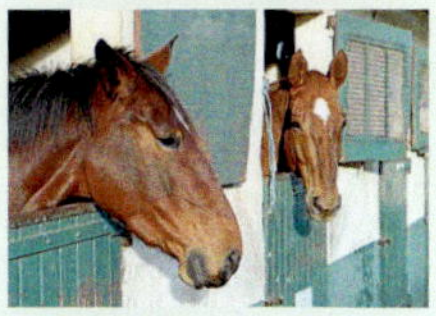

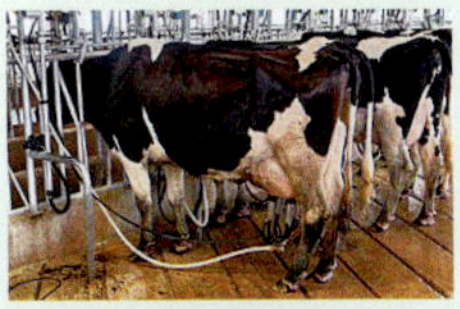

SIMPLE PRESENT Revision

→ Extra Practice, pp. 97, 116

Mit der einfachen Gegenwart (*simple present*) sagst du, was jemand immer wieder oder regelmäßig tut.

Bejahte Aussagesätze

I We You	play.
He She	plays.

Verneinte Aussagesätze

I We You	don't	play.
He She	doesn't	play.

Fragen

Do	I we you	play?
Does	he she	play?

! Diese Zeitangaben findest du oft in Sätzen im *simple present*:

every day • every Monday • every week • every month • every year • on Mondays • always • usually • often • sometimes • never

PRESENT PROGRESSIVE Revision

→ Extra Practice, p. 100

Mit der Verlaufsform der Gegenwart (*present progressive*) sagst du, was gerade passiert.

Bejahte Aussagesätze

I'm You're He's She's We're They're	reading	English now.

Verneinte Aussagesätze

I'm not You aren't He isn't She isn't We aren't They aren't	reading	French now.

Fragen

Is	he she	leaving now?
Are	we you they	leaving now?

! Diese Zeitangaben findest du oft in Sätzen im *present progessive*:

now • at the moment

Mit dieser Form kannst du auch sagen, was du planst:

I'm travelling to England next week.

SIMPLE PAST Revision

→ Extra Practice, pp. 108, 116

Mit der einfachen Vergangenheit (*simple past*) sagst du, was in der Vergangenheit geschah.

Bejahte Aussagesätze

I You He She We They	went to school yesterday.

Verneinte Aussagesätze

I You He She We They	didn't go to school yesterday.

Fragen

Did	I you he she we they	go to school yesterday?

! Regelmäßige Verben haben die Endung *-ed*:

answered, arrived, danced, finished, happened, invited, jumped, missed, needed, organized, visited, worked

! Unregelmäßige Verben haben besondere Vergangenheitsformen:

bring – brought
do – did
drink – drank
eat – ate
forget – forgot
put – put

! Diese Zeitangaben findest du oft in Sätzen im *simple past*:

last year/month/week/Friday
in July/2007
on February 14th
at 3 o'clock

PAST PROGRESSIVE

→ Extra Practice, pp. 101–102, 116

Mit der Verlaufsform der Vergangenheit (*past progressive*) sagst du, was in der Vergangenheit gerade im Gange war.

Bejahte Aussagesätze

I He She	was	reading.
You We they	were	reading.

Verneinte Aussagesätze

I He She	wasn't	reading.
You We they	weren't	reading.

Fragen

Was	I he she	reading?
Were	you we they	reading?

! Ein stummes e am Ende des Verbs fällt bei der *ing*-Form weg:
arrive – arriving   come – coming

! Bei manchen Verben wird der letzte Buchstabe verdoppelt:
stop – stopping   run – running

SUMMARY

WILL-FUTURE Revision

→ Extra Practice, p. 112

Wenn du voraussagen willst, was in der Zukunft geschehen wird, benutzt du *will* oder die Kurzform *'ll*.

Bejahte Aussagesätze

I You He/She We They	'll	go.

Verneinte Aussagesätze

I You He/She We They	won't	go.

Fragen

Will	I you he/she we they	go?

ING-FORM

→ Extra Practice, pp. 109–110

Mit der *ing*-Form kannst du über Tätigkeiten und Hobbys sprechen.

Die *ing*-Form kann Subjekt eines Satzes sein.

Camping is great.

! Die *ing*-Form folgt auf bestimmte Verben.

finish	prohibit
hate	start
like	stop
love	try

! Die *ing*-Form wird häufig nach Ausdrücken mit Präpositionen gebraucht.

She's good at dancing.

I'm against ...	It's famous for ...
I'm interested in ...	It's great for ...
I don't have a problem with ...	It's popular for ...
I look forward to ...	She's good at ...
After ...	Thanks for ...
Before ...	What about ...?

IMPERATIVE

→ Extra Practice, p. 105

Mit der Befehlsform *(imperative)* forderst du jemanden auf, etwas zu tun oder nicht zu tun. Du benutzt die Grundform des Verbs.

In einem verneinten Befehlssatz benutzt du *don't* und die Grundform des Verbs.

Close the door, please.
Come here.

Don't	worry! run!

CAN/CAN'T Revision

→ Extra Practice, p. 104

Mit *can/can't* sagst du, was jemand (nicht) tun kann oder darf.

I You He/She We They	can can't	play football.

Can I use your mobile?

HAVE TO/DON'T HAVE TO Revision

→ Extra Practice, pp. 104–105

Mit *have to* sagst du, was jemand tun muss.
Mit *don't have to* sagst du, was jemand nicht zu tun braucht.

I You We They	have to don't have to	be quiet.

He She	has to doesn't have to	be quiet.

SHOULD/SHOULDN'T

→ Extra Practice, p. 106

Mit *should/shouldn't* rätst du jemandem, etwas zu tun oder nicht zu tun.

I You He/She We They	should shouldn't	help him.

MUST/MUSTN'T

→ Extra Practice, pp. 106–107, 117

Mit *must* sagst du, was jemand tun muss.

I You He/She We They	must	go home.

Mit *mustn't* verbietest du jemandem, etwas zu tun.

I You He/She We They	mustn't	go into the water.

! you don't have to = du musst nicht

! you mustn't = du darfst nicht

SUMMARY

ADJECTIVES Revision

→ Extra Practice, pp. 108–109

Adjektive (*adjectives*) geben Informationen über eine Person oder eine Sache.

Adjektive können nach dem Verb *be* stehen.

The weather was terrible.

Adjektive stehen oft vor einem Nomen.

Our new neighbour has a big dog.

Wenn mehr als ein Adjektiv vor einem Nomen steht, kannst du ein Komma verwenden.

Mum bought a big, old house.

big – small
nice – terrible
clean – dirty
English – German
white – black
cheap – expensive
early – late
narrow – wide

Tip: Learn opposites together.

COMPARISONS Revision

→ Extra Practice, pp. 98–99

Personen, Dinge, Tiere oder Orte kann man miteinander vergleichen.

Bei einsilbigen und den meisten zweisilbigen Adjektiven auf *-y* hängst du *-er*, bzw. *-est* an das Adjektiv, um die Vergleichsformen zu bilden.

fast – faster – fastest
cheap – cheaper – cheapest
quiet – quieter – quietest
happy – happier – happiest

! Manchmal musst du bei der Schreibweise aufpassen.

hot – hotter – hottest
busy – busier – busiest
safe – safer – safest

! Diese Formen musst du auswendig lernen:

good – better – best
bad – worse – worst

Bei dreisilbigen und manchen zweisilbigen Adjektiven setzt du *more* bzw. *most* vor das Adjektiv.

interesting – more interesting – most interesting
beautiful – more beautiful – most beautiful
expensive – more expensive – most expensive
famous – more famous – most famous

ADVERBS

→ Extra Practice, pp. 113–114

Adverbien (*adverbs*) benutzt du, um zu beschreiben WIE man etwas macht. Die meisten Adverbien bildest du, indem du *-ly* an das Adjektiv anhängst.

Adjektiv	**Adverb**
quick	quickly
careful	carefully
safe	safely

! Bei Adjektiven, die auf -y enden, musst du bei der Schreibweise aufpassen.

easy	easily
angry	angrily

! Diese Formen musst du auswendig lernen:

good	well
hard	hard
fast	fast

PREPOSITIONS OF PLACE Revision

→ Extra Practice, p. 113

Räumliche Präpositionen (*prepositions of place*) sagen dir, wo etwas ist oder in welche Richtung sich etwas bewegt.

on the chair

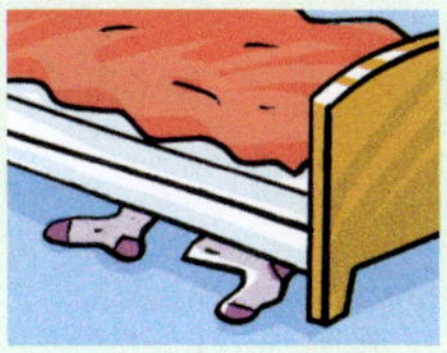

under the bed

in the cupboard

next to the bag

behind the door

between the table and the bed

at the top of the window

above the computer

opposite the chair

in front of the computer

through the door

out of the window

into the bed

down the TV

past the window

SUMMARY

WHO/THAT

→ Extra Practice, pp. 100–101

Mit den Relativpronomen *who* und *that* kannst du zusätzliche Informationen über eine Person oder eine Sache geben.

Who verwendest du nur nach Personen.

Brad Pitt is an actor who comes from Santa Monica.
They are the boys who live in Manhattan.

Ansonsten benutzt du *that*.

Surfing is a sport that is very popular in Los Angeles.
This is a day that you'll remember.

*IF-CLAUSES (Type II)

→ Extra Practice, p. 118

Mit *if*-Sätzen (Typ II) sagst du, was unter bestimmten Bedingungen geschehen würde. Es ist aber ziemlich unwahrscheinlich, dass die Bedingungen erfüllt werden.

If-Sätze bestehen aus zwei Teilen:

- einem Nebensatz (mit *if*) im *simple past*	- einem Hauptsatz mit *would* oder der Kurzform *'d* und einem Infinitiv
If I lived in the USA,	I'd speak lots of English.
If I went to New York,	I'd visit Chinatown.

Der if-Satz kann auch hinter dem Hauptsatz stehen:

I'd go to the USA if I had the money.

*PASSIVE

→ Extra Practice, p. 117

Mit dem Passiv *(passive)* sagst du, dass etwas mit einem Gegenstand oder einer Person gemacht wird oder wurde. Wichtig ist, **was** passiert ist, nicht wer es gemacht hat.

Das Passiv wird mit einer Form von *be* und dem Partizip Perfekt des Verbs gebildet.

These cars are made in Germany.
Our house was built in 2007.

Das Partizip Perfekt von regelmäßigen Verben endet auf *-ed:*
finish – finished
start – started
play – played
answer – answered

! Das Partizip Perfekt von unregelmäßigen Verben musst du auswendig lernen. Du brauchst diese Form auch für das *present perfect* und kannst sie in der *List of irregular verbs,* (dritte Spalte) auf S. 197–198 finden.

*Nur Pflichtstoff für den EK in Nordrhein-Westfalen

NUMBERS, SOUNDS, ABC

ENGLISH NUMBERS

1	**one** [wʌn]	1st	**first** [fɜːst]
2	**two** [tuː]	2nd	**second** ['sekənd]
3	**three** [θriː]	3rd	**third** [θɜːd]
4	**four** [fɔː]	4th	**fourth** [fɔːθ]
5	**five** [faɪv]	5th	**fifth** [fɪfθ]
6	**six** [sɪks]	6th	**sixth** [sɪksθ]
7	**seven** ['sevn]	7th	**seventh** ['sevnθ]
8	**eight** [eɪt]	8th	**eighth** [eɪtθ]
9	**nine** [naɪn]	9th	**ninth** [naɪnθ]
10	**ten** [ten]	10th	**tenth** [tenθ]
11	**eleven** [ɪ'levn]	11th	**eleventh** [ɪ'levnθ]
12	**twelve** [twelv]	12th	**twelfth** [twelfθ]
13	**thirteen** ['θɜː'tiːn]	13th	**thirteenth** ['θɜː'tiːnθ]
14	**fourteen** ['fɔː'tiːn]	14th	**fourteenth** ['fɔː'tiːnθ]
15	**fifteen** ['fɪf'tiːn]	15th	**fifteenth** ['fɪf'tiːnθ]
16	**sixteen** ['sɪks'tiːn]	16th	**sixteenth** ['sɪks'tiːnθ]
17	**seventeen** ['sevn'tiːn]	17th	**seventeenth** ['sevn'tiːnθ]
18	**eighteen** ['eɪ'tiːn]	18th	**eighteenth** ['eɪ'tiːnθ]
19	**nineteen** ['naɪn'tiːn]	19th	**nineteenth** ['naɪn'tiːnθ]
20	**twenty** ['twenti]	20th	**twentieth** ['twentiəθ]
21	**twenty-one** ['twenti'wʌn]	21st	**twenty-first** ['twenti'fɜːst]
...		...	
30	**thirty** ['θɜːti]	30th	**thirtieth** ['θɜːtiəθ]
40	**forty** ['fɔːti]	40th	**fortieth** ['fɔːtiəθ]
50	**fifty** ['fɪfti]	50th	**fiftieth** ['fɪftiəθ]
60	**sixty** ['sɪksti]	60th	**sixtieth** ['sɪkstiəθ]
70	**seventy** ['sevnti]	70th	**seventieth** ['sevntiəθ]
80	**eighty** ['eɪti]	80th	**eightieth** ['eɪtiəθ]
90	**ninety** ['naɪnti]	90th	**ninetieth** ['naɪntiəθ]
100	**a hundred** [ə'hʌndrəd] **one hundred** ['wʌn'hʌndrəd]	100th	**hundredth** ['hʌndrədθ]
101	**one hundred and one** [wʌnhʌndrədn'wʌn]	101st	**one hundred and first** [wʌnhʌndrədn'fɜːst]
...		...	
1000	**a thousand** [ə'θaʊznd] **one thousand** ['wʌn'θaʊznd]	1000th	**thousandth** ['θaʊznθ]

THE ENGLISH ALPHABET

a	[eɪ]	**n**	[en]
b	[biː]	**o**	[əʊ]
c	[siː]	**p**	[piː]
d	[diː]	**q**	[kjuː]
e	[iː]	**r**	[ɑː]
f	[ef]	**s**	[es]
g	[dʒiː]	**t**	[tiː]
h	[eɪtʃ]	**u**	[juː]
i	[aɪ]	**v**	[viː]
j	[dʒeɪ]	**w**	['dʌbljuː]
k	[keɪ]	**x**	[eks]
l	[el]	**y**	[waɪ]
m	[em]	**z**	[zed]

ENGLISH SOUNDS

[iː]	**eat, see, he**
[ɑː]	**ask, class, car**
[ɔː]	**or, ball, door, four**
[uː]	**ruler, blue, too, two, you**
[ɜː]	**early, her, girl, work**
[ɪ]	**in, big, England**
[e]	**yes, bed, again, breakfast**
[æ]	**animal, cat, black**
[ʌ]	**us, but, tough, colour**
[ɒ]	**on, dog, what, across**
[ʊ]	**put, good, could**
[ə]	**again, sister, today**
[i]	**radio, video, happy**
[u]	**July, museum, usually**
[eɪ]	**eight, name, play, great**
[aɪ]	**I, time, right, my**
[ɔɪ]	**boy, join, voice**
[əʊ]	**old, no, road, yellow**
[aʊ]	**our, house, now**
[ɪə]	**near, here, we're**
[eə]	**airport, share, there, their**
[ʊə]	**poor, you're, sure**
[b]	**bike, table, verb**
[p]	**pen, pupil, shop**
[d]	**day, window, good**
[t]	**ten, matter, at**
[k]	**kitchen, car, back, book**
[g]	**go, again, bag**
[ŋ]	**wrong, morning, bank**
[l]	**like, old, small**
[r]	**ruler, friend, sorry**
[v]	**very, seven, have**
[w]	**we, where, quarter**
[s]	**six, poster, yes**
[z]	**present, quiz, his, please**
[ʃ]	**she, station, English**
[tʃ]	**child, teacher, match**
[dʒ]	**job, German, orange**
[ʒ]	**usually, treasure hunt**
[j]	**yes, you, young**
[θ]	**thing, bathroom, month**
[ð]	**the, father, with**

[iː] [ɑː] [ɔː]

Dieses Wörterverzeichnis enthält neue Wörter des Buches in der Reihenfolge, in der sie im Buch zum ersten Mal vorkommen.

In der eckigen Klammer steht, wie die Wörter ausgesprochen werden.

Ein **blauer**/**roter** Pfeil heißt: Schau dir den **blauen**/**roten** Kasten rechts an.

Der graue Pfeil heißt: Schau in die rechte Spalte.

In den **roten** Kästen stehen wichtige Hinweise.

Diese Zahl gibt die Seite an, auf der die Wörter zum ersten Mal vorkommen.

Fette Wörter sind besonders wichtig.

Die **blauen** Kästen fassen Wörter in Gruppen zusammen. So lernst du sie besser.

Schräg gestellte Wörter gehören nicht zum Pflichtwortschatz.

Das **rote** Sternchen kennzeichnet unregelmäßige Verben (vgl. unten).

(AE) heißt, dass dieses Wort vor allem im amerikanischen Englisch verwendet wird.

Dieses Zeichen bedeutet: Aufgepasst!

download [ˌdaʊnˈləʊd] herunterladen
fantastic [fæn'tæstɪk] fantastisch
69 he sings **sadly** ['sædli] er singt traurig → → The song isn't really sad, but they sing it so *sadly*.
slow [sləʊ] langsam → Please drive *slowly*.
voice [vɔɪs] Stimme → I heard two different *voices*.
rhythm ['rɪðəm] Rhythmus
female ['fi:meɪl] weiblich → → a *female* cook/teacher/trainer/... [eine Köchin/Lehrerin/Trainerin/...]
Write about **yourself.** Schreibe über dich (selbst).

→ **-ly**
fight bravely
smoke nervously
ask politely
smile shyly

→ man
woman
male
female

Story
70 ***wake up** [weɪk'ʌp] aufwachen
moon [mu:n] Mond
above [ə'bʌv] über → → My flat is *above* the shop.
light switch ['laɪtswɪtʃ] Lichtschalter
mirror ['mɪrə] Spiegel
deaf [def] taub
hearing ['hɪərɪŋ] Gehör
they had come sie waren gekommen
loud [laʊd] laut
***shake: she shook me** [ʃeɪk, ʃʊk] schütteln: sie schüttelte mich → (1) We *shook* the tree, so the apples fell down. (2) She *shook* her *head*. [Sie schüttelte den Kopf.]
I see her mouth moving ich sehe, wie sich ihr Mund bewegt
mouth [maʊθ] Mund
frightening ['fraɪtnɪŋ] beängstigend, furchterregend → → That's the most *frightening* story that I've ever heard!
closet ['klɒzɪt] (AE) Wandschrank
sigh [saɪ] seufzen → Tim *sighed* because he didn't kn...

→ **über**
above the shop
across the car...
about the stor...

→ I'm frightened.
It's frightening.

! In British English *'potato'* [pə'teɪtəʊ] doesn't rhyme with 'tomato' [tə'mɑ:təʊ].
I'll have a hamburger and a cola, please.

Am Ende jeder Unit ...

... siehst du, welche Wörter im amerikanischen/britischen Englisch bevorzugt werden und wie die drei Formen der neuen unregelmäßigen Verben aus der Unit lauten.

American English vocabulary ★ ★

AE (American English)	**BE (British English)**
grade [greɪd]	year
sneaker ['sni:kə]	trainer

***Irregular verbs**

Infinitive form	**Simple past form**
hit [hɪt]	I hit [hɪt]
leave [li:v]	I left [left]
shoot [ʃu:t]	I shot [ʃɒt]

... kannst du auch überprüfen, wie gut du die neuen Wörter schon beherrschst – und wie gut du dich an bekannte Wörter erinnerst.

Test yourself
1 Find the three missing letters and finish ...
financ - - - , sal - - - , lett - - - , pri - - - ...
2 Find the opposites and write them in yo...
true – ... • quiet – ... • white bread ...

Do you remember?
Write two lists in your exercise book: a) Plac...
amusement arcade • block • brochure • chur...
holiday • hospital • museum • post office • ...

Next stop: USA

6	**stop** [stɒp]	Halt; Haltestelle	→
	Put up your hand.	Heb(t) die Hand.	
7	**state** [steɪt]	(Bundes-)Staat, Land	
	population [pɒpju'leɪʃn]	Bevölkerung(szahl)	→ Germany has a *population* of more than 80 million.
	far [fɑː]	weit →	→ The park isn't *far* from here. → near – far
	lake [leɪk]	(Binnen-)See	
	fact [fækt]	Tatsache	
8	**American** [ə'merɪkən]	amerikanisch; Amerikaner/in	→ My friend Joe is *American*, so he speaks *American* English.
	pronunciation [prənʌnsi'eɪʃn]	Aussprache	
	British ['brɪtɪʃ]	britisch; Brite/Britin	→ I met lots of *British* people on holiday in Spain.
	conversation [kɒnvə'seɪʃn]	Unterhaltung, Gespräch	
	Hi you guys. [gaɪz]	(AE) Hallo Leute.	
	Gimme five! [gɪmi'faɪv]	(AE) *Aufforderung dazu, die (erhobenen) Hände aneinander zu klatschen*	→
	How ya doin'? [haʊjə'duːɪn]	(AE) Wie geht's?	
	Have a nice day!	(AE) (Einen) Schönen Tag noch!	
	awesome ['ɔːsəm]	(AE) irre, toll	→ Billy's new CD is really *awesome*!
9	**apartment** [ə'pɑːtmənt]	(AE) Wohnung	
	store [stɔː]	(AE) Laden, Geschäft	
	sidewalk ['saɪdwɔːk]	(AE) Bürgersteig	
	cellphone ['selfəʊn]	(AE) Handy, Mobiltelefon	
	subway ['sʌbweɪ]	(AE) U-Bahn	→ The New York *subway* is as famous as the London underground.
	mix the cards **up** [mɪks]	die Karten durcheinander bringen, mischen	
	spelling ['spelɪŋ]	Rechtschreibung →	→ spell spelling

American English vocabulary ★ ★ ★ ★ ★ ★ ★ ★ ★ ★

AE (American English)	**BE (British English)**	
apartment [ə'pɑːtmənt]	flat	Wohnung
cellphone ['selfəʊn]	mobile	Handy, Mobiltelefon
sidewalk ['saɪdwɔːk]	pavement	Bürgersteig
store [stɔː]	shop	Laden, Geschäft
subway ['sʌbweɪ]	underground	U-Bahn

Can I borrow your mobile, please? – My mobile? Oh, you mean my cellphone!

Unit 1

Lerntipp 1: So lernst du englische Wörter – und behältst sie!

- Fertige ein **Wortbild** an: 
- Finde ein **Reimwort** und denke dir etwas dazu: "*cheese* – *please* = Käse, bitte!"
- Markiere **Unterschiede** zu ähnlichen deutschen Wörtern: Adresse – *add̲ress̲*.
- **Stelle** dir irgend etwas **vor**: *high* [haɪ] (= hoch) 

10	**Little Italy** [lɪtl'ɪtəli]	„Klein-Italien"	→ Kenn is a nice *little* village. [nettes kleines Dorf]
	financial [faɪ'nænʃl]	finanziell, Finanz-	
	district ['dɪstrɪkt]	Bezirk, Gebiet	
	Statue of Liberty ['stætʃu:əv'lɪbəti]	Freiheitsstatue	→
	at the top [tɒp]	ganz oben (auf), auf der Spitze	→ We had a picnic *at the top* of the hill.
11	**tour** [tʊə]	Führung, Rundgang	
	false [fɔ:ls]	falsch, unwahr →	→ right – wrong true – false
	immigrant ['ɪmɪgrənt]	Immigrant/in, Einwanderer/Einwanderin	
	neighbourhood ['neɪbəhʊd]	Viertel, Gegend	
	theatre ['θɪətə]	Theater	
	busy ['bɪzi]	**1** hektisch, belebt; **2** beschäftigt	→ My mother works in a *busy* place: She's *busy* from 10 to 5 every day.
	sightseeing ['saɪtsi:ɪŋ]	Besichtigungen	→ We did some *sightseeing* in Rome.
12	**dinner** ['dɪnə]	Abendessen →	→ breakfast lunch dinner
	pocket money ['pɒkɪtmʌni]	Taschengeld	→ Take your hand out of your *pocket*, please. [Tasche]
	deli ['deli]	(AE) Feinkostgeschäft und -imbiss	
	menu ['menju:]	Speisekarte	→ Let's look at the *menu* first.
	white bread ['waɪtbred]	Weißbrot	
	brown bread ['braʊnbred]	Graubrot	
	beef [bi:f]	Rindfleisch	→ I'm not keen on *beef*, but I like chicken.
	smoked salmon [sməʊkt'sæmən]	Räucherlachs	→ We bought some *salmon* for dinner. [Lachs] ! Aussprache: ['sæmən]
	egg [eg]	Ei	→ I love sandwiches with *egg* salad.
	lettuce ['letɪs]	(Kopf-)Salat	
	tomato, tomatoes [tə'mɑ:təʊ, tə'mɑ:təʊz]	Tomate, Tomaten	→ Let's make a salad with the lettuce and the *tomatoes*.
	potato, potatoes [pə'teɪtəʊ, pə'teɪtəʊz]	Kartoffel, Kartoffeln	→ ! In British English *'potato'* [pə'teɪtəʊ] doesn't rhyme with 'tomato' [tə'mɑ:təʊ].
	potato chips [pə'teɪtəʊtʃɪps]	(AE) Kartoffelchips	
	I'll have ...	Ich nehme ...	→ *I'll have* a hamburger and a cola, please. 
13	**line** [laɪn]	Linie	
	end [end]	Ende	
	change at 42nd Street **to** line 7	an der 42. Straße in die Linie 7 umsteigen	→ Where do I have to *change*? – At Times Square.
	block [blɒk]	Häuserblock	

Story

14	**quote** [kwəʊt]	Zitat	
	America [ə'merɪkə]	Amerika →	
	skin [skɪn]	Haut	
	in prison ['prɪzn]	im Gefängnis	
	black people, white people	Schwarze, Weiße	→ Most of the *black people* in New York City live in Brooklyn.
	kill [kɪl]	töten, umbringen	
	children's home	Kinderheim	
	lawyer ['lɔːjə]	Rechtsanwalt, -anwältin	
	at that time	damals	
	***steal** [stiːl]	stehlen	→ Somebody *stole* my bike!
	go to prison	ins Gefängnis kommen →	
	education [edʒu'keɪʃn]	Bildung, Ausbildung	
	Muslim ['mʊzlɪm]	Muslim, Muslimin	
	change his name to ...	seinen Namen ändern in ...	
	slave [sleɪv]	Sklave, Sklavin	
	***fight** [faɪt]	kämpfen; sich streiten	→ My little brothers often *fight*.
	right [raɪt]	Recht	→ We have the *right* to say what we think.
	freedom ['friːdəm]	Freiheit	
	violence ['vaɪələns]	Gewalt, Gewalttätigkeit	
	use violence **to** change things	Gewalt anwenden, um Dinge zu verändern	→ Most tourists visit New York *to* see Manhattan.
	speaker ['spiːkə]	Redner, Rednerin	
	bring about [brɪŋə'baʊt]	herbeiführen	
	change [tʃeɪndʒ]	Veränderung	
15	*Mecca* ['mekə]	Mekka	
	***lose: I lost** [luːz, lɒst]	verlieren: ich verlor	→ Here's my phone number. Don't *lose* it!

→ USA
America
American

→ **Ohne 'the'**
go to church
go to hospital
go to prison
go to school
go to town

Wordpower

16	**meat** [miːt]	Fleisch	→ I like fish and vegetables, but I don't eat *meat*.
	boyfriend ['bɔɪfrend]	(fester) Freund	
	out [aʊt]	hinaus/heraus; aus	
	say/read/explain the dates **to her**	ihr die Daten sagen/vorlesen/erklären	

Revision

17	**opposite** ['ɒpəzɪt]	Gegenteil	→ The *opposite* of 'cold' is 'hot'.
	travel ['trævl]	Reise-, Reisen	→ *Travel brochures* are interesting (and often free).

Skills training

18	**appointment** (card) [ə'pɔɪntmənt]	Termin(kärtchen)	
	mall [mɔːl]	(AE) Einkaufszentrum	
	concert ['kɒnsət]	Konzert	
	dentist ['dentɪst]	Zahnarzt, Zahnärztin	
	any ['eni]	irgendwelche	→ Now, do you have *any* questions?
19	When **should** I ...?	Wann soll ich ...?	→ *Should* I wear the red or the green T-shirt?
	movie ['muːvi]	(AE) Film	
21	**copy** ['kɒpi]	abschreiben; kopieren	→ ! he copies; he's copying; he copied
	RSVP [ɑːresviː'piː]	u.A.w.g. (= um Antwort wird gebeten)	

by October 15th	bis zum 15. Oktober	→ I need an answer *by* Monday.
message ['mesɪdʒ]	Mitteilung, Nachricht	

Look at language

22 *way of life*	Lebensweise	
I love living here.	Ich lebe sehr gern hier.	→ Pam *loves reading*, but I *love listening* to music.
win a lottery ['lɒtəri]	in einer Lotterie gewinnen	
mom [mɒm]	(AE) Mama, Mutti	
What **would** you like/miss?	Was würdest du mögen/ vermissen?	→ I'*d* (I *would*) miss healthy food. Jill *wouldn't* like the bread.

American English vocabulary ★ ★ ★ ★ ★ ★ ★ ★ ★ ★

AE (American English)	BE (British English)	
mall [mɔ:l]	shopping centre	Einkaufszentrum
mom [mɒm]	mum	Mama, Mutti
movie ['mu:vi]	film	Film
potato chips [pə'teɪtəʊtʃɪps]	crisps	Kartoffelchips

* Irregular verbs

Infinitive form	Simple past form	Present perfect form
fight [faɪt]	I fought [fɔ:t]	I've fought [fɔ:t]
lose [lu:z]	I lost [lɒst]	I've lost [lɒst]
steal [sti:l]	I stole [stəʊl]	I've stolen ['stəʊlən]

Test yourself

1 Find the three missing letters and finish the words in your exercise book.
financ - - -, sal - - -, lett - - -, pri - - -, viole - - -, oppos - - -, mess - - -

2 Find the opposites and write them in your exercise book.
true – ... • quiet – ... • white bread – ... • find – ...

Tipp:
Schau dir die vorangegangenen Wortlisten gut an.

3 Find and write in your exercise book:

1 a word for 'highest point'
2 a place where actors work
3 an evening meal
4 a list of food and drinks
5 a fish
6 a green vegetable

4 Make sentences with these words and write them in your exercise book.

1 I'll – some – sandwich – water, – a – beef – have – please. – and
2 Most – to – here – tourists – skiing. – come – go
3 I – Thursday. – have – by – to – article – finish – the

Do you remember?
Write two lists in your exercise book: a) Places in the city; b) Travel words.
amusement arcade • block • brochure • church • cinema • district • guide • holiday • hospital • museum • post office • sightseeing • theatre • tour • tourist • traveller • trip

Are your answers right? Check on page 198.

Unit 2

Lerntipp 2: Planvoll lernen

Um erfolgreich Vokabeln zu lernen, solltest du bestimmte Voraussetzungen schaffen. Du brauchst:

- **Ruhe**: Keine Ablenkung durch andere Menschen, laute Musik, Fernseher oder SMS.
- **Zeit**: Keinen Termindruck und keine anderen dringenden Arbeiten.
- **Pausen**: Finde deinen Rhythmus, z. B. 10 Minuten Lernen – 3 Minuten Pause usw.
- **ein Ziel**: Lege jeden Tag fest, was du schaffen willst, z. B. einen bestimmten Abschnitt, eine bestimmte Menge *irregular verbs*, Wiederholung bestimmter Wörter.
- **einen Weg**: Überlege dir, wie du am besten vorgehst, um dein heutiges Ziel zu erreichen (vgl. auch Lerntipp 1 auf S. 142).

24	**surfer** ['sɜːfə]	Surfer, Surferin	
	stall [stɔːl]	(Verkaufs-)Stand	→ I like the food *stalls* at the pier.
25	**boardwalk** ['bɔːdwɔːk]	(hölzerne) Strandpromenade	→ 
	homeless ['həʊmləs]	heimatlos; obdachlos	
27	**the media** ['miːdiə]	die Medien →	
	less [les]	weniger	→ I'd like to have more free time and *less* homework.
	What kind of programmes? [kaɪnd]	Was für Sendungen?	→ *What kind of* music do you like best? – Hip hop.
	prefer [prɪ'fɜː]	vorziehen	→ ! I prefe**rr**ed
	chat show ['tʃætʃəʊ]	Talkshow	
	series ['sɪəriːz]	Serie; Reihe	→ There's a new family *series* on TV.
	comedy ['kɒmədi]	Komödie, humorvoller Film/Roman	
	romance [rəʊ'mæns]	Liebesfilm, Liebesroman	
	between [bɪ'twiːn]	zwischen	

→ **The media**
newspapers
radio
the Internet
TV

Story

28	**Lucky thing!** ['lʌki'θɪŋ]	Der/Die Glückliche! Du Glückliche/r!	
	he was waiting	er wartete (gerade) →	 → When Tim arrived, his friends *were watching* TV.
	freeway ['friːweɪ]	Autobahn *(in den USA)*	
	remember [rɪ'membə]	daran denken	→ *Remember:* You must drive on the left in England!
	role [rəʊl]	Rolle	
	it **could** be [kʊd]	es könnte sein	→ If you like, we *could* go to Spain this summer.
	career (in TV) [kə'rɪə]	(Fernseh-)Karriere, berufliche Laufbahn (im Fernsehen)	
	audition [ɔː'dɪʃn]	Vorsprechen, Vorsingen	→ About 500 actors queued for the *audition*.
	studio ['stjuːdiəʊ]	Studio	
	it had sent	es hatte geschickt	
	jog [dʒɒg]	joggen	→ I *jogged* through the park in one hour.
	grass [grɑːs]	Gras, Rasen	
	wait in line [ɪn'laɪn]	(AE) Schlange stehen	→ I hate long *lines*. [(AE) Warteschlangen]
	(for) a long time	lange	→ We danced together *for a long time*.
	director [də'rektə]	Regisseur, Regisseurin	

→ **was/were -ing**
I was listening
you were reading
he/she was eating
we were drawing
they were talking

	photo shoot ['fəʊtəʊʃu:t]	Fotosession, Fotoshooting	
29	**wave** [weɪv]	Welle	→ 
	wetsuit ['wetsu:t]	Surf-/Tauch(schutz)anzug	
	(surfing) gear ['sɜ:fɪŋgɪə]	**1** (Surf-)Kleidung, Klamotten; **2** (Surf-)Ausrüstung	→ (1) Tina is wearing her disco *gear*. (2) We bought some camping *gear* for the holidays.
	surf [sɜ:f]	surfen	
	photographer [fə'tɒgrəfə]	Fotograf, Fotografin	
	make-up artist ['meɪkʌpɑ:tɪst]	Visagist, Visagistin	
	take photos [teɪk'fəʊtəʊz]	Fotos machen, fotografieren	 → Can you *take a photo* of me and my sister, please?
	turn to the left	sich nach links drehen	
	on the beach	am Strand	
	model ['mɒdl]	(Foto-)Modell →	
	a job **like that**	so ein Job	→ Look! I'd like a car *like that.*

→ Careers in TV
actor
director
make-up artist
model
photographer

Wordpower

30	**definition** [defɪ'nɪʃn]	Definition	
	What do you call ...? [kɔ:l]	Wie nennt/bezeichnet man ...?	→ *What do you call* somebody who reads? – A reader!

Training

31	**context** ['kɒntekst]	Zusammenhang, Kontext	
	meaning ['mi:nɪŋ]	Bedeutung	→ What are the two *meanings* of the word "gear"?
	entry ['entri]	Eintrag	→ Find the *entry* for "gear" in a dictionary.

Skills training

32	**phone message** ['fəʊnmesɪdʒ]	Telefonnotiz; telefonische Nachricht	
	phone call ['fəʊnkɔ:l]	Anruf	
	call [kɔ:l]	anrufen	
	Can I take a message?	Kann ich (ihm/ihr) etwas ausrichten?	
	answer the phone	ans Telefon gehen	→ Can you *answer the phone,* please? I'm busy.
33	**call/phone back**	zurückrufen	
35	**against** [ə'genst]	gegen	→ Lots of people are *against* the new airport.
	drug [drʌg]	Droge	
	relax [rɪ'læks]	(sich) entspannen	→ After work Sue *relaxes* with a cup of tea.
	main point ['meɪn'pɔɪnt]	Schwerpunkt	
	useful ['ju:sfl]	nützlich	→ If you live in the country, a car is very *useful.*
	On the one hand, ... On the other hand, ...	Einerseits ... Andererseits ...	→ *On the one hand,* I'd like to have a job. *On the other hand,* I like my free time too. ...
	all in all	insgesamt	→ ... *All in all* I need the money. So I'll look for a weekend job!

Look at language

36	**uncool** [ʌn'ku:l]	nicht cool, uncool	
	ride [raɪd]	**1** „Fahrattraktion", Fahrgeschäft; **2** Fahrt	→ There are some cool *rides* at the funfair this year.
	pirate ['paɪrət]	Pirat, Piratin	
	camera ['kæmərə]	Fotoapparat, Kamera →	
	fireworks ['faɪəwɜ:ks]	Feuerwerk	

→
camera
film
photo
photographer
take photos

American English vocabulary ★ ★ ★ ★ ★ ★ ★ ★ ★ ★

AE (American English)	**BE (British English)**	
line [laɪn]	queue [kjuː]	(Warte-)Schlange
wait in line	queue (up)	Schlange stehen

Test yourself

1 Write the plural forms of these words in your exercise book.
movie – ... • comedy – ... • model – ... • message – ... • drug – ...

2 Odd word out: One word isn't OK. Write it in your exercise book.
1 **wetsuit • stall • wave • surfer**
2 **comedy • action film • romance • camera**
3 **phone message • audition • mobile • phone call**
4 **entry • film • series • programme**

Tipp:
Schau dir die vorangegangenen Wortlisten gut an.

3 Word families: Find the new words in this unit and write them in your exercise book.
1 **home** (noun) – **homeless** (adjective)
2 **romantic** (adjective) – ... (noun)
3 **jogger** (noun) – ... (verb)
4 **mean** (verb) – ... (noun)
5 **use** (verb) – ... (adjective)
6 **cool** (adjective) – ... (the opposite)

4 Make sentences with these words and write them in your exercise book.
1 **you – kind – like – of – what – do – films – best**
2 **for – jogged – a – through – time – we – field – long – a**
3 **on – took – we – of – holiday – lots – photos**

Do you remember?
Write the answers in your exercise book. What do you call ...
a) something that you write in every day?
b) something that you write to invite people?
c) a time to relax between lessons or appointments?
d) a conversation between two people?

Are your answers right? Check on page 198.

Unit 3

Lerntipp 3: Englische Rechtschreibung (1)

In der englischen Rechtschreibung gibt es einige Besonderheiten. Zwei Beispiele:

- **-el** und **-le**: Wörter wie *travel* oder *model* enden auf -el, das ist einfach. Aber du kennst viel mehr englische Wörter, die mit -le am Ende geschrieben werden, wie *table* oder *article*. Denke z. B. an die englischen Wörter für ‚Apfel', ‚Titel' oder ‚schrecklich, furchtbar'. Fallen dir noch mehr Beispiele ein?
- **-er** und **-re**: Das einfache -er am Ende kennst du vor allem für Personen, z. B. *reader*, *photographer* oder *sister*. Es gibt aber auch einige (nicht sehr viele!) Fälle, in denen es -re heißen muss, wie bei *centre*, *metre* oder *theatre*. (Nur im amerikanischen Englisch werden auch diese Wörter mit -er am Ende geschrieben.)

Tipp: Führe Listen über Wörter mit besonderen Schreibweisen!

VOCABULARY

38	**high school** ['haɪsku:l]	Oberschule *(in den USA)*	→ "Sullivan High" means "Sullivan *High School*".
	student ['stju:dnt]	(AE) Schüler, Schülerin	
	grade 9 [greɪd]	(AE) 9. Klasse	
	as [əz]	als	→ My sister works *as* a courier.
	English as a Second Language	Englisch als Zweitsprache	→ We speak French at home, but I learn *English as a Second Language* at school.
	extra classes ['klɑ:sɪz]	Förderunterricht	
	medical ['medɪkl]	Medizin-; medizinisch	
	locker ['lɒkə]	Schließfach, Spind	→ We always put our things in *lockers* before sport.
	cheerleader ['tʃɪəli:də]	*Person, die das Publikum bei einem Wettkampf zum Beifall anfeuert*	
	security check [sɪ'kjʊərətitʃek]	Sicherheitskontrolle	
39	**first aid** [fɜ:st'eɪd]	erste Hilfe	
40	**court** [kɔ:t]	Spielfeld, Platz	
	hoop [hu:p]	(Basketball-)Korb	
	equipment [ɪ'kwɪpmənt]	Ausstattung, Ausrüstung	
	shorts [ʃɔ:ts]	Shorts, kurze Hosen →	→ I need some new *shorts* for the summer!
	free throw [fri:'θrəʊ]	Freiwurf	
	shot [ʃɒt]	Korbwurf	
	touch [tʌtʃ]	berühren, anfassen	→ She didn't hear me, so I *touched* her arm.
	kick [kɪk]	kicken, treten	
	YMCA [waɪemsi:'eɪ]	CVJM	
	happy ending [hæpi'endɪŋ]	Happy End	→ I like love stories with a *happy ending*.
	I spent [spent]	ich verbrachte	
	I have no clue [klu:]	ich habe keine Ahnung	
	I got [gɒt]	(AE) ich habe	
	gotta find me a place ['gɒtə]	(ich) muss einen Ort finden	
	***shoot** [ʃu:t]	schießen; werfen	→ Before I could *shoot*, I lost the ball.
	dreams of being like ... ['bi:ɪŋ]	Träume, in denen ich wie ... bin	
	a ball's no good	ein Ball nützt nichts	
	till [tɪl]	bis	
	(it) so happened to be ...	zufälligerweise war es ...	
	score [skɔ:]	Spielstand, Punktzahl	→ What's the *score* now? [Wie steht's jetzt?]
	it was tied [taɪd]	es war unentschieden	
	three on the **clock** [klɒk]	drei (Minuten) auf der Uhr	→ Sorry I'm late. The kitchen *clock* isn't working.
	it's (= it was) up to me	es lag an mir	
	sky-high [skaɪ'haɪ]	himmelhoch	
	release [rɪ'li:s]	loslassen	
	everything for young men to enjoy [ɪn'dʒɔɪ]	alles, was jungen Männern gefällt	
	hang out [hæŋ'aʊt]	herumhängen	
	you can get yourself clean	du kannst dich waschen	
	meal [mi:l]	Mahlzeit, Essen	
	you can do whatever you feel [wɒt'evə]	du kannst tun, wonach dir gerade ist	
41	**sneaker** ['sni:kə]	(AE) Sportschuh	
	brand [brænd]	Marke	→ We all know lots of *brand* names from TV.
	each [i:tʃ]	jede, jeder, jedes	→ Grandad gave *each* child a little present.
	soccer ['sɒkə]	Fußball	→ *Soccer* (or football) is the most popular sport in Germany.

Nicht mit "a"
some jeans
some shorts

basketball

American football

baseball

	expert ['ekspɜːt]	Fachmann/-frau, Experte/ Expertin	
	print out [prɪnt'aʊt]	ausdrucken	

Story

42	she felt **confident** ['kɒnfɪdənt]	sie war zuversichtlich	
	move [muːv]	(sich) bewegen	→ Don't *move* now!
	***throw (at): I threw (at)** [θrəʊ, θruː]	werfen (auf): ich warf (auf)	→ Basketball players don't kick the ball, they *throw* it.
	cheer [tʃɪə]	jubeln, hurra rufen →	
	half-time [hɑːf'taɪm]	Halbzeit	
	score [skɔː]	(Punkte) erzielen, (Tor) schießen	→ I tried, but I didn't *score*.
	it was 24–18 to North ['twenti'fɔːreɪ'tiːn]	es stand 24:18 für North	→ What's the score? – *It's 2–1 to* England.
	Too bad! ['tuː'bæd]	Schade!	→ Sorry, I can't come tonight. – *Too bad!*
	Well done! ['wel'dʌn]	Gut gemacht!	
	Good luck! ['gʊd'lʌk]	Viel Glück!	
	***hit: I hit** [hɪt, hɪt]	schlagen: ich schlug →	
43	**referee** [refə'riː]	Schiedsrichter, -richterin	
	miss [mɪs]	daneben treffen; daneben gehen	→ I threw the ball, but it *missed* the hoop.
	play by the rules	sich an die Spielregeln halten	→ You can join us if you *play by the rules*.
	self-control [selfkən'trəʊl]	Selbstbeherrschung	→ I lost my *self-control* and I hit her – in my dream.

→ cheer
cheerleader

→ hit
kick
shoot
throw

Wordpower

44	**imperative** [ɪm'perətɪv]	Befehlsform, Imperativ	! Aussprache: [ɪm'perətɪv]

Skills training

46	**Giving orders** [gɪvɪŋ'ɔːdəz]	Anweisungen geben, Befehle erteilen	
	in the school car park	auf dem Schulparkplatz	
	tray [treɪ]	Tablett	
	***leave** [liːv]	(liegen) lassen, vergessen	→ Oh no! I *left* my mobile in the cafe!
	over there [əʊvə'ðeə]	da/dort drüben (hin)	→ Let's sit *over there* and have a chat.
	exchange [ɪks'tʃeɪndʒ]	Austausch-; Tausch-	
49	**fix** [fɪks]	reparieren	
	if [ɪf]	ob	→ Ask Pam *if* she can come to my party, please.

Look at language

50	**paramedic** [pærə'medɪk]	Rettungssanitäter/in	→ The *paramedics* took my father to hospital.
	academy [ə'kædəmi]	Akademie	
	give first aid	erste Hilfe leisten	
	become sick [sɪk]	(AE) krank werden	
	on the weekend	(AE) am Wochenende	
	panic ['pænɪk]	durchdrehen, in Panik geraten	→ ! he panics, but: he's panicking, he panicked
	difficult ['dɪfɪkəlt]	schwierig, schwer	→ Swimming isn't *difficult*. It's really easy!
	emotional [ɪ'məʊʃənl]	gefühlsbetont	
	earn [ɜːn]	verdienen	

American English vocabulary ★ ★ ★ ★ ★ ★ ★ ★ ★ ★		
AE (American English)	**BE (British English)**	
grade [greɪd]	year	Klasse
sneaker ['sni:kə]	trainer	Sportschuh
student ['stju:dnt]	pupil	Schüler, Schülerin

* Irregular verbs		
Infinitive form	**Simple past form**	**Present perfect form**
hit [hɪt]	I hit [hɪt]	I've hit [hɪt]
leave [li:v]	I left [left]	I've left [left]
shoot [ʃu:t]	I shot [ʃɒt]	I've shot [ʃɒt]
throw [θrəʊ]	I threw [θru:]	I've thrown [θrəʊn]

Test yourself

1 *Schreibe die Grundform dieser Verben in dein Heft.*

I cheered – cheer • I fixed – ... • I hit – ... • I kicked – ... • I left – ... • I missed – ... • I panicked – ... • I shot – ... • I threw – ... • I touched – ...

2 *Bilde Kommentare aus den Wörtern und schreibe die Dialoge in dein Heft.*

bad • done • good • luck • too • well

1 **I scored lots of points in the game. – ... ...!**
2 **I'll try to score lots of points in the game. – ... ...!**
3 **I didn't score lots of points in the game. – ... ...!**

Tipp:
Schau dir die vorangegangenen Wortlisten gut an.

Do you remember?

Pick the right word and finish the sentences in your exercise book.

gear • point • rules • sign

1 I don't know softball. What are the ...?
2 You get one ... for each right answer.
3 Give me a ... when you're ready.
4 I can't surf – I don't have the right ...

Are your answers right? Check on page 198.

Unit 4

Lerntipp 4: Englische Rechtschreibung (2)

Hier sind zwei weitere Beispiele für Besonderheiten der englischen Rechtschreibung.

- **-ea-** und **-ee-**: Diese beiden Buchstabenpaare im Wort werden zwar oft gleich ausgesprochen *(mean, meet)*, aber eben unterschiedlich geschrieben. Sammle Beispiele!
- **-gh und -ght**: Einige englische Wörter hören mit den Buchstaben -gh *(laugh, through)* oder -ght *(right, fight)* auf. Fertige eine Liste an!

52	*evergreen* ['evəgri:n]	immergrün
	Washington State [wɒʃɪŋtən'steɪt]	der Bundesstaat Washington
	forest ['fɒrɪst]	Wald, Waldgebiet

	bear [beə]	Bär	
	deer [dɪə]	Hirsch, Hirsche	→ We saw lots of *deer* in the national park.
	cougar ['ku:gə]	(AE) Puma	
	reservation [rezə'veɪʃn]	(Indianer-)Reservation, Reservat	→ We stayed in a hotel *on the reservation.* [in der Reservation]
	festival ['festɪvl]	Festival; Fest	
	tree [tri:]	Baum	
53	**go whale watching** ['weɪlwɒtʃɪŋ]	auf Walbeobachtungstour gehen	→ We went *whale watching* in Canada. *Whale watching* is very popular there. [Walbeobachtung]
	island ['aɪlənd]	Insel	
	hike; hiking [haɪk, 'haɪkɪŋ]	wandern; (das) Wandern →	→ *Hiking* is great. I *hiked* all weekend.
54	**fire** ['faɪə]	Feuer; Brand	
	smoke; smoking [sməʊk, 'sməʊkɪŋ]	rauchen; (das) Rauchen	→ I don't *smoke*. I think *smoking* is stupid.
	campfire ['kæmpfaɪə]	Lagerfeuer	
	campground ['kæmpgraʊnd]	(AE) Campingplatz, Zeltplatz	
	noise [nɔɪz]	Lärm; Geräusch	
	***keep** [ki:p]	halten, behalten	
	prohibited [prə'hɪbɪtɪd]	verboten	→ Look, swimming is *prohibited* here.
	as many **as**	so viele wie	→ I think Mike isn't *as* nice *as* his brother.
55	**wall** [wɔ:l]	Wand; Mauer	
	beaver ['bi:və]	Biber	
	entrance fee ['entrənsfi:]	Eintrittspreis	
	person ['pɜ:sn]	Person, Mensch	→ All the people were quiet. Only one *person* was talking. ! Aussprache: ['pɜ:sn]

→ **-ing**
Reading is fun.
I've finished drawing.
He's good at singing.

Story

56	**root** [ru:t]	Wurzel	
	tent [tent]	Zelt	
	they were looking forward to getting out of town ['fɔ:wəd]	sie freuten sich darauf, aus der Stadt herauszukommen	→ *I'm* really *looking forward to seeing* you again.
	After leaving Port Townsend, they drove ...	Nachdem sie Port Townsend verlassen hatten, fuhren sie ...	→ *After finishing* my homework, I went to bed.
	*drive: **I drove** [drəʊv]	fahren: ich fuhr	→ I love driving. Last week I *drove* to London.
	***put up a tent** [pʊt'ʌp]	ein Zelt aufstellen	
	*eat: **I ate** [et]	essen: ich aß	
	Native American ['neɪtɪvə'merɪkən]	amerik. Ureinwohner/in, Indianer/in	→ About 100 *Native Americans* live on the reservation that we visited.
	grandparents ['grænpeərənts]	Großeltern →	
57	*the Makah people* [mə'kɑ:]	das Volk der Makah	
	tepee ['ti:pi:]	Tipi	
	longhouse ['lɒŋhaʊs]	Langhaus	
	uncle ['ʌŋkl]	Onkel →	
	hunt; hunting [hʌnt, 'hʌntɪŋ]	jagen; (das) Jagen	→ For some people, *hunting* is a sport.
	*bring: **I brought** [brɔ:t]	bringen: ich brachte	
	illness ['ɪlnəs]	Krankheit	
	prohibit [prə'hɪbɪt]	verbieten	
	fish [fɪʃ]	fischen, angeln	→ 
	ocean ['əʊʃn]	Ozean; Meer	
	*forget: **I forgot** [fə'gɒt]	vergessen: ich vergaß	→ Where's Ben? – Oh sorry, I *forgot* to phone him.

→ grandparents
grandma
grandad

→ aunt
uncle
cousin

Wordpower

58	**adjective** ['ædʒɪktɪv]	Adjektiv, Eigenschaftswort →	→ An alphabet of *adjectives*: angry, big, cheap, dirty, easy, fast, ...

→ noun
verb
adjective

Training

59	**mind map** ['maɪndmæp]	Mindmap *(eine Art Gedankenkarte)*	→ A *mind map* can help you to remember things.
	look after [lʊk'ɑ:ftə]	sich kümmern um, aufpassen auf	→ I can't come tomorrow. I have to *look after* my little brother.
	***lead** [li:d]	führen	→ This road *leads* to the beach.
	get lost [get'lɒst]	sich verirren	→ We *got lost* on our way to the hotel in London.

Skills training

60	**European** [jʊərə'pi:ən]	europäisch; Europäer, Europäerin →	
61	**Can I help you?**	Kann ich Ihnen behilflich sein?	→ *Can I help you?*
	recommend [rekə'mend]	empfehlen	→ For French food I can *recommend* the 'Café Paris'.
	kayaking ['kaɪækɪŋ]	Kajakfahren	
63	**apply (for/to)** [ə'plaɪ]	sich bewerben (um/bei)	→ I *applied for* a job as a courier, but I didn't get it.
	part-time [pɑ:t'taɪm]	Teilzeit, Teilzeit-	→ Pat works *part-time* in a disco.
	sales clerk ['seɪlzklɑ:k]	(AE) Verkäufer/in	→ ! Aussprache: BE [klɑ:k], AE [klɜ:rk]
	per [pɜ:]	pro	→ We spent about 10 pounds *per* person for drinks.
	résumé ['rezjumeɪ]	(AE) Lebenslauf	→ ! Aussprache: BE ['rezjumeɪ], AE ['rezəmeɪ]
	family name	Nachname, Familienname	→ Sorry, Martin is my *family name* –
	first name	Vorname	→ my *first name* is Richard.
	(work) experience [ɪk'spɪəriəns]	(Berufs-)Erfahrung	
	cashier [kæ'ʃɪə]	Kassierer, Kassiererin →	→ My mum works as a *cashier*.
	cover letter ['kʌvəletə]	(AE) Anschreiben, Begleitbrief	
	Yours truly, ... [jɔ:z'tru:li]	(AE) Mit freundlichen Grüßen ...	
	cleaner ['kli:nə]	Putzhilfe, Raumpfleger/in	→ My uncle is a *cleaner*.
	assistant [ə'sɪstənt]	Assistent, Assistentin	

→ American
Asian
European

→ **In a shop**
cashier
customer
detective
shop assistant
shopper
shoplifter

Look at language

64	**animal rights** ['ænɪml'raɪts]	Tierrechte, Tierschutz-	→ I love my pets, so I joined an *animal rights* group.
	tradition [trə'dɪʃn]	Tradition	
	oil [ɔɪl]	Öl	
	cook; cooking [kʊk, 'kʊkɪŋ]	kochen; (das) Kochen	→ I'm not a good cook. In fact, I hate *cooking*.
	lamp [læmp]	Lampe	
	nearly ['nɪəli]	fast	
	extinct [ɪk'stɪŋkt]	ausgestorben	
	trouble ['trʌbl]	Unruhe	
	there was lots of activity	es war viel los, es gab viel Trubel	
	protest [prə'test]	protestieren	
	save [seɪv]	retten	→ The paramedics *saved* my friend's life.
	grey whale ['greɪ'weɪl]	Grauwal	

American English vocabulary ★ ★ ★ ★ ★ ★ ★ ★ ★ ★ ★

AE (American English)	BE (British English)	
campground ['kæmpgraʊnd]	campsite ['kæmpsaɪt]	Campingplatz, Zeltplatz
cougar ['ku:gə]	puma ['pju:mə]	Puma
cover letter ['kʌvəletə]	covering letter ['kʌvərɪŋletə]	Anschreiben, Begleitbrief
résumé ['rezjumeɪ]	CV ['si:'vi:]	Lebenslauf
sales clerk ['seɪlzklɑ:k]	shop assistant	Verkäufer/in
Yours truly [jɔ:z'tru:li]	Yours sincerely [jɔ:zsɪn'sɪəli]	Mit freundlichen Grüßen

*Irregular verbs

Infinitive form	Simple past form	Present perfect form
bring [brɪŋ]	I brought [brɔ:t]	I've brought [brɔ:t]
drive [draɪv]	I drove [drəʊv]	I've driven ['drɪvn]
eat [i:t]	I ate [et]	I've eaten ['i:tn]
forget [fə'get]	I forgot [fə'gɒt]	I've forgotten [fə'gɒtn]
keep [ki:p]	I kept [kept]	I've kept [kept]
lead [li:d]	I led [led]	I've led [led]
put [pʊt]	I put [pʊt]	I've put [pʊt]

Test yourself

1 Word families: Find the new words and write them in your exercise book.

1 **aunt** (woman) – **uncle** (man)
2 **ill** (adjective) – ... (noun)
3 **fishing** (noun) – ... (verb)
4 **Europe** (noun) – ... (adjective)
5 **clean** (adjective) – ... (noun/job)
6 **cook** (noun) – ... (verb)

Tipp:
Schau dir die vorangegangenen Wortlisten gut an.

2 Make sentences with these words and write them in your exercise book.

1 **looking – is – mum – forward – you – my – meeting – to**
2 **to – after – really – was – I – driving – London, – tired**
3 **have – after – I – little – my – to – cousins – look**

Do you remember?

Write two lists in your exercise book: a) The environment; b) Outdoor activities.

camping • cycling • fishing • forest • hiking • hunting • island • kayaking • lake • mountain • ocean • river • sea • skiing • swimming • walking

Are your answers right? Check on page 198.

Unit 5

Lerntipp 5: The alphabet game

Am meisten Spaß macht das Spiel zu dritt oder zu viert!

Spielablauf: In jeder Runde wird ein Buchstabe genannt. Alle schreiben so schnell wie möglich 5 englische Wörter auf, die mit diesem Buchstaben beginnen. Wer zuerst fertig ist, ruft „Stop!" und erhält 5 Extrapunkte. Alle anderen erhalten pro Wort 5 Punkte. Dann wird gemeinsam im **Dictionary** (S.160–179) überprüft, ob die Wörter richtig geschrieben sind; für jeden Fehler wird wieder ein Punkt abgezogen. Wer hat nach 5 Runden die meisten Punkte?

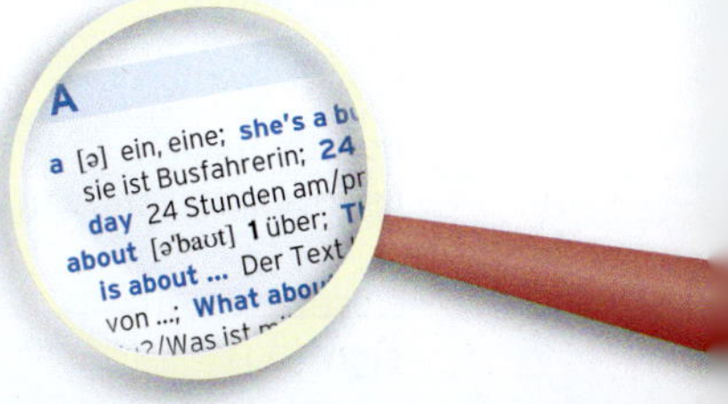

	English	German	Example
66	**Spanish** ['spænɪʃ]	spanisch; Spanisch; Spanier, Spanierin(nen)	Luis and Maria live in Spain, but they aren't *Spanish*.
	Little Havana [hə'vænə]	„Klein-Havanna"	
	men playing games	Männer, die Spiele spielen	
	crime [kraɪm]	Verbrechen	
	on stage [steɪdʒ]	auf der Bühne	
	award [ə'wɔːd]	Preis, Auszeichnung	The band won many *awards*.
67	**Hispanic** [hɪ'spænɪk]	Hispano-Amerikaner/in; hispanisch; spanisch-sprachig	
	% = per cent [pə'sent]	Prozent	
	musician [mju'zɪʃn]	Musiker, Musikerin	
	umbrella [ʌm'brelə]	Schirm	
68	**male** [meɪl]	männlich	My favourite *male* actor is Daniel Radcliffe.
	general ['dʒenrəl]	allgemein	
	piano [pi'ænəʊ]	Klavier	I can't play the *piano*, but I can play the guitar.
	hip [hɪp]	Hüfte	
	lie [laɪ]	lügen	That wasn't true. He *lied*. ! he lies, he's lying
	Colombia [kə'lɒmbiə]	Kolumbien	
	***spend** [spend]	verbringen	
	in front of [frʌnt]	vor	Tim spends all his free time *in front of* the TV.
	download [daʊn'ləʊd]	herunterladen	
	fantastic [fæn'tæstɪk]	fantastisch	
69	he sings **sadly** ['sædli]	er singt traurig	The song isn't really sad, but they sing it so *sadly*.
	slow [sləʊ]	langsam	Please drive *slowly*.
	voice [vɔɪs]	Stimme	I heard two different *voices*.
	rhythm ['rɪðəm]	Rhythmus	
	female ['fiːmeɪl]	weiblich	a *female* cook/teacher/trainer/... [eine Köchin/Lehrerin/Trainerin/...]
	Write about **yourself.**	Schreibe über dich (selbst).	

→ Britain – British
Spain – Spanish

→ crime
violence
steal
fight
kill
police officer
prison

→ **-ly**
fight bravely
smoke nervously
ask politely
smile shyly

→ man
woman
male
female

Story

	English	German	Example
70	***wake up** [weɪk'ʌp]	aufwachen	
	moon [muːn]	Mond	
	above [ə'bʌv]	über	My flat is *above* the shop.
	light switch ['laɪtswɪtʃ]	Lichtschalter	
	mirror ['mɪrə]	Spiegel	
	deaf [def]	taub	
	hearing ['hɪərɪŋ]	Gehör	
	they had come	sie waren gekommen	
	loud [laʊd]	laut	
	***shake: she shook me** [ʃeɪk, ʃʊk]	schütteln: sie schüttelte mich	(1) We *shook* the tree, so the apples fell down. (2) She *shook her head*. [Sie schüttelte den Kopf.]
	I see her mouth moving	ich sehe, wie sich ihr Mund bewegt	
	mouth [maʊθ]	Mund	
	frightening ['fraɪtnɪŋ]	beängstigend, furcht-erregend	That's the most *frightening* story that I've ever heard!
	closet ['klɒzɪt]	(AE) Wandschrank	
	sigh [saɪ]	seufzen	Tim *sighed* because he didn't know what he should do.
	I've been thinking that	ich habe das (immer wieder) gedacht	

→ **über**
above the shop
across the canal
about the story

→ I'm frightened.
It's frightening.

kiss [kɪs]	(sich) küssen	
key [ki:]	Schlüssel	
she shouts something at him	sie ruft ihm etwas zu	
ear [ɪə]	Ohr	
opposite ['ɒpəzɪt]	gegenüber (von)	→ The supermarket is *opposite* the museum.
alarm [ə'lɑ:m]	Alarmanlage	
71 **feeling** ['fi:lɪŋ]	Gefühl →	→ He hates talking about his *feelings*.

→ feel
feeling

Wordpower

72 **preposition** [prepə'zɪʃn]	Präposition, Verhältniswort	→ Words like 'under' or 'between' are *prepositions*.

Skills training

74 **hurricane** ['hʌrɪkən]	Orkan	→
theme park ['θi:mpɑ:k]	Themenpark	
12° Celsius (= 12 degrees Celsius) [dɪ'gri:z, 'selsiəs]	12 Grad Celsius	! 1 degree, 2 degree**s**
space [speɪs]	Weltraum →	→ Imagine you could travel through *space*.
astronaut ['æstrənɔ:t]	Astronaut, Astronautin	
Just a minute.	Einen Augenblick.	
75 **Do you mind if I** sit here? [maɪnd]	Haben Sie etwas dagegen, wenn ich mich hier hinsetze?	→ *Do you mind if I* open the window?
Go ahead. [ə'hed]	Mach(t) / Machen Sie nur.	→ Can I open my presents now? – Yes, *go ahead*.
You're welcome.	Nichts zu danken; Bitte schön.	→ Thanks for your help. – *You're welcome.*
77 **reason** ['ri:zn]	Grund	
in my opinion [ə'pɪnjən]	meiner Meinung nach	→ *In my opinion*, that's a great idea.
believe [bɪ'li:v]	glauben	→ You shouldn't *believe* everything that you hear.

→ **Ohne 'the'**
at church
at school
in Elm Street
in hospital
in space
in prison
on stage

Look at language

78 ***grow** [grəʊ]	wachsen	→ The tree *hasn't grown* in the last year.
economy [ɪ'kɒnəmi]	Wirtschaft	
illegal [ɪ'li:gl]	ungesetzlich, illegal	→ It's *illegal* to smoke here.
papers ['peɪpəz]	(Ausweis-)Papiere	
Mexico ['meksɪkəʊ]	Mexiko	
employer [ɪm'plɔɪə]	Arbeitgeber, Arbeitgeberin	→ This firm is one of the largest *employers* in the area.
power ['paʊə]	Macht; Stärke	
79 **adverb** ['ædvɜ:b]	Adverb, Umstandswort	

*** Irregular verbs**

Infinitive form	Simple past form	Present perfect form
grow [grəʊ]	I grew [gru:]	I've grown [grəʊn]
shake [ʃeɪk]	I shook [ʃʊk]	I've shaken ['ʃeɪkən]
spend [spend]	I spent [spent]	I've spent [spent]
wake up [weɪk'ʌp]	I woke up [wəʊk'ʌp]	I've woken up [wəʊkən'ʌp]

Hinweis:
"Test yourself" findest du auf S.156.

Test yourself

1 Find the opposites and write them in your exercise book.
male – … • behind – … • happily – … • fast – … • sun – … • quiet – …

2 Who or what is it? Find and write in your exercise book a word for:
1 a big musical instrument
2 say something that isn't true
3 somebody who travels in space
4 somebody who gives people jobs

3 Find the missing words and write them in your exercise book.
1 She's great! Of course she'll win an …
2 It's raining. You'll need an …
3 He can't hear you. He's …
4 I can't open the door. I don't have a …
5 Nobody will steal my car. It has a car …
6 This king doesn't have much …

Do you remember?
Write two lists in your exercise book: a) Music; b) Prepositions.
above • behind • between • concert • guitar • in front of • into • musical instrument • musician • near • onto • opposite • piano • singer • song • sound • stage • through • title • towards

Are your answers right? Check on page 198.

Tipp: Schau dir die vorangegangenen Wortlisten gut an.

Unit 6

80	*before* [bɪ'fɔ:]	vor	
	it was called	es wurde genannt ➔	➔ it's called – it was called; they're sent – they were sent
	trail [treɪl]	Pfad, Weg	
	pioneer [paɪə'nɪə]	Pionier, Pionierin	
81	*wagon train* ['wægəntreɪn]	Zug von Planwagen	
	camp [kæmp]	lagern, zelten ➔	→ Last summer we *camped* at the river. ➔ camp, campfire, camping, tent
	Indian ['ɪndiən]	Indianer, Indianerin; indianisch	
	buffalo, buffaloes ['bʌfələʊ, 'bʌfələʊz]	Büffel ➔	→  ➔ bear, beaver, buffalo, cougar, deer
	California [kælɪ'fɔ:niə]	Kalifornien	
82	*scan* [skæn]	überfliegen	→ I only *scanned* the newspaper today.
	If I had the money, …	Wenn ich das Geld hätte, …	
	enough [ɪ'nʌf]	genug	→ We don't have *enough* time to stop.
	e-pal ['i:pæl]	E-Mail-Freund/-Freundin	
	county fair [kaʊnti'feə]	*eine Art Landwirtschaftsschau*	
	coast [kəʊst]	Küste	→ *on the coast* [an der Küste]
	I'd teach you to ride [ti:tʃ]	ich würde dir das Reiten beibringen ➔ ➔	➔ teach – I taught – I've/I had taught; ➔ teach, teacher
	ride [raɪd]	reiten ➔	➔ ride – I rode – I've/I had ridden
	excited [ɪk'saɪtɪd]	aufgeregt, begeistert	
83	*Historical Society* [hɪ'stɒrɪklsə'saɪəti]	Geschichtsverein	
	they were built [bɪlt]	sie wurden gebaut ➔	➔ build – I built – I've/I had built
	establish [ɪ'stæblɪʃ]	einrichten; eröffnen	
	name [neɪm]	nennen	→ I had to *name* five wild animals in the quiz.
	Farewell Bend [feə'welbend]	„Lebewohl-Biegung“	
	change to	ändern in	→ Her name was Mayer, but she *changed* it *to* May.
	encyclopedia [ɪnsaɪklə'pi:diə]	Lexikon, Enzyklopädie	

	search engine ['sɜːtʃendʒɪn]	Suchmaschine	
	nickname ['nɪkneɪm]	Spitzname	→ I'm Jack. My *nickname* in school is "Jackster".
	skunk [skʌŋk]	Stinktier, Skunk	
	jackalope ['dʒækələʊp]	*amerikanisches Fabeltier*	
	disc golf ['dɪskgɒlf]	Discgolf („Scheibengolf")	→ 

Story

84	*the flight was twelve hours* [flaɪt]	der Flug dauerte zwölf Stunden	
	highway ['haɪweɪ]	(AE) Fernstraße	
	speed limit ['spiːdlɪmɪt]	Geschwindigkeitsbegrenzung	
	kilometres per hour	Stundenkilometer	→ The speed limit is 50 *kilometres per hour.*
	barn [bɑːn]	Scheune	
	tractor ['træktə]	Traktor →	
	almost ['ɔːlməʊst]	fast	→ Don't go! Dinner is *almost* ready.
	typical ['tɪpɪkl]	typisch	! Aussprache: ['tɪpɪkl]
	diner ['daɪnə]	(AE) Imbissstube, Café	
	soda ['səʊdə]	(AE) Limonade	
	refill ['riːfɪl]	Nachfüllung	→ Most diners offer *refills* of drinks.
85	*feel homesick* ['həʊmsɪk]	Heimweh haben	
	tubing ['tjuːbɪŋ]	*Benutzung eines Reifenschlauchs als Floß*	
	tube [tjuːb]	Reifenschlauch	
	all the time [ɔːlðə'taɪm]	die ganze Zeit	
	s'mores [smɔːz]	*amerikanischer Lagerfeuersnack*	
	grill [grɪl]	grillen	→ We *grilled* sausages on our campfire.
	cracker ['krækə]	Kräcker	
	surprised [sə'praɪzd]	überrascht	→ I wasn't *surprised* when they told me the news.

→ barn
farm
farmer
field
tractor

Wordpower

86	*fizzy drink* [fɪzi'drɪŋk]	Limonade	→ Would you like a *fizzy drink*?
	passive ['pæsɪv]	Passiv	

Training

87	*reading log* ['riːdɪŋlɒg]	Lesetagebuch	
	character ['kærəktə]	Figur, Person	→ The most important *character* in the book is Ron.
	review [rɪ'vjuː]	Besprechung, Rezension	

Skills training

88	*book* [bʊk]	buchen, reservieren (lassen)	→  I've just *booked* the flights for our holiday.
	double room [dʌbl'ruːm]	Doppelzimmer	
	form [fɔːm]	Formular	
	fill in [fɪl'ɪn]	ausfüllen	→ You have to *fill in* a form on their website.
	leave [liːv]	abreisen	
	single room [sɪŋgl'ruːm]	Einzelzimmer	
	wildfire ['waɪldfaɪə]	Großflächenbrand	
	dry [draɪ]	trocken	! dry – drier – driest
89	*receptionist* [rɪ'sepʃənɪst]	Empfangschef, -dame →	

→ **Hotel/Motel**
single/double room
receptionist
book a room
fill in a form
arrive – leave

	Enjoy your stay. [ɪn'dʒɔɪ, steɪ]	Einen angenehmen Aufenthalt.	
90	*hero, heroes* ['hɪərəʊ, 'hɪərəʊz]	Held/Heldin, Helden/Heldinnen	→ Everybody called the brave girl a *hero*.
91	*describe* [dɪ'skraɪb]	beschreiben	

American English vocabulary ★ ★ ★ ★ ★ ★ ★ ★ ★ ★

AE (American English)	BE (British English)	
diner ['daɪnə]	cafe	Imbissstube, Café
highway ['haɪweɪ]	trunk road ['trʌŋkrəʊd]	Fernstraße
soda ['səʊdə]	fizzy drink [fɪzi'drɪŋk]	Limonade

Extra Practice · Unit 1

97	*design* [dɪ'zaɪn]	entwerfen
	all the time [ɔ:lðə'taɪm]	die ganze Zeit →
98	*comparison* [kəm'pærɪsn]	Vergleich →
	joke [dʒəʊk]	Witz, Scherz
	World Trade Center [wɜ:ld'treɪdsentə]	Welthandelszentrum
	skyscraper ['skaɪskreɪpə]	Wolkenkratzer, Hochhaus
	they flew [flu:]	sie flogen
	hole [həʊl]	Loch
99	*in the background/foreground* ['bækgraʊnd, 'fɔ:graʊnd]	im Hintergrund/Vordergrund →

→ all the pupils
all the time
all weekend

→ compare
comparison

→ in the background
in the foreground
on the right
on the left

Extra Practice · Unit 2

100	*describe* [dɪ'skraɪb]	beschreiben →
	surfing ['sɜ:fɪŋ]	Surfen, Wellenreiten →
103	*Who can teach me?* [ti:tʃ]	Wer kann es mir beibringen?
	she has put an advert in the newspaper	sie hat eine Anzeige in die Zeitung gesetzt
	anything ['eniθɪŋ]	irgendetwas →
	Subject: ... ['sʌbdʒɪkt]	Betreff: ...

→ describe
description

→ surf
surfboard
surfer
surfing
surfing gear

→ something
anything
nothing

Extra Practice · Unit 3

104	*Lake Michigan* [leɪk'mɪʃɪgən]	Michigansee
	field [fi:ld]	Sportplatz
105	*sell* [sel]	sich verkaufen
	library ['laɪbrəri]	Bücherei →
106	*advice* [əd'vaɪs]	Rat
	yearbook ['jɪəbʊk]	Jahrbuch
107	*homecoming* ['həʊmkʌmɪŋ]	Ehemaligentreffen

→ book
bookshop
library

	dance [dɑːns]	Tanzveranstaltung, Ball
	decorate ['dekəreɪt]	schmücken
	king [kɪŋ]	König →
	object ['ɒbdʒɪkt]	Gegenstand, Objekt
	shirt [ʃɜːt]	Hemd →

→ king
queen

→ shirt
T-shirt
jacket

Extra Practice · Unit 4

108	*table* ['teɪbl]	Tabelle
	infinitive [ɪn'fɪnətɪv]	Infinitiv →
	building ['bɪldɪŋ]	Gebäude
109	*they thought of making Leavenworth a German town*	sie kamen darauf, aus Leavenworth eine deutsche Stadt zu machen
	Bavaria [bə'veəriə]	Bayern
	ski [skiː]	Ski fahren
110	*raven* ['reɪvn]	Rabe
	crow [krəʊ]	Krähe
111	*Subject: ...* ['sʌbdʒɪkt]	Betreff: ...
	Dear Sir/Madam, ... [sɜː, 'mædəm]	Sehr geehrte Damen und Herren, ...

→ **-ive**
adjective
detective
expensive
imperative
infinitive
past/present progressive

Extra Practice · Unit 5

112	*Independence Day* [ɪndɪ'pendənsdeɪ]	Unabhängigkeitstag
	hope [həʊp]	Hoffnung →
	celebration [selɪ'breɪʃn]	Feier →
	at 10th Street and Ocean Drive	an der Ecke 10. Straße und Ocean Drive
114	*rewrite* [riː'raɪt]	umschreiben

→ **1** hope (verb)
2 hope (noun)

→ celebration
festival
party

Extra Practice · Unit 6

116	*dune* [djuːn]	Düne →
	dune buggy ['djuːnbʌgi]	„Strandbuggy" *(offenes Freizeitauto)*
117	*in the 1860s* [eɪtiːn'sɪkstiz]	in den sechziger Jahren des 19. Jahrhunderts
	take [teɪk]	einnehmen
	land [lænd]	Land
	he was shown [ʃəʊn]	es wurde ihm gezeigt
	away [ə'weɪ]	weg, fort →
	war [wɔː]	Krieg
118	*if-clause* ['ɪfklɔːz]	if-Satz
	type [taɪp]	Typ
119	*penfriend* ['penfrend]	Brieffreund, Brieffreundin →

→ ocean
sea
shore
beach
dune

→ go away – come back

→ **Friends**
boyfriend
girlfriend
penfriend
e-pal

Alphabetische Liste der Wörter aus den Bänden 1–4 (Englisch – Deutsch)

mit Fundstellenangaben für den Lernwortschatz aus Band 4, z. B.
Next: 6 = Next stop: USA, S. 6 oder U5: 70 = Unit 5, S. 70

WF (wahlfrei): nicht zum Lernwortschatz gehörende Wörter
→ verweist auf die Grundform eines Wortes
(AE): überwiegend im amerikanischen Englisch benutzte Vokabeln; Schreibweise und Aussprache entsprechen generell dem britischen Englisch.

A

a [ə] ein, eine; **she's a bus driver** sie ist Busfahrerin; **24 hours a day** 24 Stunden am/pro Tag
about [ə'baʊt] **1** über; **The text is about ...** Der Text handelt von ...; **What about you?** Und du?/Was ist mit dir? **2** ungefähr
above [ə'bʌv] über U5: 70
academy [ə'kædəmi] Akademie WF
accident ['æksɪdənt] Unfall
accordion [ə'kɔːdiən] Akkordeon WF
across [ə'krɒs] über; hinüber, herüber
act [ækt]: **Act the dialogue.** Spielt das Gespräch nach.
action film ['ækʃnfɪlm] Actionfilm
activity [æk'tɪvəti] Beschäftigung, Aktivität; **there was lots of activity** es war viel los, es gab viel Trubel WF
actor ['æktə] Schauspieler/in
address [ə'dres] Adresse
adjective ['ædʒɪktɪv] Adjektiv, Eigenschaftswort U4: 58
adult ['ædʌlt] Erwachsene, Erwachsener
adverb ['ædvɜːb] Adverb, Umstandswort U5: 79
advert ['ædvɜːt] Anzeige
advice [əd'vaɪs] Rat WF
afraid [ə'freɪd]: **I'm afraid ...** Leider ...
Africa ['æfrɪkə] Afrika
after ['ɑːftə] **1** nach; **after school** nach der Schule; **after a ball** hinter einem Ball her; **After that ...** Danach ... WF; **2** nachdem U4: 56
afternoon ['ɑːftə'nuːn] Nachmittag; **in the afternoon** am Nachmittag, nachmittags
again [ə'gen] noch einmal, (schon) wieder
against [ə'genst] gegen U2: 35
age [eɪdʒ] Alter
ago [ə'gəʊ]: **two years ago** vor zwei Jahren
agree [ə'griː]: **I agree (with you).** Ich stimme (dir) zu. Ich bin derselben Meinung (wie du).
ahead [ə'hed]: **Go ahead.** Mach(t) / Machen Sie nur. U5: 75
aid [eɪd]: **first aid** erste Hilfe U3: 39
airport ['eəpɔːt] Flughafen; **at Exeter Airport** am Flughafen Exeter
alarm [ə'lɑːm] Alarmanlage U5: 70
alarm clock [ə'lɑːmklɒk] Wecker WF
alcohol ['ælkəhɒl] Alkohol
alcoholic [ælkə'hɒlɪk] alkoholisch WF
all (the) [ɔːl] alle; **all in all** insgesamt U2: 35; **all the time** die ganze Zeit WF U6; **all weekend** das ganze Wochenende
almost ['ɔːlməʊst] fast WF U6
alone [ə'ləʊn] allein
along [ə'lɒŋ] entlang
alphabet ['ælfəbet] Alphabet
alphabetical [ælfə'betɪkl] alphabetisch
always ['ɔːlweɪz] immer
a.m. [eɪ'em] morgens, vormittags
am [æm] bin; **I'm (= I am) Sarah.** Ich heiße Sarah. **I'm from London.** Ich komme aus London. **How are you? - I'm fine, thanks.** Wie geht's? - Danke, gut. **Are you ...? - Yes, I am./ No, I'm not.** Bist du ...? - Ja./ Nein.
America [ə'merɪkə] Amerika U1: 14
American [ə'merɪkən] amerikanisch; Amerikaner/in Next: 8
amusement arcade [ə'mjuːzməntɑːkeɪd] Spielhalle
an [ən] ein, eine
and [ænd, ənd] und; **at 10th Street and Ocean Drive** an der Ecke 10. Straße und Ocean Drive WF
angry (with) ['æŋgri] böse, wütend (auf)
animal ['ænɪml] Tier; **animal rights** Tierrechte, Tierschutz- U4: 64
another [ə'nʌðə] **1** noch ein, eine, einer, eins; **2** ein anderer/anderes, eine andere
answer ['ɑːnsə] **1** (be)antworten; **answer the phone** ans Telefon gehen U2: 32; **2** Antwort
any ['eni] irgendein, -eine, -eines WF; irgendwelche U1: 18; **not ... any** kein, keine
anything ['eniθɪŋ] irgendetwas WF; **not ... anything** nichts
anywhere ['eniweə] überall WF; **not ... anywhere** nirgendwo, nirgendwohin, nirgendwoher
apartment [ə'pɑːtmənt] (AE) Wohnung Next: 9
apple ['æpl] Apfel
apply (for/to) [ə'plaɪ] sich bewerben (um/bei) U4: 63
appointment [ə'pɔɪntmənt] Termin, Verabredung U1: 18; **appointment card** (Patienten-) Terminkärtchen U1: 18
April ['eɪprəl] April
are [ɑː] bist; seid; sind; **aren't (= are not)** bist/seid/sind nicht; **How are you?** Wie geht's? **What are they in German?** Wie heißen sie auf Deutsch?
area ['eəriə] Gegend
arm [ɑːm] Arm
around [ə'raʊnd]: **around them** um sie herum WF
arrangement [ə'reɪndʒmənt] Absprache; **make an arrangement** eine Absprache treffen
arrive [ə'raɪv] ankommen
art [ɑːt] Kunst
article ['ɑːtɪkl] Artikel
artist ['ɑːtɪst] Künstler/in WF
arts and crafts [ɑːtsənd'krɑːfts]: **arts and crafts club** Bastel-AG WF
as [æz, əz] **1** als U3: 38; **2** wie WF; **as many/... as** so viele/... wie U4: 54
Asia ['eɪʃə] Asien
Asian ['eɪʃn] asiatisch; Asiat/in
ask [ɑːsk] fragen; **ask a question** eine Frage stellen; **ask for** bitten um

assistant [ə'sɪstənt] Assistent, Assistentin U4: 63; **shop assistant** Verkäufer, Verkäuferin
astronaut ['æstrənɔːt] Astronaut, Astronautin U5: 74
at [æt, ət] bei; an; in; **at eight o'clock** um acht/zwanzig Uhr; **at Exeter Station** im Bahnhof Exeter; **at home** zu Hause, daheim; **at last** endlich WF; **at night** nachts, in der Nacht; **at the moment** zurzeit, im Moment; **at the weekend** am Wochenende; **she's at school** sie ist in der Schule; sie geht zur Schule
ate [et] (→ eat): **I ate** ich aß, ich habe gegessen U4: 56
athletics [æθ'letɪks] Leichtathletik
audio ['ɔːdiəʊ]: **audio device** akustisches Gerät WF
audition [ɔː'dɪʃn] Vorsprechen, Vorsingen U2: 28
August ['ɔːgəst] August; **August 20th** 20. August
aunt [ɑːnt] Tante
Austria ['ɒstriə] Österreich
auto feeder ['ɔːtəfiːdə] automatischer Papiereinzug WF
autograph ['ɔːtəgrɑːf] Autogramm
autumn ['ɔːtəm] Herbst
available [ə'veɪləbl] erhältlich WF
award [ə'wɔːd] Preis, Auszeichnung U5: 66
away [ə'weɪ] weg, fort WF
awesome ['ɔːsəm] (AE) irre, toll Next: 8

B

baby ['beɪbi] Baby WF U6
babysitter ['beɪbisɪtə] Babysitter, Babysitterin WF
back [bæk] zurück; **back from school** aus der Schule zurück; **I'm back!** Ich bin wieder da! **at the back of the book** hinten im Buch
background ['bækgraʊnd] Hintergrund WF
backwards ['bækwədz] rückwärts WF
bacon ['beɪkən] Speck WF
bad [bæd] schlecht; schlimm; **Too bad!** Schade! U3: 42
badminton ['bædmɪntən] Badminton, Federball(spiel)
bag [bæg] (Schul-)Tasche
bagel ['beɪgl] Bagel *(eine Art ringförmiges, festes Brötchen)* WF
baggage handler ['bægɪdʒhændlə] Gepäckabfertiger/Gepäckabfertigerin
baker ['beɪkə] Bäcker, Bäckerin WF
ball [bɔːl] Ball
banana [bə'nɑːnə] Banane
band [bænd] Band, (Musik-)Gruppe
bank [bæŋk] Bank, Sparkasse
barn [bɑːn] Scheune WF U6
baseball ['beɪsbɔːl] Baseball U3: 41
basketball ['bɑːskɪtbɔːl] Basketball
bass guitar [beɪsgɪ'tɑː] Bassgitarre WF
bathroom ['bɑːθruːm] Badezimmer, Bad
battery ['bætri] Batterie WF
battery pack ['bætripæk] Akku WF
Bavaria [bə'veəriə] Bayern WF
be [biː, bi] (I/he was, you were; I've been) sein
beach [biːtʃ] Strand; **on the beach** am Strand U2: 29
bean [biːn] Bohne WF
bear [beə] Bär U4: 52
beard [bɪəd] Bart WF
beat [biːt] schlagen WF
beautiful ['bjuːtɪfl] schön, wunderschön
beaver ['biːvə] Biber U4: 55
became [bɪ'keɪm] (→ become): **I became** ich wurde, ich bin geworden
because [bɪ'kɒz] weil
become [bɪ'kʌm] (I became, I've become) werden; **I've become** ich bin geworden
bed [bed] Bett
bedroom ['bedruːm] Schlafzimmer
beef [biːf] Rindfleisch U1: 12
been [biːn, bɪn] (→ be): **I've been** ich bin gewesen; **I've been thinking that** ich habe das (immer wieder) gedacht WF
beep [biːp] piepen WF
beer [bɪə] Bier
before [bɪ'fɔː] **1** bevor; **2** vor WF U6
behind [bɪ'haɪnd] hinter
being ['biːɪŋ]: **dreams of being like ...** Träume, in denen ich wie ... bin WF
Belgium ['beldʒəm] Belgien
believe [bɪ'liːv] glauben U5: 77
belong to [bɪ'lɒŋtə] gehören WF
best [best] beste, bester, bestes; am besten U1: 11; **Best wishes, ...** Viele Grüße ...
better ['betə] besser
between [bɪ'twiːn] zwischen U2: 27
beverage ['bevərɪdʒ] Getränk WF
beware [bɪ'weə]: **Beware of ...** Nimm dich in Acht vor ... WF
big [bɪg] groß
bike [baɪk] Fahrrad, Rad
biology [baɪ'ɒlədʒi] Biologie WF
bird [bɜːd] Vogel
birthday ['bɜːθdeɪ] Geburtstag; **It's my birthday.** Ich habe Geburtstag.
biscuit ['bɪskɪt] Keks, Plätzchen WF
black [blæk] schwarz; **Black Forest** Schwarzwald WF; **black people** Schwarze U1: 14
blanket ['blæŋkɪt] Decke WF
block [blɒk] Häuserblock U1: 13
blog [blɒg] Blog *(von Weblog; hier eine Art Online-Tagebuch)*
blogger ['blɒgə] Blogger, Bloggerin *(Autor/in eines Blogs)*
blogging ['blɒgɪŋ] Bloggen *(ein Blog führen und auf andere Blogs reagieren)*
blonde [blɒnd] blond
blue [bluː] blau
board [bɔːd] **1** Tafel; **2** Board, Brett
boardwalk ['bɔːdwɔːk] (hölzerne) Strandpromenade U2: 25
boat [bəʊt] Boot; Schiff
book [bʊk] **1** Buch; Heft; **2** buchen, reservieren (lassen) WF U6
bookshop ['bʊkʃɒp] Buchladen, Buchhandlung
boot [buːt] Stiefel WF
border ['bɔːdə] Grenze
bored [bɔːd] gelangweilt; **I'm bored** ich langweile mich
boring ['bɔːrɪŋ] langweilig
born [bɔːn]: **I was born ...** ich wurde ... geboren
borrow ['bɒrəʊ]: **borrow a pen** sich einen Füller (aus)leihen
bought [bɔːt] (→ buy): **I bought** ich kaufte, ich habe gekauft; **I've bought** ich habe gekauft
box [bɒks] Kiste, Kasten
boy [bɔɪ] Junge
boyfriend ['bɔɪfrend] (fester) Freund U1: 16
brain [breɪn] Gehirn WF
brand [brænd] Marke U3: 41
brave [breɪv] mutig, tapfer
bread [bred] Brot
break [breɪk] Pause
breakfast ['brekfəst] Frühstück; **have breakfast** frühstücken
bridge [brɪdʒ] Brücke
bring [brɪŋ] (I brought, I've brought) bringen; **bring about** herbeiführen WF

Britain ['brɪtn] Großbritannien

British ['brɪtɪʃ] britisch; Brite/Britin Next: 8

broccoli ['brɒkəli] Brokkoli WF

brochure ['brəʊʃə] Broschüre

brother ['brʌðə] Bruder; **brothers and sisters** Geschwister

brought [brɔːt] (→ bring): **I brought** ich brachte, ich habe gebracht U4: 57; **I've brought** ich habe gebracht U4: 153

brown [braʊn] braun; **brown bread** Graubrot U1: 12

buddy ['bʌdi] „Kumpel" *(ältere/r Schüler/in, der/die jüngeren hilft)*

buffalo, buffaloes ['bʌfələʊ, 'bʌfələʊz] Büffel WF U6

builder's helper ['bɪldəz'helpə] Baugehilfe, Baugehilfin WF

building ['bɪldɪŋ] Gebäude WF

building site ['bɪldɪŋsaɪt] Baustelle WF

built [bɪlt]: **she built** sie baute WF; **they were built** sie wurden gebaut WF U6

bully ['bʊli] Tyrann, „Mobber/in"

bullying ['bʊliɪŋ] Schikanieren, Mobbing; **text bullying** SMS-Terror

bus [bʌs] Bus

bus driver ['bʌsdraɪvə] Busfahrer, Busfahrerin

business ['bɪznəs] Betrieb, Geschäft(s-)

bus stop ['bʌstɒp] Bushaltestelle

busy ['bɪzi] beschäftigt; hektisch, belebt U1: 11; **a busy road** eine viel befahrene Straße

but [bʌt] aber

button ['bʌtn] Knopf; Taste

buy [baɪ] (I bought, I've bought) kaufen

by [baɪ] **1** an, in der Nähe von, neben; **2** von; durch; **by bike/bus/car/...** mit dem Rad/Bus/Auto/...; **by his arms** an den Armen; **by October 15th** bis zum 15. Oktober U1: 21; **Learn it by heart.** Lerne es auswendig. **play by the rules** sich an die Spielregeln halten U3: 43

Bye. [baɪ] Tschüs. Wiedersehen.

C

cabin ['kæbɪn] Hütte WF

cable ['keɪbl] Kabel WF

cafe ['kæfeɪ] Café

cake [keɪk] Kuchen

California [kælɪ'fɔːniə] Kalifornien WF U6

call [kɔːl] **1** anrufen; (herbei)rufen U2: 32; **call back** zurückrufen U2: 33; **call me at ...** ruf mich unter ... an WF; **2** nennen, bezeichnen U2: 30; **What do you call ...?** Wie nennt/bezeichnet man ...? U2: 30; **3 phone call** Anruf U2: 32

calling ['kɔːlɪŋ]: **Thanks for calling.** Danke für den Anruf.

came [keɪm] (→ come): **I came** ich kam, ich bin gekommen

camera ['kæmərə] Fotoapparat, Kamera U2: 36

camp [kæmp] lagern, zelten WF U6

campfire ['kæmpfaɪə] Lagerfeuer U4: 54

campground ['kæmpgraʊnd] (AE) Campingplatz, Zeltplatz U4: 54

camping ['kæmpɪŋ] Camping

can [kæn, kən] können, dürfen; **can't** [kɑːnt] nicht können; **Can you ...? - Yes, I can./No, I can't.** Kannst du ...? - Ja./Nein.

canal [kə'næl] Kanal

canoe [kə'nuː] Kanu

canoeing [kə'nuːɪŋ] Kanufahren, Paddeln

cap [kæp] Kappe

capital ['kæpɪtl] Hauptstadt

captain ['kæptɪn] Spielführer/in, Mannschaftskapitän/in WF

car [kɑː] Auto

card [kɑːd] Karte

career [kə'rɪə] **1** Beruf, Berufs- U3: 50; **2 career (in TV)** (Fernseh-)Karriere, berufliche Laufbahn (im Fernsehen) U2: 28

careful ['keəfl] vorsichtig

carnival ['kɑːnɪvl] Karneval

car park ['kɑːpɑːk] Parkplatz

carry ['kæri] tragen WF

cashier [kæ'ʃɪə] Kassierer, Kassiererin U4: 63

castle ['kɑːsl] Schloss; Burg

cat [kæt] Katze

catch [kætʃ] fangen WF

category ['kætəgəri] Kategorie WF

cauliflower ['kɒliflaʊə] Blumenkohl WF

CD [siː'diː] CD

celebration [selɪ'breɪʃn] Feier WF

cellphone ['selfəʊn] (AE) Handy, Mobiltelefon Next: 9

cent [sent] Cent U1: 12

centre ['sentə] Zentrum; Mitte

chair [tʃeə] Stuhl; Sessel

chairperson ['tʃeəpɜːsn] Vorsitzende, Vorsitzender

change [tʃeɪndʒ] **1** (sich) ändern, (sich) verändern; **change to** ändern in WF; **2** umsteigen U1: 13; **change at 42nd Street to line 7** an der 42. Straße in die Linie 7 umsteigen U1: 13; **3** Veränderung WF

character ['kærəktə] Figur, Person WF U6

charge [tʃɑːdʒ] aufladen WF

charged up [tʃɑːdʒd'ʌp]: **it's charged up** es ist aufgeladen

charger ['tʃɑːdʒə] (Batterie-)Ladegerät

chat [tʃæt]: **have a chat** sich unterhalten

chat show ['tʃætʃəʊ] Talkshow U2: 27

cheap [tʃiːp] billig, preiswert

check [tʃek] kontrollieren, überprüfen

cheer [tʃɪə] (zu)jubeln, hurra rufen U3: 42

cheerleader ['tʃɪəliːdə] *Person, die das Publikum bei einem Wettkampf zum Beifall anfeuert* U3: 38

cheese [tʃiːz] Käse

cherry ['tʃeri] Kirsche WF

chess [tʃes] Schach WF

chicken ['tʃɪkɪn] Huhn; (Brat-)Hähnchen

child, children [tʃaɪld, 'tʃɪldrən] Kind, Kinder

chips [tʃɪps] Pommes frites

chocolate ['tʃɒklət] Schokolade

choir ['kwaɪə] Chor WF

Christmas ['krɪsməs] Weihnachten

church [tʃɜːtʃ] Kirche

cider ['saɪdə] Apfelwein

cinema ['sɪnəmə] Kino

city ['sɪti] Stadt, Großstadt

clarinet [klærə'net] Klarinette WF

class [klɑːs] Klasse; **extra classes** Förderunterricht U3: 38

classical ['klæsɪkl] klassisch WF

classroom ['klɑːsruːm] Klassenzimmer

class teacher ['klɑː'tiːtʃə] Klassenlehrer, Klassenlehrerin

clean [kliːn] sauber

cleaner ['kliːnə] Putzhilfe, Raumpfleger/in U4: 63

clear [klɪə]: **clear tables** Tische abräumen WF

cliff [klɪf] Klippe, Felsen

climb (a hill) [klaɪm] (auf einen Hügel) klettern

climber ['klaɪmə] Kletterer, Kletterin
clock [klɒk] Uhr U3: 40
close [kləʊz] zumachen, schließen
closed [kləʊzd] geschlossen, zu
closet ['klɒzɪt] (AE) Wandschrank WF
clothes [kləʊðz] Kleidung, Kleider
cloud [klaʊd] Wolke
cloudy ['klaʊdi] bewölkt
club [klʌb] **1** Klub, Arbeitsgemeinschaft; Verein; **2** Disko
clue [klu:]: **I have no clue** ich habe keine Ahnung WF
coach [kəʊtʃ] Coach U3: 42
coast [kəʊst] Küste WF U6; **on the coast** an der Küste WF U6
coffee shop ['kɒfiʃɒp] Selbstbedienungscafé WF
cola ['kəʊlə] Cola
cold [kəʊld] kalt
collect [kə'lekt] sammeln
Colombia [kə'lɒmbiə] Kolumbien U5: 68
colour ['kʌlə] Farbe; **What colour is your room?** Welche Farbe hat dein Zimmer?
combine harvester [kɒmbaɪn'hɑ:vɪstə] Mähdrescher WF
come [kʌm] (I came, I've come) kommen; mitkommen; **I've come** ich bin gekommen; **come in** hereinkommen; **come first in ...** Erste/Erster werden bei ...
comedy ['kɒmədi] Komödie, humorvoller Film/Roman U2: 27
comic ['kɒmɪk] Comic WF
communications [kəmju:nɪ'keɪʃnz]: **information and communications technology** Informatik WF
compare [kəm'peə] vergleichen
comparison [kəm'pærɪsn] Vergleich WF
competition [kɒmpə'tɪʃn] Wettbewerb
complain [kəm'pleɪn] sich beschweren
complete [kəm'pli:t] vollständig
computer [kəm'pju:tə] Computer, Rechner
concerned (about) [kən'sɜ:nd] besorgt (wegen) WF
concert ['kɒnsət] Konzert U1: 18
confident ['kɒnfɪdənt] zuversichtlich, selbstsicher U3: 42
Congratulations! [kəngrætʃu'leɪʃnz] Herzlichen Glückwunsch!
connect [kə'nekt] anschließen, verbinden WF
context ['kɒntekst] Zusammenhang, Kontext U2: 31
conversation [kɒnvə'seɪʃn] Unterhaltung, Gespräch Next: 8
cook [kʊk] **1** kochen U4: 64; **2** Koch, Köchin
cool [ku:l] cool, toll
copy ['kɒpi] **1** abschreiben; kopieren U1: 21; **2** Kopie, Fotokopie WF
correct [kə'rekt] korrigieren, berichtigen
cost [kɒst] Preis WF
cotton ['kɒtn] Baumwolle WF
cougar ['ku:gə] (AE) Puma U4: 52
could [kʊd]: **I could(n't)** **1** ich konnte (nicht); **2** ich könnte (nicht) U2: 28
council ['kaʊnsl]: **school council** Schülermitverwaltung WF
country ['kʌntri] Land; **in the country** auf dem Land
county fair [kaʊnti'feə] *eine Art Landwirtschaftsschau* WF U6
courier ['kʊriə] Kurier/Kurierin, Bote/Botin
course [kɔ:s]: **of course** natürlich, selbstverständlich
court [kɔ:t] Spielfeld, Platz U3: 40
courtroom drama ['kɔ:tru:mdrɑ:mə] Gerichtsshow, -sendung WF
cousin ['kʌzn] Cousin, Cousine
cover ['kʌvə] **1** Abdeckung WF; **2** Umschlag WF
cover letter ['kʌvəletə] Anschreiben, Begleitbrief U4: 63
cow [kaʊ] Kuh
coward ['kaʊəd] Feigling WF
cowboy ['kaʊbɔɪ] Cowboy WF
cracker ['krækə] Kräcker WF U6
crash [kræʃ] abstürzen WF
crawl [krɔ:l] kriechen; **crawl in** hineinkriechen
credit ['kredɪt] Guthaben
crime [kraɪm] Verbrechen U5: 66
crisps [krɪsps] Kartoffelchips
crow [krəʊ] Krähe WF
cry [kraɪ] weinen
cup [kʌp] Tasse; **a cup of tea** eine Tasse Tee
cupboard ['kʌbəd] Schrank
cycling ['saɪklɪŋ] Radfahren
Czech Republic [tʃekrɪ'pʌblɪk] Tschechische Republik

D

dad [dæd] Papa, Vati
dance [dɑ:ns] **1** tanzen; **2** Tanzveranstaltung, Ball WF
dancer ['dɑ:nsə] Tänzer/in U5: 68
dancing ['dɑ:nsɪŋ]: **go dancing** tanzen gehen
dangerous ['deɪndʒərəs] gefährlich
dare [deə] Mutprobe
date [deɪt] Datum
daughter ['dɔ:tə] Tochter
day [deɪ] Tag
deaf [def] taub U5: 70
deal [di:l] (I dealt, I've dealt): **deal with bags** sich um Taschen kümmern
dear [dɪə]: **Dear ...** Liebe/Lieber ...; **Dear Sir/Madam, ...** Sehr geehrte Damen und Herren, ... WF
December [dɪ'sembə] Dezember
decorate ['dekəreɪt] schmücken WF
deer [dɪə] Hirsch, Hirsche U4: 52
definition [defɪ'nɪʃn] Definition U2: 30
degree [dɪ'gri:] Grad U5: 74
deli ['deli] (AE) Feinkostgeschäft und -imbiss U1: 12
deliver [dɪ'lɪvə] austragen WF
Denmark ['denmɑ:k] Dänemark
dentist ['dentɪst] Zahnarzt, Zahnärztin U1: 18
department store [dɪ'pɑ:tməntstɔ:] Kaufhaus
depressed [dɪ'prest] deprimiert WF
describe [dɪ'skraɪb] beschreiben WF U6
description [dɪ'skrɪpʃn] Beschreibung
design [dɪ'zaɪn] entwerfen WF
designated ['dezɪgneɪtɪd] gekennzeichnet WF
destination [destɪ'neɪʃn] (Reise-)Ziel WF
detail ['di:teɪl] Detail WF
detective [dɪ'tektɪv] Detektiv/in
devastated ['devəsteɪtɪd] erschüttert, am Boden zerstört
device [dɪ'vaɪs] Gerät WF
dialogue ['daɪəlɒg] Dialog, Gespräch
diary ['daɪəri] Tagebuch; **homework diary** Hausaufgabenheft; Schülerkalender
dictionary ['dɪkʃənri] Wörterbuch; Wörterverzeichnis
did [dɪd] (→ do): **I did** ich machte, ich habe gemacht
die [daɪ] sterben
difference ['dɪfrəns]: **make a difference** etwas bewegen, etwas verändern WF
different ['dɪfrənt] verschieden; anders; andere, anderer, anderes; **different from** anders als

difficult ['dɪfɪkəlt] schwierig, schwer U3: 50
diner ['daɪnə] (AE) Imbissstube, Café WF U6
dinner ['dɪnə] Abendessen U1: 12
director [də'rektə] Regisseur, Regisseurin U2: 28
dirty ['dɜ:ti] schmutzig
disc golf ['dɪskgɒlf] Discgolf („Scheibengolf") WF U6
dislike [dɪs'laɪk] Abneigung
district ['dɪstrɪkt] Bezirk, Gebiet U1: 10
disturb [dɪ'stɜ:b] stören WF
DJ ['di:dʒeɪ] DJ (= Discjockey)
do [du:] (he does; I did, I've done) 1 tun, machen; schaffen; 2 **I don't (= do not)/He doesn't (= does not) live here.** Ich wohne/Er wohnt nicht hier. **Do you/Does he live here? – Yes, I do./No, I don't./Yes, he does./No, he doesn't.** Wohnst du/Wohnt er hier? – Ja./Nein. **Don't eat.** Iss nicht.
document ['dɒkjumənt] Dokument, Schriftstück WF
documentary [dɒkju'mentri] Dokumentarfilm WF
does [dʌz] → do
dog [dɒg] Hund
doing ['du:ɪŋ]: **What are you doing?** Was machst du (da)? **How ya doin'?** (AE) Wie geht's? WF
dollar ($) ['dɒlə] Dollar *(Währung)* U1: 12
dolphin ['dɒlfɪn] Delfin
done [dʌn] (→ do): **I've done** ich habe gemacht
door [dɔ:] Tür
double-decker bus [dʌbldekə'bʌs] Doppeldecker WF
double room [dʌbl'ru:m] Doppelzimmer WF U6
down [daʊn] hinunter/herunter, hinab/herab
download [daʊn'ləʊd] herunterladen U5: 68
drama ['drɑ:mə]: **courtroom drama** Gerichtsshow, Gerichtssendung WF; **family drama** Familienfilm WF
drank [dræŋk] (→ drink): **I drank** ich trank, ich habe getrunken
draw [drɔ:] (I drew, I've drawn) zeichnen
dream [dri:m] 1 träumen; 2 Traum
dressing ['dresɪŋ] Anziehen WF

drink [drɪŋk] 1 (I drank, I've drunk) trinken; 2 Getränk
drive [draɪv] (I drove, I've driven) fahren
driven ['drɪvn] (→ drive): **I've driven** ich bin gefahren U4: 153
driver ['draɪvə] (Auto-)Fahrer, Fahrerin
drove [drəʊv] (→ drive): **I drove** ich fuhr, ich bin gefahren U4: 56
drug [drʌg] Droge U2: 35
drug-free [drʌg'fri:] drogenfrei WF
drums [drʌmz] Trommeln; Schlagzeug WF
dry trocken WF U6
Dubliner ['dʌblɪnə] Dubliner, Dublinerin
dumb [dʌm] dumm, blöd WF
dune [dju:n] Düne WF
dune buggy ['dju:nbʌgi] „Strandbuggy" *(offenes Freizeitauto)* WF
DVD [di:vi:'di:] DVD
DVD player [di:vi:'di:pleɪə] DVD-Player

E

each [i:tʃ] jede, jeder, jedes U3: 41
ear [ɪə] Ohr U5: 70
early ['ɜ:li] früh
earn [ɜ:n] verdienen WF
east [i:st] Osten; Ost-; östlich
easy ['i:zi] einfach, leicht
eat [i:t] (I ate, I've eaten) essen; fressen
eaten ['i:tn] (→ eat): **I've eaten** ich habe gegessen U4: 153
economy [ɪ'kɒnəmi] Wirtschaft U5: 78
education [edʒu'keɪʃn] Bildung, Ausbildung WF
egg [eg] Ei U1: 12
eighteensixties [eɪti:n'sɪkstiz]: **in the 1860s** in den sechziger Jahren des 19. Jahrhunderts WF
electric [ɪ'lektrɪk] elektrisch
electricity [ɪlek'trɪsəti] Strom, Elektrizität
electronic [ɪlek'trɒnɪk] elektronisch
e-mail ['i:meɪl] E-Mail
embarrassed [ɪm'bærəst] verlegen
emotional [ɪ'məʊʃənl] gefühlsbetont WF
employer [ɪm'plɔɪə] Arbeitgeber, Arbeitgeberin U5: 78
encyclopedia [ɪnsaɪklə'pi:diə] Lexikon, Enzyklopädie WF U6
end [end] Ende U1: 13; **in the end** letztendlich; schließlich

ending ['endɪŋ] Schluss; **happy ending** Happy End U3: 40
energy ['enədʒi] Energie; Kraft; **full of energy** energiegeladen WF
England ['ɪŋglənd] England
English ['ɪŋglɪʃ] englisch; Englisch; Engländer/Engländerin(nen); **English teacher** Englischlehrer/-lehrerin
enjoy [ɪn'dʒɔɪ] genießen WF; **Enjoy your stay.** Einen angenehmen Aufenthalt. WF U6; **everything for young men to enjoy** alles, was jungen Männern gefällt WF
enough [ɪ'nʌf] genug WF U6
entrance fee ['entrənsfi:] Eintrittspreis U4: 55
entry ['entri] Eintrag U2: 31
environment [ɪn'vaɪrənmənt] Umwelt; Umgebung
environmental studies [ɪnvaɪrən'mentl'stʌdiz] Umweltlehre WF
e-pal ['i:pæl] E-Mail-Freund/Freundin WF U6
equipment [ɪ'kwɪpmənt] Ausstattung, Ausrüstung U3: 40
errand ['erənd]: **run errands** Besorgungen machen WF
escape [ɪ'skeɪp] fliehen, entkommen WF
establish [ɪ'stæblɪʃ] einrichten; eröffnen WF U6
euro (€) ['jʊərəʊ] Euro
Europe ['jʊərəp] Europa
European [jʊərə'pi:ən] europäisch; Europäer, Europäerin U4: 60
evening ['i:vnɪŋ] Abend; **in the evening** am Abend, abends
event [ɪ'vent] Veranstaltung WF
ever ['evə] schon einmal, jemals; **the lowest price ever** der niedrigste Preis, den es je gab WF
evergreen ['evəgri:n] immergrün WF
every ['evri] jede, jeder, jedes
everybody ['evribɒdi] jeder, alle
everyone ['evriwʌn] jeder, alle WF
everything ['evriθɪŋ] alles
everywhere ['evriweə] überall, überallhin, überallher
exactly [ɪg'zæktli] genau WF
example [ɪg'zɑ:mpl] Beispiel
exchange [ɪks'tʃeɪndʒ] Austausch-; Tausch- U3: 46
excited [ɪk'saɪtɪd] aufgeregt, begeistert WF U6
exciting [ɪk'saɪtɪŋ] aufregend, spannend

excuse [ɪk'skjuːz]: **Excuse me, ...** Entschuldigen Sie, ...
exercise ['eksəsaɪz] Übung
exercise book ['eksəsaɪzbʊk] Schulheft
exhibition [eksɪ'bɪʃn] Ausstellung
expensive [ɪk'spensɪv] teuer
experience [ɪk'spɪəriəns] Erfahrung U4: 63; **do work experience** ein Berufspraktikum machen WF
expert ['ekspɜːt] Fachmann/-frau, Experte/Expertin U3: 41
explain [ɪk'spleɪn] erklären; **explain something to her** ihr etwas erklären U1: 16
extinct [ɪk'stɪŋkt] ausgestorben WF
extra ['ekstrə]: **extra classes** Förderunterricht U3: 38
eye [aɪ] Auge

F

face [feɪs] Gesicht
fact [fækt] Tatsache Next: 7; **In fact, it was better.** Es war sogar besser.
factory ['fæktri] Fabrik
fair [feə]: **county fair** *eine Art Landwirtschaftsschau* WF U6
fair play [feə'pleɪ] Fair Play U3: 42
fall [fɔːl] (I fell, I've fallen) fallen
false [fɔːls] falsch, unwahr U1: 11
family ['fæməli] Familie; **family name** Nachname, Familienname U4: 63
famous ['feɪməs] berühmt
fan [fæn] Fan, Anhänger/in
fantastic [fæn'tæstɪk] fantastisch U5: 68
fantasy film ['fæntəsifɪlm] Fantasyfilm WF
far [fɑː] weit Next: 7
Farewell Bend [feə'welbend] „Lebewohl-Biegung" WF U6
farm [fɑːm] Bauernhof, Hof
farmer ['fɑːmə] Bauer, Bäuerin
fast [fɑːst] schnell
fast food [fɑːst'fuːd] Fastfood *(schnell verzehrbare Gerichte)*
father ['fɑːðə] Vater
favourite ['feɪvərɪt] Lieblings-; Favorit, Favoritin
February ['februəri] Februar
feed [fiːd] (I fed, I've fed) füttern, zu essen geben
feel [fiːl] (I felt, I've felt) (sich) fühlen
feeling ['fiːlɪŋ] Gefühl U5: 71
feet [fiːt] Füße (→ foot)
fell [fel] (→ fall): **I fell** ich fiel, ich bin gefallen
felt [felt] (→ feel): **I felt** ich fühlte (mich), ich habe (mich) gefühlt; **I've felt** ich habe (mich) gefühlt
female ['fiːmeɪl] weiblich U5: 69
festival ['festɪvl] Festival; Fest U4: 52
field [fiːld] Feld, Wiese; Sportplatz WF
fight [faɪt] (I fought, I've fought) kämpfen; sich streiten U1: 14
file [faɪl] Karteikarte; Akte; Aktenordner WF
fill in [fɪl'ɪn] ausfüllen WF U6
film [fɪlm] Film
final ['faɪnl] Finale WF
financial [faɪ'nænʃl] finanziell, Finanz- U1: 10
find [faɪnd] (I found, I've found) finden; **find out** herausfinden
fine [faɪn] gut, schön; **How are you? – I'm fine, thanks.** Wie geht's? – Danke, gut.
finish ['fɪnɪʃ] aufhören (mit); beenden; **To finish, ...** Um zum Ende zu kommen, ...
fire ['faɪə] Feuer; Brand U4: 54
fireworks ['faɪəwɜːks] Feuerwerk U2: 36
first [fɜːst] **1** erste, erster, erstes; **first aid** erste Hilfe U3: 39; **first name** Vorname U4: 63; **2** zuerst
firstly ['fɜːstli] erstens
fish [fɪʃ] **1** Fisch, Fische; **2** fischen, angeln U4: 57
fish and chip shop [fɪʃən'tʃɪpʃɒp] *Schnellimbiss für Fisch und Pommes frites*
fishing ['fɪʃɪŋ] Fischen, Angeln
fit [fɪt] fit U3: 50
fix [fɪks] reparieren U3: 49
fizzy drink [fɪzi'drɪŋk] Limonade WF U6
flag [flæg] Fahne, Flagge
flat [flæt] Wohnung
flew [fluː]: **they flew** sie flogen WF
flight [flaɪt] Flug WF U6
flip phone ['flɪpfəʊn] Klapphandy
floor [flɔː] Fußboden, Boden
flyer ['flaɪə] Handzettel WF
follow ['fɒləʊ] folgen, verfolgen
food [fuːd] Essen; Lebensmittel
foot, feet [fʊt, fiːt] Fuß, Füße; **on foot** zu Fuß
football ['fʊtbɔːl] Fußball; **American football** American Football *(ähnlich wie Rugby)* U3: 41
for [fɔː, fə] **1** für; **2** zu; **3** denn WF; **for 14 years** 14 Jahre lang; **for a long time** lange U2: 28; **for breakfast** zum Frühstück; **stay for long** lange bleiben
foreground ['fɔːgraʊnd] Vordergrund WF
forest ['fɒrɪst] Wald, Waldgebiet U4: 52
forget [fə'get] (I forgot, I've forgotten) vergessen
forgot [fə'gɒt] (→ forget): **I forgot** ich vergaß, ich habe vergessen U4: 57
forgotten [fə'gɒtn] (→ forget): **I've forgotten** ich habe vergessen U4: 153
form [fɔːm] **1** Form; **2** Formular WF U6
forward ['fɔːwəd]: **I'm looking forward to hearing from you** ich freue mich darauf, von Ihnen zu hören U4: 56
forwards ['fɔːwədz] vorwärts WF
fought [fɔːt] (→ fight): **I fought** ich kämpfte, ich habe gekämpft U1: 144; **I've fought** ich habe gekämpft U1: 144
foul [faʊl] Foul U3: 40
found [faʊnd] (→ find): **I found** ich fand, ich habe gefunden; **I've found** ich habe gefunden; **If they found her ...** Wenn sie sie fänden ... WF
fountain ['faʊntən] Brunnen WF
France [frɑːns] Frankreich
freak [friːk] Freak *(jemand, der sich sehr für etwas begeistert)*
free [friː] **1** frei; **2** kostenlos; **free throw** Freiwurf U3: 40; **free time** Freizeit
freedom ['friːdəm] Freiheit U1: 14
freeway ['friːweɪ] Autobahn *(in den USA)* U2: 28
French [frentʃ] französisch; Französisch; Franzose(n), Französin(nen)
Friday ['fraɪdeɪ, 'fraɪdi] Freitag
friend [frend] Freund, Freundin
friendly ['frendli] freundlich
frightened ['fraɪtnd]: **I'm frightened** ich habe Angst
frightening ['fraɪtnɪŋ] beängstigend, Furcht erregend U5: 70
from [frɒm, frəm] aus; von; **I'm from London.** Ich komme aus London.
front [frʌnt]: **in front of** vor U5: 68
fruit [fruːt] Obst, Früchte

full [fʊl] voll; vollständig WF
fun [fʌn] Spaß; **It's fun.** Es macht Spaß.
funfair ['fʌnfeə] Kirmes, Jahrmarkt
funny ['fʌni] lustig, komisch
furniture ['fɜːnɪtʃə] Möbel
future ['fjuːtʃə] Zukunft

G

Gaelic ['gælɪk] Gälisch *(keltische Sprache)*
game [geɪm] Spiel; **game show** Spielshow WF
gang [gæŋ] Gang, Bande, Clique
garage ['gærɑːʒ] Autowerkstatt WF
garden ['gɑːdn] Garten
gardener ['gɑːdnə] Gärtner/in
gas [gæs] (AE) Benzin WF
gate [geɪt] Tor
gave [geɪv] (→ give): **I gave** ich gab, ich habe gegeben
gear [gɪə] **1** Gang *(Fahrrad, Auto)*; **2** Ausrüstung U2: 29; **safety gear** Sicherheitsausrüstung; **3** Kleidung, Klamotten U2: 29
general ['dʒenrəl] allgemein U5: 68
geography [dʒi'ɒgrəfi] Erdkunde, Geografie
German ['dʒɜːmən] deutsch; Deutsch; Deutsche, Deutscher
Germany ['dʒɜːməni] Deutschland
get [get] (I got, I've got) **1** bekommen; **2** holen; **3** kommen, gelangen; **get lost** sich verirren U4: 59; **get on the bus** in den Bus einsteigen WF; **get out** rausgehen WF **I have to get out of this place.** Ich muss hier raus. **get up** aufstehen; **you can get yourself clean** du kannst dich waschen WF
ghost [gəʊst] Geist, Gespenst
Gimme five! [gɪmi'faɪv] (AE) *Aufforderung dazu, die (erhobenen) Hände aneinander zu klatschen* WF
girl [gɜːl] Mädchen
girlfriend ['gɜːlfrend] (feste) Freundin
give [gɪv] (I gave, I've given) geben; **Give the book to Tim.** Gib Tim das Buch. **give first aid** erste Hilfe leisten WF; **give to the poor** die Armen beschenken WF
give up [gɪv'ʌp] aufgeben; **give up TV** auf den Fernseher verzichten WF
given ['gɪvn] (→ give): **I've given** ich habe gegeben

giving ['gɪvɪŋ]: **Giving orders** Anweisungen geben, Befehle erteilen U3: 46
glass [glɑːs] Glas, Trinkglas
glove [glʌv] Handschuh WF
go [gəʊ] (I went, I've gone) gehen; fahren; fliegen; führen; **go in** hineingehen; **Go ahead.** Mach(t) / Machen Sie nur. U5: 75
goalkeeper ['gəʊlkiːpə] Torwart WF
going to ['gəʊɪŋtu, 'gəʊɪŋtə]: **I'm going to win** ich werde gewinnen, ich gewinne; **I'm going to be a ranger.** Ich werde Ranger.
golf [gɒlf] Golf
good [gʊd] gut; **good at** gut in; **a ball's no good** ein Ball nützt nichts WF; **Good evening/ morning/night.** Gute(n) Abend/ Morgen/Nacht. **Good luck!** Viel Glück! U3: 42
Goodbye. [gʊd'baɪ] Auf Wiedersehen.
goose [guːs] Gans WF
got [gɒt] (→ get): **I got 1** ich bekam, ich habe bekommen; **2** (AE) ich habe WF; **I've got** ich habe bekommen
gotta ['gɒtə]: **gotta find me a place** (ich) muss einen Ort finden WF
government ['gʌvənmənt] Regierung WF
grade [greɪd]: **grade 9** (AE) 9. Klasse U3: 38
grandad ['grændæd] Opa, Großvater
granddaughter ['grændɔːtə] Enkeltochter, Enkelin WF
grandma ['grænmɑː] Oma, Großmutter
grandparents ['grænpeərənts] Großeltern U4: 56
grass [grɑːs] Gras, Rasen U2: 28
grave [greɪv] Grab
great [greɪt] toll, großartig
great-grandmother ['greɪt'grænmʌðə] Urgroßmutter WF
Greektown ['griːktaʊn] „Griechenstadt" WF
green [griːn] grün
grew [gruː] (→ grow): **I grew** ich wuchs, ich bin gewachsen U5: 156
grey [greɪ] grau WF
grey whale ['greɪ'weɪl] Grauwal WF
grill [grɪl] grillen WF U6
grilled [grɪld] gegrillt WF
ground [graʊnd] Boden
grounded ['graʊndɪd]: **I'm grounded** ich habe Hausarrest/ Stubenarrest

group [gruːp] Gruppe
grow [grəʊ] (I grew, I've grown) wachsen U5: 78
grown [grəʊn] (→ grow): **I've grown** ich bin gewachsen U5: 156
guard [gɑːd]: **security guard** Wachfrau, Wachmann
guess [ges] raten; erraten
guest [gest] Gast WF
guide [gaɪd] **1** führen WF; **2** Führer/in *(für Sehenswürdigkeiten)*
guitar [gɪ'tɑː] Gitarre
guys [gaɪz]: **Hi you guys.** (AE) Hallo Leute. Next: 8
gym [dʒɪm] Turnhalle; Fitnessstudio

H

had [hæd, həd] (→ have): **I had** ich hatte, ich habe gehabt; **I've had** ich habe gehabt; **he had told** er hatte erzählt WF; **it had sent** es hatte geschickt U2: 28; **they had brought/sold/taken** sie hatten gebracht/verkauft/mitgenommen WF; **they had come** sie waren gekommen WF; **If I had the money, ...** Wenn ich das Geld hätte, ... WF U6
hair [heə] Haar, Haare
hairdresser ['heədresə] Friseur/in
half [hɑːf]: **half past nine** halb zehn; **three and a half** dreieinhalb
half-time [hɑːf'taɪm] Halbzeit U3: 42
Halloween [hæləʊ'iːn] Halloween
ham [hæm] Schinken
hamburger ['hæmbɜːgə] Hamburger
hamster ['hæmstə] Hamster
hand [hænd] Hand; **On the one hand, ... On the other hand, ...** Einerseits ... Andererseits ... U2: 35
hand out [hænd'aʊt] verteilen WF
hand signal ['hændsɪgnəl] Handzeichen
hang out [hæŋ'aʊt] herumhängen WF
happen ['hæpən] passieren, geschehen; **(it) so happened to be ...** zufälligerweise war es ... WF
happy ['hæpi] glücklich, froh; **I'm happy for her** ich freue mich für sie; **Happy birthday!** Herzlichen Glückwunsch zum Geburtstag! **happy ending** Happy End U3: 40
hard [hɑːd] hart; schwer

harvest ['hɑ:vɪst] ernten WF
has [hæz, həz] → have
hate [heɪt] hassen, nicht ausstehen können
hate-free [heɪt'fri:] hassfrei WF
Havana [hə'vænə] Havanna U5: 66
have [hæv, həv] (he has; I had, I've had) **1** haben; **I'll have ...** Ich nehme ... *(Bestellung)* U1: 12; **have a chat** sich unterhalten; **have a cola** eine Cola trinken; **have a party** eine Party geben; **have a picnic** ein Picknick machen; **have an ice cream** ein Eis essen; **have breakfast** frühstücken; **Have a nice day!** (AE) (Einen) Schönen Tag noch! Next: 8; **2 I've (= I have)/he has finished** ich habe/er hat beendet; **I haven't (= have not)/he hasn't (= has not) finished** ich habe/er hat nicht beendet; **Have you ever ...? – Yes, I have./No, I haven't.** Bist/Hast du schon einmal ...? – Ja./Nein.
have to ['hævtu, 'hævtə] (I had to, I've had to) müssen
he [hi:] er; **he's (= he is)** er ist
head [hed] Kopf
heading ['hedɪŋ] Rubrik; Überschrift
healthy ['helθi] gesund
hear [hɪə] (I heard, I've heard) hören
heard [hɜ:d] (→ hear): **I heard** ich hörte, ich habe gehört; **I've heard** ich habe gehört
hearing ['hɪərɪŋ] Gehör WF
heart [hɑ:t]: **Learn it by heart.** Lerne es auswendig.
held [held] (→ hold): **I held** ich hielt, ich habe gehalten; **I've held** ich habe gehalten
Hello. [hə'ləʊ] Hallo. (Guten) Tag.
helmet ['helmɪt] Helm
help [help] **1** helfen; **Can I help you?** Kann ich Ihnen behilflich sein? U4: 61; **2** Hilfe
helper ['helpə] Helfer, Helferin
her [hɜ:] **1** ihr, ihre; **2** ihr, sie
here [hɪə] hier; hierher; **Here you are.** Hier, bitte.
hero, heroes ['hɪərəʊ, 'hɪərəʊz] Held/Heldin, Helden/Heldinnen WF U6
Hi. [haɪ] Hallo.
high [haɪ] hoch
high jump ['haɪdʒʌmp] Hochsprung
highlight ['haɪlaɪt] Höhepunkt WF
high school ['haɪsku:l] Oberschule *(in den USA)* U3: 38
highway ['haɪweɪ] (AE) Fernstraße WF U6
hike [haɪk] wandern U4: 53
hiker ['haɪkə] Wanderer, Wanderin U4: 59
hill [hɪl] Hügel, (kleiner) Berg
him [hɪm] ihm, ihn
hip [hɪp] Hüfte U5: 68
hire ['haɪə] mieten; vermieten
his [hɪz] sein, seine
Hispanic [hɪ'spænɪk] Hispano-Amerikaner/in; hispanisch; spanischsprachig U5: 67
Historical Society [hɪ'stɒrɪklsə'saɪəti] Geschichtsverein WF U6
history ['hɪstri] Geschichte
hit [hɪt] **1** (I hit, I've hit) schlagen U3: 42; **I hit** ich schlug, ich habe geschlagen U3: 42; **I've hit** ich habe geschlagen U3: 150; **2** Hit U5: 77
hobby ['hɒbi] Hobby
hockey ['hɒki] Hockey
hold [həʊld] (I held, I've held) halten; (MP3-Player:) speichern
hole [həʊl] Loch WF
holiday, holidays ['hɒlədeɪ, -z] Ferien, Urlaub; **go on holiday** in den Urlaub fahren; **she's on holiday** sie macht Urlaub, sie ist im Urlaub
home [həʊm] Heim, Zuhause; **at home** zu Hause, daheim; **go home** nach Hause gehen; **children's home** Kinderheim WF
homecoming ['həʊmkʌmɪŋ] Ehemaligentreffen WF
home economics ['həʊmi:kə'nɒmɪks] Hauswirtschaftslehre WF
homeless ['həʊmləs] heimatlos; obdachlos U2: 25
home-made [həʊm'meɪd] selbst gemacht
homesick ['həʊmsɪk]: **feel homesick** Heimweh haben WF U6
homework ['həʊmwɜ:k] Hausaufgaben, Schularbeiten; **I do my homework.** Ich mache (meine) Hausaufgaben.
homework diary [həʊmwɜ:k'daɪəri] Hausaufgabenheft; Schülerkalender
hoop [hu:p] (Basketball-)Korb U3: 40
hope [həʊp] **1** hoffen; **2** Hoffnung WF
horror ['hɒrə] Horror
horse [hɔ:s] Pferd
horse riding ['hɔ:sraɪdɪŋ] Reiten
hospital ['hɒspɪtl] Krankenhaus
hot [hɒt] heiß
hot dog ['hɒtdɒg] Hot Dog WF U6
hotel [həʊ'tel] Hotel
hour ['aʊə] Stunde
house [haʊs] **1** Haus; **at Tim's house** bei Tim (zu Hause); **Let's go to my house.** Gehen wir zu mir (nach Hause). **2** House *(Musikrichtung)* U1: 21
how [haʊ] wie; **how to find us** wie man uns findet; **How much is/are ...?** Was kostet/kosten ...? **How ya doin'?** (AE) Wie geht's? WF
hundred ['hʌndrəd] hundert
hungry ['hʌŋgri] hungrig; **I'm hungry.** Ich habe Hunger.
hunt [hʌnt] jagen U4: 57
hunter ['hʌntə] Jäger, Jägerin U4: 60
hurling ['hɜ:lɪŋ] Hurling *(irische Sportart; ähnlich wie Hockey)*
hurricane ['hʌrɪkən] Orkan U5: 74
hurry ['hʌri]: **Hurry up!** Beeil dich!
hurt [hɜ:t] (I hurt, I've hurt) verletzen, wehtun; **I hurt my hand** ich verletzte mir die Hand, ich habe mir die Hand verletzt

I

I [aɪ] ich; **I'd like ...** Ich möchte .../Ich hätte gern ...; **I'd like to go/...** Ich möchte gehen/...; **I'll (= I will) go** ich werde gehen; **I'll give you your invitations in the break.** Ich gebe euch eure Einladungen in der Pause. **I'll have ...** Ich nehme ... *(Bestellung)* U1: 12; **I'm (= I am)** ich bin
ice cream [aɪs'kri:m] (Speise-)Eis
idea [aɪ'dɪə] Idee, Einfall
idol ['aɪdl] Idol WF
if [ɪf] **1** wenn, falls; **2** ob U3: 49
if-clause ['ɪfklɔ:z] if-Satz WF
ill [ɪl] krank
illegal [ɪ'li:gl] ungesetzlich, illegal U5: 78
illness ['ɪlnəs] Krankheit U4: 57
illuminations [ɪlu:mɪ'neɪʃnz] Festbeleuchtung
imagine [ɪ'mædʒɪn] sich (etwas) vorstellen
immigrant ['ɪmɪgrənt] Immigrant/Immigrantin, Einwanderer/Einwanderin U1: 11
imperative [ɪm'perətɪv] Befehlsform, Imperativ U3: 44
important [ɪm'pɔ:tnt] wichtig

in [ɪn] in; **in 1971** (im Jahre) 1971; **in April** im April; **In fact, it was better.** Es war sogar besser. **in Fairfield Road** in der Fairfield Road; **in front of** [ɪn'frʌntəv] vor U5: 68; **in German** auf Deutsch; **in the car park** auf dem Parkplatz U3: 46; **in the country** auf dem Land; **in the morning/afternoon/evening** am Morgen/Nachmittag/Abend; **in the picture** auf dem Bild; **in the playground** auf dem Schulhof; **in the same place** am selben Ort; **in the street** auf der Straße; **in the world** auf der (ganzen) Welt; **in winter** im Winter; **come in** hereinkommen; **go in** hineingehen

Independence Day [ɪndɪ'pendənsdeɪ] Unabhängigkeitstag WF

Indian ['ɪndiən] Indianer, Indianerin; indianisch WF U6

indie (music) ['ɪndi] „Indie-Musik" *(von großen Plattenfirmen unabhängige Musik)* WF

indoors [ɪn'dɔːz] in der Halle, drinnen

infinitive [ɪn'fɪnətɪv] Infinitiv WF

information [ɪnfə'meɪʃn] Informationen, Informations-; **information and communications technology** Informatik WF

in-line skating [ɪnlaɪn'skeɪtɪŋ] Inlineskating WF

insert [ɪn'sɜːt] einlegen WF

instead of [ɪn'stedəv] statt

instructions [ɪn'strʌkʃnz] Gebrauchsanweisung

instrument ['ɪnstrəmənt] Instrument

intercom ['ɪntəkɒm] Sprechanlage

interest ['ɪntrəst] Interesse

interested (in) ['ɪntrəstɪd] interessiert (an)

interesting ['ɪntrəstɪŋ] interessant

international [ɪntə'næʃnəl] international

Internet ['ɪntənet] Internet; **on the Internet** im Internet

Internet kiosk ['ɪntənetkiːɒsk] Internet-Kiosk *(öffentlich zugängliches Internet-Terminal)*

interpreting [ɪn'tɜːprɪtɪŋ] Dolmetschen

interview ['ɪntəvjuː] **1** Interview WF; **2** Vorstellungsgespräch WF

interviewer ['ɪntəvjuːə] Gesprächsleiter/in eines Vorstellungsgesprächs WF

into ['ɪntu, 'ɪntə] in (... hinein/herein); **into the street** auf die Straße (hinaus)

invitation [ɪnvɪ'teɪʃn] Einladung

invite (for) [ɪn'vaɪt] einladen (zu)

Ireland ['aɪələnd] Irland

Irish ['aɪrɪʃ] irisch; Irisch; Ire(n), Irin(nen)

is [ɪz] ist; **isn't (= is not)** ist nicht; **What colour is your room?** Welche Farbe hat dein Zimmer?

island ['aɪlənd] Insel U4: 53

it [ɪt] **1** es *(nicht bei Personen:* er, sie); **2** ihm, es *(nicht bei Personen*: ihm, ihn; ihr, sie); **it's (= it is)** es ist; **it's 24–18 to North** es steht 24 : 18 für North U3: 42; **It's my birthday.** Ich habe Geburtstag. **It's Sarah.** Hier spricht Sarah.

Italy ['ɪtəli] Italien U1: 10

its [ɪts] sein, seine; ihr, ihre

J

jackalope ['dʒækələʊp] *amerikanisches Fabeltier* WF U6

jacket ['dʒækət] Jacke

January ['dʒænjuəri] Januar

jealous (of) ['dʒeləs] neidisch (auf); eifersüchtig (auf)

jeans [dʒiːnz] Jeans

job [dʒɒb] **1** Aufgabe, Arbeit; **2** Arbeitsstelle; Beruf

jog [dʒɒg] joggen U2: 28

jogger ['dʒɒgə] Jogger, Joggerin

jogging ['dʒɒgɪŋ] Jogging

jogging trousers ['dʒɒgɪŋtraʊzəz] Jogginghose WF

join [dʒɔɪn]: **join a club** einem Klub beitreten, Mitglied in einem Klub werden; **join us for a party** an unserer Party teilnehmen WF

joke [dʒəʊk] Witz, Scherz WF

judo ['dʒuːdəʊ] Judo

juice [dʒuːs] Saft

July [dʒu'laɪ] Juli

jump [dʒʌmp] springen; **(the) high jump** Hochsprung

June [dʒuːn] Juni

junior ['dʒuːniə]: **junior ranger** Junior-Ranger U4: 54

jury ['dʒʊəri] Jury WF

just [dʒʌst] **1** gerade, soeben; **2** einfach WF; **Just a minute.** Einen Augenblick. U5: 74; **just before** kurz (be)vor

K

kayaking ['kaɪækɪŋ] Kajakfahren U4: 61

keen [kiːn]: **I'm not keen on it** ich habe nicht viel dafür übrig

keep [kiːp] (I kept, I've kept) halten, behalten U4: 54

kept [kept] (→ keep): **I kept** ich hielt, ich habe gehalten U4: 153; **I've kept** ich habe gehalten U4: 153

key [kiː] Schlüssel U5: 70

keyboard ['kiːbɔːd] Keyboard WF

kick [kɪk] kicken, treten U3: 40

kid [kɪd] Kind; Jugendliche/r

kill [kɪl] töten, umbringen U1: 14

kilometre ['kɪləmiːtə] Kilometer; **kilometres per hour** Stundenkilometer WF U6

kilt [kɪlt] Kilt *(Schottenrock)*

kind [kaɪnd]: **What kind of programmes?** Was für Sendungen? U2: 27

king [kɪŋ] König WF

kiosk ['kiːɒsk]: **Internet kiosk** Internet-Kiosk *(öffentlich zugängliches Internet-Terminal)*

kiss [kɪs] (sich) küssen U5: 70

kitchen ['kɪtʃɪn] Küche

knew [njuː] (→ know): **I knew** ich wusste, ich habe gewusst

know [nəʊ] (I knew, I've known) wissen; kennen; **he wanted to know her better** er wollte sie besser kennen lernen WF

L

label ['leɪbl] Schildchen, Etikett

lad [læd] Junge WF

laid [leɪd]: **he laid** er legte WF

lake [leɪk] (Binnen-)See Next: 7; **Lake Michigan** [leɪk'mɪʃɪgən] Michigansee WF

lamb [læm] Lamm(fleisch) WF

lamp [læmp] Lampe WF

land [lænd] Land WF

landmark ['lændmɑːk] Wahrzeichen WF

language ['læŋgwɪdʒ] Sprache

laptop ['læptɒp] Laptop

last [lɑːst] letzte, letzter, letztes; **at last** endlich WF

late [leɪt] spät; zu spät, verspätet; **He's late (for school).** Er kommt zu spät (zur Schule).

laugh [lɑːf] lachen

law [lɔː] Gesetz WF

lawn [lɔ:n] Rasen WF
lawyer ['lɔ:jə] Rechtsanwalt, Rechtsanwältin WF
lead [li:d] (I led, I've led) führen U4: 59
lead singer [li:d'sɪŋə] Leadsänger, Leadsängerin WF
lean [li:n] sich lehnen WF; **lean forwards/backwards** sich vorbeugen/zurücklehnen WF
learn [lɜ:n] lernen; **learn about London** etwas über London erfahren; **Learn it by heart.** Lerne es auswendig.
leave [li:v] (I left, I've left) **1** verlassen, weggehen (von); abreisen WF U6; **2** (stehen/liegen) lassen, vergessen U3: 46
led [led] (→ lead): **I led** ich führte, ich habe geführt U4: 153; **I've led** ich habe geführt U4: 153
leek [li:k] Lauch/Porree(stange)
left [left] links; **on the left** auf der linken Seite; **on your left** links (von Ihnen)
left [left] (→ leave): **I left** ich verließ, ich habe verlassen; **I've left** ich habe verlassen U3: 150
lemonade [lemə'neɪd] (Zitronen-)Limonade
less [les] weniger U2: 27
lesson ['lesn] (Unterrichts-)Stunde
let [let]: **Let's finish.** Lasst uns aufhören./Hören wir auf.
letter ['letə] **1** Brief; **2** Buchstabe
letterboxing ['letəbɒksɪŋ] „Letterboxing" *(eine Art Schatzsuche)*
lettuce ['letɪs] (Kopf-)Salat U1: 12
library ['laɪbrəri] Bücherei WF
lie [laɪ] lügen U5: 68
life [laɪf] Leben
lift [lɪft] anheben WF
light [laɪt] Licht, Lampe
light switch ['laɪtswɪtʃ] Lichtschalter U5: 70
like [laɪk] **1** mögen, gern haben; **I like it.** Ich mag es./Es gefällt mir. **I (don't) like walking.** Ich laufe (nicht) gern. **I'd like ...** Ich möchte .../Ich hätte gern ...; **I'd like to go/...** Ich möchte gehen/...; **Who likes it best?** Wem gefällt es am besten? **2** wie; **like that/this** so U5: 68; **a job like that/this** so ein Job U2: 29; **What does she look like?** Wie sieht sie aus? **what the book is like** wie das Buch ist
likes and dislikes ['laɪksən'dɪslaɪks] Vorlieben und Abneigungen
line [laɪn] **1** Zeile; **2** Linie U1: 13; (AE) (Warte-)Schlange U2: 145; **wait in line** (AE) Schlange stehen U2: 28; **line of gear** Kollektion WF
link [lɪŋk] Link; Verbindung U5: 73
lip [lɪp] Lippe
list [lɪst] Liste
listen ['lɪsn] zuhören; **listen to** hören, sich anhören
litter ['lɪtə] Abfall
little ['lɪtl] klein U1: 10; **Little Italy** „Klein-Italien" U1: 10
live [lɪv] wohnen, leben
live [laɪv] live WF
living room ['lɪvɪŋru:m] Wohnzimmer
local ['ləʊkl] örtlich, einheimisch WF
locker ['lɒkə] Schließfach, Spind U3: 38
lonely ['ləʊnli] einsam
long [lɒŋ] lang; lange
longhouse ['lɒŋhaʊs] Langhaus WF
look [lʊk] **1** schauen, sehen; **look after** [lʊk'ɑ:ftə] sich kümmern um, aufpassen auf U4: 59; **look at** ansehen, sich ansehen; **look for** suchen; **I'm looking forward to hearing from you** ich freue mich darauf, von Ihnen zu hören U4: 56; **2** aussehen; **What does she look like?** Wie sieht sie aus?
lose [lu:z] (I lost, I've lost) verlieren U1: 15
lost [lɒst] **1** (→ lose): **I lost** ich verlor, ich habe verloren U1: 15; **I've lost** ich habe verloren U1: 144; **2 get lost** sich verirren U4: 59
lots [lɒts]: **lots of** viele; viel
lottery ['lɒtəri]: **win a lottery** in einer Lotterie gewinnen WF
lotto ['lɒtəʊ] Lotto; **win the lotto** im Lotto gewinnen
loud [laʊd] laut U5: 70
love [lʌv] **1** lieben, sehr mögen; **I love reading.** Ich lese sehr gern. U1: 22; **2** Liebe; **(Lots of) Love, ...** (Viele) Liebe Grüße ...
luck [lʌk]: **Good luck!** Viel Glück! U3: 42
lucky ['lʌki]: **Lucky thing!** Der/Die/Du Glückliche/r! U2: 28
lunch [lʌntʃ] Mittagessen
lunch break ['lʌntʃbreɪk] Mittagspause
lunchtime ['lʌntʃtaɪm] Mittagszeit; Mittagspause
Luxembourg ['lʌksəmbɜ:g] Luxemburg

M

machine [mə'ʃi:n] Maschine, Gerät
madam ['mædəm]: **Dear Sir/Madam, ...** Sehr geehrte Damen und Herren, ... WF
made [meɪd] (→ make): **I made** ich machte, ich habe gemacht; **I've made** ich habe gemacht; **if they made me say goodbye** wenn man mich zwänge, mich zu verabschieden; **she made them feel happy** sie machte sie glücklich WF
magazine [mægə'zi:n] Zeitschrift
main point ['meɪn'pɔɪnt] Schwerpunkt U2: 35
make [meɪk] (I made, I've made) machen, herstellen; **make a difference** etwas bewegen, etwas verändern WF; **make an arrangement** eine Absprache treffen; **make groups** Gruppen bilden; **Make notes.** Mach dir Notizen. **nobody can make me eat this** keiner kann mich dazu zwingen, dies zu essen
make-up ['meɪkʌp] Make-up U2: 30
make-up artist ['meɪkʌpɑ:tɪst] Visagist, Visagistin U2: 29
male [meɪl] männlich U5: 68
mall [mɔ:l] (AE) Einkaufszentrum U1: 18
man, men [mæn, men] Mann, Männer
many ['meni] viele; **many a man** so manchen Mann WF
map [mæp] Landkarte, Karte; Plan U1: 13
March [mɑ:tʃ] März
market ['mɑ:kɪt] Markt WF
married ['mærid] verheiratet
marshmallow [mɑ:ʃ'mæləʊ] Marshmallow („Mäusespeck") WF U6
master ['mɑ:stə] Herr WF
match [mætʃ] **1** Spiel, Wettkampf; **2 Match the words with the pictures.** Ordne den Wörtern die Bilder zu.
maths [mæθs] Mathe(matik)
maximum ['mæksɪməm] Höchst- WF
May [meɪ] Mai
maybe ['meɪbi] vielleicht
me [mi:] **1** mir, mich; **2** ich
meal [mi:l] Mahlzeit, (zubereitetes) Essen WF
mean [mi:n] (I meant, I've meant) meinen; bedeuten

meaning ['miːnɪŋ] Bedeutung U2: 31
meant [ment] (→ mean): **I meant** ich meinte, ich habe gemeint; **I've meant** ich habe gemeint
meat [miːt] Fleisch U1: 16
Mecca ['mekə] Mekka WF
media ['miːdiə]: **the media** die Medien U2: 27
medical ['medɪkl] Medizin-; medizinisch U3: 38
meet [miːt] (I met, I've met) **1** (sich) treffen (mit); **2** kennen lernen; **Nice to meet you.** Schön, dich/Sie kennen zu lernen.
melon ['melən] Melone WF
men [men] Männer (→ man)
menu ['menjuː] Speisekarte U1: 12
message ['mesɪdʒ] Mitteilung, Nachricht U1: 21; **Can I take a message?** Kann ich (ihm/ihr) etwas ausrichten? U2: 32; **phone message** Telefonnotiz; telefonische Nachricht U2: 32
met [met] (→ meet): **I met** ich traf, ich habe getroffen
metal ['metl] Metal *(Musikrichtung)* U5: 68
metre ['miːtə] Meter
Mexico ['meksɪkəʊ] Mexiko U5: 78
mile [maɪl] Meile
milk [mɪlk] Milch
milking machine ['mɪlkɪŋməʃiːn] Melkmaschine WF
million ['mɪljən] Million
mind [maɪnd]: **Do you mind if I sit here?** Haben Sie etwas dagegen, wenn ich mich hier hinsetze? U5: 75
mind map ['maɪndmæp] Mindmap *(eine Art Gedankenkarte)* U4: 59
minute ['mɪnɪt] Minute
mirror ['mɪrə] Spiegel U5: 70
miss [mɪs] **1** vermissen; **2** daneben treffen; daneben gehen U3: 43
missing ['mɪsɪŋ]: **the missing words** die fehlenden Wörter
mix up [mɪks'ʌp] durcheinander bringen, mischen Next: 9
mobile (phone) ['məʊbaɪl] Handy
mobile home [məʊbaɪl'həʊm] (Stand-)Wohnwagen
model ['mɒdl] (Foto-)Modell U2: 29
modern ['mɒdn] modern
mom [mɒm] (AE) Mama, Mutti U1: 22
moment ['məʊmənt] Moment; **at the moment** zurzeit, im Moment
Monday ['mʌndeɪ, 'mʌndi] Montag
money ['mʌni] Geld
monster ['mɒnstə] Monster
month [mʌnθ] Monat
moon [muːn] Mond U5: 70
moor [mɔː] (Hoch-)Moor
more [mɔː] mehr, weitere; **more expensive** teurer
morning ['mɔːnɪŋ] Morgen; **in the morning** am Morgen, morgens; **Monday morning** Montagmorgen
moss [mɒs] Moos WF
most [məʊst] der/die/das meiste, die meisten; **most expensive** teuerste/teuerster/teuerstes, am teuersten
motel [məʊ'tel] Motel WF U6
mother ['mʌðə] Mutter
motorbike ['məʊtəbaɪk] Motorrad
mountain ['maʊntən] Berg; **in the mountains** im Gebirge
mountain bike ['maʊntənbaɪk] Mountainbike
mountain biking ['maʊntənbaɪkɪŋ] Mountainbikefahren
mountain board ['maʊntənbɔːd] Mountainboard *(eine Art Gelände-Skateboard)*
mountain boarding ['maʊntənbɔːdɪŋ] Mountainboardfahren
mourn [mɔːn]: **mourn for his life** um sein Leben trauern WF
mouth [maʊθ] Mund U5: 70
move [muːv] **1** (sich) bewegen U3: 42; **2** umziehen
movie ['muːvi] (AE) Film U1: 19
movie theater ['muːviθɪətə] (AE) Kino WF
mow [məʊ] mähen WF
MP3 player [empiː'θriːpleɪə] MP3-Player
Mr ['mɪstə]: **Mr Dunn** Herr Dunn
Mrs ['mɪsɪz]: **Mrs Jones** Frau Jones
Ms [mɪz, məz]: **Ms Brown** Frau Brown
much [mʌtʃ] viel
mum [mʌm] Mama, Mutti
museum [mju'ziːəm] Museum
mushroom ['mʌʃruːm] Champignon, Pilz WF
music ['mjuːzɪk] Musik
musical instrument [mjuːzɪkl'ɪnstrəmənt] Musikinstrument
musician [mju'zɪʃn] Musiker, Musikerin U5: 67
Muslim ['mʊzlɪm] Muslim, Muslimin U1: 14
must [mʌst] müssen
mustn't ['mʌsnt] nicht dürfen
my [maɪ] mein, meine

N

name [neɪm] **1** Name; **What's your name?** Wie heißt du? **2** nennen WF U6
narrow ['nærəʊ] schmal, eng
national park ['næʃnəl'pɑːk] Nationalpark
Native American ['neɪtɪvə'merɪkən] amerik. Ureinwohner/in, Indianer/Indianerin U4: 56
natural ['nætʃrəl] natürlich WF
navy (blue) ['neɪvi] marineblau WF
NBA (National Basketball Association) [enbiː'eɪ] Nationaler Basketball-Verband *(in den USA)* WF
near [nɪə] in der Nähe (von); nah
nearest ['nɪərɪst]: **the nearest airport** der nächste Flughafen
nearly ['nɪəli] fast WF
need [niːd] brauchen
neighbour ['neɪbə] Nachbar, Nachbarin
neighbourhood ['neɪbəhʊd] Viertel, Gegend U1: 11
nervous ['nɜːvəs] nervös, ängstlich
net [net] Netz WF
Netherlands ['neðələndz] Niederlande
network ['netwɜːk] Netz; Wortnetz, Wörternetz
never ['nevə] (noch) nie, niemals
new [njuː] neu
news [njuːz] Nachricht(en); Neuigkeit(en)
newspaper ['njuːzpeɪpə] Zeitung
next [nekst] nächste, nächster, nächstes
next to ['nekstu, 'nekstə] neben
nice [naɪs] nett; schön
nickname ['nɪkneɪm] Spitzname WF U6
night [naɪt] Nacht; **at night** nachts, in der Nacht
no [nəʊ] **1** nein; **2** kein, keine; **There's no such thing.** So etwas gibt es nicht.
nobody ['nəʊbədi] niemand
noise [nɔɪz] Lärm; Geräusch U4: 54
nominee [nɒmɪ'niː] Kandidat, Kandidatin WF
nonsense ['nɒnsns] Unsinn, Blödsinn
north [nɔːθ] Norden; Nord-; nördlich; **in the north** im Norden

North Star [nɔ:θ'stɑ:] Nordstern WF
(the) north-west [nɔ:θ'west] (der) Nordwesten U4: 52
northern ['nɔ:ðən] Nord-, nördlich
Northern Ireland ['nɔ:ðən'aɪələnd] Nordirland
not [nɒt] nicht
note [nəʊt] Notiz
nothing ['nʌθɪŋ] (gar) nichts
noticeboard ['nəʊtɪsbɔ:d] Anschlagbrett, Schwarzes Brett
noun [naʊn] Nomen
November [nəʊ'vembə] November
now [naʊ] nun, jetzt
number ['nʌmbə] Nummer; Zahl; Ziffer; Anzahl WF U6

O

object ['ɒbdʒɪkt] Gegenstand, Objekt WF
ocean ['əʊʃn] Ozean; Meer U4: 57
o'clock [ə'klɒk]: **at eight o'clock** um acht/zwanzig Uhr
October [ɒk'təʊbə] Oktober
of [ɒv, əv] von; **a picture of my dog** ein Bild meines Hundes; **a cup of tea** eine Tasse Tee; **think of** denken an
of course [əv'kɔ:s] natürlich, selbstverständlich
off [ɒf] von; **jump on and off** rein- und rausspringen WF
offer ['ɒfə] **1** anbieten; **2** Angebot; **special offer** Sonderangebot
office ['ɒfɪs] Büro WF; **tourist office** Touristeninformation, Fremdenverkehrsbüro
officer ['ɒfɪsə]: **police officer** Polizist/Polizistin, Polizeibeamter/-beamtin
off-road ['ɒfrəʊd] abseits der Straße, im Gelände
often ['ɒfn] oft
oil [ɔɪl] Öl WF
OK [əʊ'keɪ] okay, (schon) gut, in Ordnung; **Are you OK?** Ist alles in Ordnung bei dir? **That's OK.** Schon gut./Bitte.
old [əʊld] alt
Olympics [ə'lɪmpɪks]: **the Olympics** die Olympischen Spiele
on [ɒn] **1** auf; **2** an, eingeschaltet; **on August 5th** am 5. August; **on a reservation** in einer Reservation U4: 151; **on Dartmoor** in Dartmoor; **on foot** zu Fuß; **on holiday** in/im Urlaub; **on Saturdays** samstags; **on school days** an Schultagen; **on special offer** im Sonderangebot; **on the beach** am Strand U2: 29; **on the board** an der Tafel; **on the bus** im Bus; **on the coast** an der Küste WF U6; **on the intercom** über die Sprechanlage; **on the Internet** im Internet; **On the one hand, ... On the other hand, ...** Einerseits ... Andererseits ... U2: 35; **on the phone** am Telefon; **on the road** unterwegs; **on the weekend** (AE) am Wochenende WF; **on TV** im Fernsehen; **get on the team** in die Mannschaft kommen; **jump on and off** rein- und rausspringen WF
one [wʌn] ein, eine, einer, eines; **one day** eines Tages
online [ɒn'laɪn] online U2: 34
only ['əʊnli] nur, bloß; erst
onto ['ɒntʊ, 'ɒntə] auf (... hinauf/herauf)
open ['əʊpən] **1** öffnen, aufmachen; **2** sich öffnen, aufgehen; **3** offen, geöffnet
opening act ['əʊpənɪŋækt] Vorgruppe WF
opinion [ə'pɪnjən] Meinung U5: 77; **in my opinion** meiner Meinung nach U5: 77
opposite ['ɒpəzɪt] **1** Gegenteil U1: 17; **2** gegenüber (von) U5: 70
or [ɔ:] oder
orange ['ɒrɪndʒ] Orange
order ['ɔ:də] **1** Reihenfolge; **2** Anweisung, Befehl U3: 46; **out of order** außer Betrieb WF
organize ['ɔ:gənaɪz] ordnen; organisieren
orphan ['ɔ:fn] Waise WF
other ['ʌðə] andere, weitere
our ['aʊə] unser, unsere
out [aʊt] hinaus/heraus, aus U1: 16; **find out** herausfinden
out of ['aʊtəv] aus (... hinaus/heraus); **out of order** außer Betrieb WF; **I have to get out of this place.** Ich muss hier raus.
outdoor ['aʊtdɔ:]: **outdoor activity** Beschäftigung im Freien; **outdoor store** (AE) Geschäft mit Artikeln für Sport und Freizeit im Freien U4: 63
outdoors [aʊt'dɔ:z] im Freien, draußen
outlaw ['aʊtlɔ:] Bandit, Banditin WF
over ['əʊvə] vorbei, zu Ende, aus; **Come on over!** Komm vorbei! WF; **over there** da drüben, dort drüben (hin) U3: 46
own [əʊn]: **your own room** dein eigenes Zimmer

P

Pacific [pə'sɪfɪk] pazifisch WF
pack [pæk] packen, einpacken
page [peɪdʒ] Seite
paid [peɪd] (→ pay): **I paid** ich zahlte, ich habe gezahlt
pain [peɪn] Schmerzen; **Parents are a pain!** Eltern nerven!
palm tree ['pɑ:mtri:] Palme WF
panic ['pænɪk] durchdrehen, in Panik geraten U3: 50
paper ['peɪpə] Papier WF
papers ['peɪpəz] (Ausweis-)Papiere U5: 78
paragraph ['pærəgrɑ:f] Absatz
paramedic [pærə'medɪk] Rettungssanitäter, Rettungssanitäterin U3: 50
parent, parents ['peərənt, 'peərənts] Elternteil, Eltern
park [pɑ:k] Park
part [pɑ:t] Teil
partner ['pɑ:tnə] Partner, Partnerin
part-time [pɑ:t'taɪm] Teilzeit, Teilzeit- U4: 63
party ['pɑ:ti] Party
pass [pɑ:s] vergehen WF
passage ['pæsɪdʒ] Gang, Korridor
passive ['pæsɪv] Passiv WF U6
past [pɑ:st] Vergangenheit
past [pɑ:st]: **past the house** am Haus vorbei; **five past ten** fünf nach zehn; **half past nine** halb zehn
past progressive [pɑ:stprə'gresɪv] Verlaufsform der Vergangenheit U2: 37
pasta ['pæstə] Nudeln WF
pavement ['peɪvmənt] Bürgersteig, Gehsteig
pay [peɪ] **1** (I paid, I've paid) zahlen, bezahlen; **2** Bezahlung; Lohn WF
PE [pi:'i:] **(= physical education)** Sport(unterricht) WF
pear [peə] Birne WF
peer mediation ['pɪəmi:di'eɪʃn] Streitschlichtung WF
pen [pen] Füller
pence (p) [pens] Pence *(britische Währung)*

pencil ['pensl] Bleistift
pencil case ['penslkeɪs] Federmäppchen, Schreibetui
penfriend ['penfrend] Brieffreund, Brieffreundin WF
people ['pi:pl] **1** Leute, Menschen; **black/white people** Schwarze/Weiße U1: 14; **2** Volk WF; **the Makah people** das Volk der Makah WF
pepper ['pepə] Paprikaschote WF
per [pɜ:] pro U4: 63
per cent [pə'sent] Prozent U5: 67
percussion [pə'kʌʃn]: **percussion instrument** Schlaginstrument WF
permitted [pə'mɪtɪd] erlaubt WF
person ['pɜ:sn] Person, Mensch U4: 55
pet [pet] Haustier, zahmes Tier
pet shop ['petʃɒp] Zoohandlung, Tierhandlung
petrol station ['petrəlsteɪʃn] Tankstelle WF
phone [fəʊn] **1** anrufen, telefonieren; **phone back** zurückrufen U2: 33; **2** Telefon; **on the phone** am Telefon
phone call ['fəʊnkɔ:l] Anruf U2: 32
phone message ['fəʊnmesɪdʒ] Telefonnotiz; telefonische Nachricht U2: 32
photo ['fəʊtəʊ] Foto; **take photos** Fotos machen, fotografieren U2: 29
photocopier ['fəʊtəʊkɒpiə] Fotokopierer, Kopiergerät WF
photographer [fə'tɒgrəfə] Fotograf, Fotografin U2: 29
photo shoot ['fəʊtəʊʃu:t] Fotosession, Fotoshooting U2: 28
phrase [freɪz] Ausdruck
piano [pi'ænəʊ] Klavier U5: 68
pick [pɪk] aussuchen, wählen
pick up [pɪk'ʌp] **1** aufheben, hochheben; **2** abholen
picnic ['pɪknɪk] Picknick
picture ['pɪktʃə] Bild, Foto
pier [pɪə] Pier, Anlegestelle
pig [pɪg] Schwein
pink [pɪŋk] rosa, pink
pioneer [paɪə'nɪə] Pionier/in WF U6
pirate ['paɪrət] Pirat, Piratin U2: 36
pita ['pi:tə] Pita (Fladenbrot) WF
pizza ['pi:tsə] Pizza
place [pleɪs] **1** Ort, Stelle, Platz; **a place to meet** ein Treffpunkt; **2** unterbringen WF
plan [plæn] **1** planen, vorhaben; **2** Plan
plane [pleɪn] Flugzeug
planner ['plænə] Planer, Planerin
play [pleɪ] spielen; **play by the rules** sich an die Spielregeln halten U3: 43; **play sports** Sport treiben; **play the guitar** Gitarre spielen; **men playing games** Männer, die Spiele spielen U5: 66
player ['pleɪə] **1** Spieler, Spielerin; **2** Abspielgerät U3: 47
playground ['pleɪgraʊnd] Schulhof; **in the playground** auf dem Schulhof
please [pli:z] bitte
plug in [plʌg'ɪn] anschließen WF
plum [plʌm] Pflaume WF
p.m. [pi:'em] nachmittags, abends
pocket ['pɒkɪt] Tasche U1: 142
pocket money ['pɒkɪtmʌni] Taschengeld U1: 12
poem ['pəʊɪm] Gedicht
poet ['pəʊɪt] Dichter, Dichterin
point [pɔɪnt] Punkt
Poland ['pəʊlənd] Polen
police [pə'li:s] Polizei-
police officer [pə'li:sɒfɪsə] Polizist/in, Polizeibeamter/-beamtin
polite [pə'laɪt] höflich
pollution [pə'lu:ʃn] Umweltverschmutzung WF
pony ['pəʊni] Pony
poor [pʊə] arm U1: 11; **Poor you!** Du Arme!/Du Armer! **the poor** die Armen WF
pop [pɒp] **1** Pop(musik) U5: 68; **2** (AE) Papa, Vati WF
popcorn ['pɒpkɔ:n] Popcorn U1: 19
popular ['pɒpjələ] beliebt
population [pɒpju'leɪʃn] Bevölkerung, Bevölkerungszahl Next: 7
pork [pɔ:k] Schweinefleisch WF
porter ['pɔ:tə] Gepäckträger/in WF
portfolio [pɔ:t'fəʊliəʊ] Portfolio
postcard ['pəʊstkɑ:d] Postkarte, Ansichtskarte
poster ['pəʊstə] Poster
post office ['pəʊstɒfɪs] Post(amt)
potato, potatoes [pə'teɪtəʊ, pə'teɪtəʊz] Kartoffel, Kartoffeln U1: 12
potato chips [pə'teɪtəʊtʃɪps] (AE) Kartoffelchips U1: 12
pound (£) [paʊnd] Pfund *(britische Währung)*
power ['paʊə] Macht; Stärke U5: 78
power button ['paʊəbʌtn] An-/Ausschalter WF
power cord ['paʊəkɔ:d] Netzkabel WF
practise ['præktɪs] üben; trainieren
prefer [prɪ'fɜ:] vorziehen U2: 27
preposition [prepə'zɪʃn] Präposition, Verhältniswort U5: 72
present [prɪ'zent] präsentieren
present ['preznt] **1** Geschenk; **2 simple present** einfache Gegenwart
present progressive [prezntprə'gresɪv] Verlaufsform der Gegenwart
press [pres] drücken WF
price [praɪs] Preis
print out [prɪnt'aʊt] ausdrucken U3: 41
prison ['prɪzn] Gefängnis U1: 14; **go to prison** ins Gefängnis kommen U1: 14; **in prison** im Gefängnis U1: 14
prize [praɪz] Preis, Gewinn
problem ['prɒbləm] Problem
produce [prə'dju:s] herstellen, produzieren
programme ['prəʊgræm] (Radio-, Fernseh-)Sendung
progressive [prə'gresɪv]: **past progressive** Verlaufsform der Vergangenheit U2: 37; **present progressive** Verlaufsform der Gegenwart
prohibit [prə'hɪbɪt] verbieten U4: 57
prohibited [prə'hɪbɪtɪd] verboten U4: 54
project ['prɒdʒekt] Projekt, Projektarbeit
pronunciation [prənʌnsi'eɪʃn] Aussprache Next: 8
protector [prə'tektə] Protektor, Schützer
protest [prə'test] protestieren WF
punk [pʌŋk] Punk(musik) U5: 68
pupil ['pju:pl] Schüler, Schülerin
push [pʊʃ] drücken
put [pʊt] (I put, I've put) stellen; legen; (an einen Platz) tun; **I put** ich tat, ich habe getan; **I've put** ich habe getan U4: 153; **put in the right order** in die richtige Reihenfolge bringen; **she has put an advert in the newspaper** sie hat eine Anzeige in die Zeitung gesetzt WF
put in [pʊt'ɪn] **1** einfügen, hinzufügen; **2** eingeben WF
put up [pʊt'ʌp]: **put up a tent** ein Zelt aufstellen U4: 56; **Put up your hand.** Heb(t) die Hand. Next: 6

Q

quad (bike) [kwɒd, 'kwɒdbaɪk] Quad *(eine Art vierrädriges Gelände-Motorrad)*
quality ['kwɒləti]: **NBA quality sneakers** (AE) Sportschuhe in NBA-Qualität WF
quarter ['kwɔːtə]: **quarter to/past one** Viertel vor/nach eins
queen [kwiːn] Königin
question ['kwestʃən] Frage
questionnaire [kwestʃə'neə] Fragebogen
queue (up) [kjuː] Schlange stehen
quickly ['kwɪkli] schnell
quiet ['kwaɪət] ruhig
quietly ['kwaɪətli] leise WF
quiz [kwɪz] Quiz
quote [kwəʊt] Zitat U1: 14

R

R & B [ɑːrən'biː] R & B *(Musikrichtung)* U5: 68
racket ['rækɪt] Schläger WF
radiator ['reɪdieɪtə] Heizkörper
radio ['reɪdiəʊ] Radio
railings ['reɪlɪŋz] Geländer
railway line ['reɪlweɪlaɪn] Eisenbahnstrecke, Gleis
rain [reɪn] regnen
ran [ræn] (→ run): **I ran** ich rannte, ich bin gerannt
ranch [rɑːntʃ] Ranch WF U6
ranger ['reɪndʒə] Ranger *(Aufseher/in in Nationalparks)*
rap [ræp] Rap(musik)
rapper ['ræpə] Rapper/in, Rapsänger/in U1: 16
rat [ræt] Ratte
raven ['reɪvn] Rabe WF
RE [ɑː'riː] **(= religious education)** Religionslehre WF
read [riːd] (I read, I've read) lesen, vorlesen; **read something to her** ihr etwas vorlesen U1: 16
read [red] (→ read): **I read** ich las, ich habe gelesen; **I've read** ich habe gelesen
read out [riːd'aʊt] vorlesen, ablesen
reader ['riːdə] Leser, Leserin
reading log ['riːdɪŋlɒg] Lesetagebuch WF U6
reading week ['riːdɪŋwiːk] Lesewoche
ready ['redi] fertig, bereit
reality show [ri'æləti∫əʊ] Realityshow *(Unterhaltungssendung, die wahre Begebenheiten zeigt oder nachstellt)* WF
really ['riːəli] wirklich, eigentlich
reason ['riːzn] Grund U5: 77
receptionist [rɪ'sepʃənɪst] Empfangschef, -dame WF U6
recommend [rekə'mend] empfehlen U4: 61
recorder [rɪ'kɔːdə] Blockflöte WF
recording contract [rɪ'kɔːdɪŋkɒntrækt] Plattenvertrag WF
red [red] rot
referee [refə'riː] Schiedsrichter, Schiedsrichterin U3: 43
refill ['riːfɪl] Nachfüllung WF U6
reggae ['regeɪ] Reggae(musik) WF
relax [rɪ'læks] (sich) entspannen U2: 35
relaxed [rɪ'lækst] entspannt WF
release [rɪ'liːs] loslassen WF
remember [rɪ'membə] **1** sich erinnern (an); **2** daran denken U2: 28
rent [rent] mieten; ausleihen
repeat [rɪ'piːt] nachsprechen
report [rɪ'pɔːt] Bericht
reservation [rezə'veɪʃn] (Indianer-)Reservation, Reservat U4: 52; **on a reservation** in einer Reservation U4: 151
resort [rɪ'zɔːt] Urlaubsort WF
respectful [rɪ'spektfl] respektvoll WF
rest [rest] ruhen, sich ausruhen WF
restart [riː'stɑːt]: **restart the computer** einen Neustart machen WF
restaurant ['restrɒnt] Restaurant
result [rɪ'zʌlt] Ergebnis, Folge
résumé ['rezjumeɪ] (AE) Lebenslauf U4: 63
retirement home [rɪ'taɪəmənthəʊm] Seniorenheim WF
review [rɪ'vjuː] Besprechung, Rezension WF U6
reward [rɪ'wɔːd] Belohnung WF
rewrite [riː'raɪt] umschreiben WF
Rhine [raɪn] Rhein
rhyme (with) [raɪm] (sich) reimen (auf)
rhythm ['rɪðəm] Rhythmus U5: 69
rice [raɪs] Reis WF
rich [rɪtʃ]: **the rich** die Reichen WF
ridden ['rɪdn] (→ ride): **I've ridden** ich bin gefahren
ride [raɪd] **1** (I rode, I've ridden) reiten WF U6; **ride a bike/mountain board/quad** (mit einem) Rad/Mountainboard/Quad fahren; **2** Fahrt; **3** Fahrgeschäft, „Fahrattraktion" U2: 36
riding ['raɪdɪŋ]: **horse riding** Reiten; **quad/Trikke/... riding** Quadfahren/Trikkefahren/...
right [raɪt] **1** richtig; **You're right.** Du hast Recht. **2** Recht U1: 14; **animal rights** Tierrechte, Tierschutz- U4: 64; **3** rechts; **on the right** auf der rechten Seite; **on your right** rechts (von Ihnen)
ringtone ['rɪŋtəʊn] Klingelton
river ['rɪvə] Fluss; **the River Exe** der Exe
road [rəʊd] Straße; **in Fairfield Road** in der Fairfield Road; **on the road** unterwegs
road safety ['rəʊdseɪfti] Verkehrssicherheit
rob [rɒb] berauben WF; **rob a bank** eine Bank ausrauben WF
rock [rɒk] **1** Fels, großer Stein; **2** Rock(musik) WF
rock climber ['rɒkklaɪmə] Kletterer, Kletterin
rock climbing ['rɒkklaɪmɪŋ] Klettern
rodeo ['rəʊdiəʊ] Rodeo WF U6
role [rəʊl] Rolle U2: 28; **role card** Rollen(spiel)karte U2: 33
roll [rəʊl] Brötchen
roller coaster ['rəʊləkəʊstə] Achterbahn
romance [rəʊ'mæns] Liebesfilm, Liebesroman U2: 27
romantic [rəʊ'mæntɪk] romantisch
Rome [rəʊm] Rom
room [ruːm] Raum, Zimmer
root [ruːt] Wurzel U4: 56
round [raʊnd] um (... herum) WF
royal (blue) ['rɔɪəl] königsblau WF
RSVP [ɑːresviː'piː] u.A.w.g. (= um Antwort wird gebeten) U1: 21
rubber ['rʌbə] Radiergummi
rugby ['rʌgbi] Rugby
rule [ruːl] Regel, Vorschrift; **play by the rules** sich an die Spielregeln halten U3: 43
ruler ['ruːlə] Lineal
run [rʌn] (I ran, I've run) rennen, laufen; **run errands** Besorgungen machen WF
runner ['rʌnə] Läufer, Läuferin
running ['rʌnɪŋ] Laufen

S

sad [sæd] traurig
safe [seɪf] sicher, in Sicherheit
safety ['seɪfti]: **road safety** Verkehrssicherheit
safety gear ['seɪftigɪə] Sicherheitsausrüstung
said [sed] (→ say): **I said** ich sagte, ich habe gesagt; **I've said** ich habe gesagt
salad ['sæləd] Salat
sales clerk ['seɪlzklɑ:k] (AE) Verkäufer, Verkäuferin U4: 63
salmon ['sæmən] Lachs U1: 142
same [seɪm]: **the same** der-/die-/dasselbe, der/die/das gleiche
sandwich ['sænwɪtʃ] Sandwich *(belegtes Brot)*
sang [sæŋ] (→ sing): **I sang** ich sang, ich habe gesungen
sat [sæt] (→ sit): **I sat** ich saß, ich habe gesessen
Saturday ['sætədeɪ, 'sætədi] Samstag, Sonnabend
sausage ['sɒsɪdʒ] Wurst, Würstchen
save [seɪv] **1** sparen; **2** retten U4: 64
saw [sɔ:] (→ see): **I saw** ich sah, ich habe gesehen
saxophone ['sæksəfəʊn] Saxofon WF
say [seɪ] (I said, I've said) sagen; **say something to her** ihr etwas sagen U1: 16; **say goodbye to ...** sich von ... verabschieden; **Say hi to Dawn, please.** Grüße Dawn, bitte. **say sorry** sich entschuldigen
scan [skæn] überfliegen WF U6
scan in [skæn'ɪn] einscannen WF
scanner ['skænə] Scanner WF
scary ['skeəri] unheimlich WF
scene [si:n] Szene; Ansicht
school [sku:l] Schule; **she's at school** sie ist in der Schule; sie geht zur Schule
school band ['sku:lbænd] Schulorchester WF
school council ['sku:l'kaʊnsl] Schülermitverwaltung WF
school day ['sku:ldeɪ] Schultag
science ['saɪəns] Naturwissenschaft
science fiction [saɪəns'fɪkʃn] Science-Fiction WF
score [skɔ:] **1** (Punkte) erzielen, (Tor) schießen U3: 42; **2** Spielstand, Punktzahl U3: 40; **What's the score?** Wie steht's? U3: 148

Scotland ['skɒtlənd] Schottland
Scots [skɒts] Schottisch *(engl. Dialekt)*
Scottish ['skɒtɪʃ] schottisch; Schotte(n), Schottin(nen)
scream [skri:m] schreien
sea [si:] Meer
seal pup ['si:lpʌp] Seehundjunges WF
search engine ['sɜ:tʃendʒɪn] Suchmaschine WF U6
seashell ['si:ʃel] Muschel
seashore ['si:ʃɔ:] Küste, Strand
season ['si:zn] Jahreszeit
second ['sekənd]: **English as a Second Language** Englisch als Zweitsprache U3: 38
security check [sɪ'kjʊərətitʃek] Sicherheitskontrolle U3: 38
security guard [sɪ'kjʊərətigɑ:d] Wachfrau, Wachmann
see [si:] (I saw, I've seen) sehen; **I see her mouth moving** ich sehe, wie sich ihr Mund bewegt WF; **See you.** Bis dann. **See you tomorrow/...** Bis morgen/...; **..., you see.** ..., verstehst du?
seen [si:n] (→ see): **I've seen** ich habe gesehen
self-control [selfkən'trəʊl] Selbstbeherrschung U3: 43
sell [sel] (I sold, I've sold) verkaufen; sich verkaufen WF
send [send] (I sent, I've sent) senden, schicken
sent [sent] (→ send): **I sent** ich sendete, ich habe gesendet; **I've sent** ich habe gesendet
sentence ['sentəns] Satz
September [sep'tembə] September
series ['sɪəri:z] Serie; Reihe U2: 27
serve [sɜ:v] servieren WF
shake [ʃeɪk] (I shook, I've shaken) schütteln U5: 70; **she shakes her head** sie schüttelt den Kopf U5: 154
shaken ['ʃeɪkən] (→ shake): **I've shaken** ich habe geschüttelt U5: 156
share [ʃeə]: **share a room** sich ein Zimmer teilen
she [ʃi:] sie; **she's (= she is)** sie ist
sheep [ʃi:p] Schaf, Schafe
shelf, shelves [ʃelf, ʃelvz] Regal, Regale
sheriff ['ʃerɪf] Sheriff WF U6
ship [ʃɪp] Schiff
shirt [ʃɜ:t] Hemd WF
shoe [ʃu:] Schuh

shook [ʃʊk] (→ shake): **I shook** ich schüttelte, ich habe geschüttelt U5: 70
shoot [ʃu:t] (I shot, I've shot) schießen; werfen U3: 40
shop [ʃɒp] Laden, Geschäft
shop assistant ['ʃɒpəsɪstənt] Verkäufer, Verkäuferin
shoplifter ['ʃɒplɪftə] Ladendieb/in
shopper ['ʃɒpə] Käufer, Käuferin
shopping ['ʃɒpɪŋ] Einkaufen U1: 11; **go shopping** einkaufen gehen
shopping centre ['ʃɒpɪŋsentə] Einkaufszentrum
shore [ʃɔ:] Ufer, Strand WF
short [ʃɔ:t] kurz; klein
shorts [ʃɔ:ts] Shorts, kurze Hosen U3: 40
shot [ʃɒt] Korbwurf U3: 40
shot [ʃɒt] (→ shoot): **I shot** ich schoss, ich habe geschossen U3: 150; **I've shot** ich habe geschossen U3: 150; **he was shot** er wurde erschossen WF
should [ʃʊd, ʃəd]: **you should** du solltest, du müsstest; **When should I ...?** Wann soll ich ...? U1: 19
shoulder ['ʃəʊldə] Schulter WF
shout [ʃaʊt] laut rufen, schreien; **she shouts something at him** sie ruft ihm etwas zu U5: 70
show [ʃəʊ] **1** (I showed, I've shown) zeigen; **2** Show
shown [ʃəʊn]: **he was shown** es wurde ihm gezeigt WF
Shut up! [ʃʌt'ʌp] Halt den Mund!
shuttle ['ʃʌtl] Shuttle U5: 74
shy [ʃaɪ] schüchtern
sick [sɪk]: **become sick** (AE) krank werden WF
side [saɪd] Seite
sidewalk ['saɪdwɔ:k] (AE) Bürgersteig Next: 9
sigh [saɪ] seufzen U5: 70
sightseeing ['saɪtsi:ɪŋ] Besichtigungen U1: 11
sign [saɪn] Schild; Zeichen
signal ['sɪgnəl] Zeichen, Signal
silly ['sɪli] dumm, albern
silver ['sɪlvə] silbern WF
simple past [sɪmpl'pɑ:st] einfache Vergangenheit
simple present [sɪmpl'preznt] einfache Gegenwart
sing [sɪŋ] (I sang, I've sung) singen
Singapore ['sɪŋəpɔ:] Singapur
singer ['sɪŋə] Sänger, Sängerin
single room ['sɪŋglru:m] Einzelzimmer WF U6

sir [sɜː]**: Dear Sir/Madam, ...** Sehr geehrte Damen und Herren, ... WF
sister ['sɪstə] Schwester; **brothers and sisters** Geschwister
sit [sɪt] (I sat, I've sat) sitzen; sich setzen
sitcom ['sɪtkɒm] „Situationskomödie", Comedy-Serie WF
skateboard ['skeɪtbɔːd] Skateboard U3: 47
skateboarder ['skeɪtbɔːdə] Skateboarder, Skateboarderin
skater ['skeɪtə] Skater, Skaterin
ski [skiː] Ski fahren WF
skiing ['skiːɪŋ] Skifahren
skin [skɪn] Haut WF
skunk [skʌŋk] Stinktier, Skunk WF U6
sky [skaɪ] Himmel WF
sky-high [skaɪ'haɪ] himmelhoch WF
skyscraper ['skaɪskreɪpə] Wolkenkratzer, Hochhaus WF
slave [sleɪv] Sklave, Sklavin WF
sleep [sliːp] (I slept, I've slept) schlafen
slept [slept]**: he/she slept** er/sie schlief, er/sie hat geschlafen WF
slip [slɪp] ausrutschen
slow [sləʊ] langsam U5: 69
small [smɔːl] klein
smile [smaɪl] lächeln
smog [smɒg] Smog U2: 25
smoke [sməʊk] rauchen U4: 54
smoked salmon [sməʊkt'sæmən] Räucherlachs U1: 12
s'mores [smɔːz] *amerikanischer Lagerfeuersnack mit Marshmallows* WF U6
sneaker ['sniːkə] (AE) Sportschuh U3: 41
sneaker wave ['sniːkəweɪv] überraschend hohe Uferwelle WF
snowboarder ['snəʊbɔːdə] Snowboarder, Snowboarderin
so [səʊ] so, also; daher
soap [səʊp] Seifenoper, Unterhaltungsserie WF
soccer ['sɒkə] Fußball U3: 41
social studies ['səʊʃl'stʌdiz] Gesellschaftslehre WF
soda ['səʊdə] (AE) Limonade WF U6
softball ['sɒftbɔːl] Softball *(ähnlich wie Baseball)* U3: 41
software ['sɒftweə] Software
sold [səʊld]**: they had sold** sie hatten verkauft WF
Somalia [sə'mɑːliə] Somalia
some [sʌm] **1** einige, ein paar; **2** etwas
somebody ['sʌmbədi] jemand
something ['sʌmθɪŋ] etwas; **something different** etwas anderes
sometimes ['sʌmtaɪmz] manchmal
song [sɒŋ] Lied
soon [suːn] bald
sorry ['sɒri]**: Sorry./I'm sorry.** Tut mir leid. **I'm sorry I ...** Tut mir leid, dass ich ...; **she felt sorry for him** er tat ihr leid WF
sound [saʊnd] **1** klingen, sich anhören; **2** Geräusch
soundtrack ['saʊndtræk] Filmmusik WF
soup [suːp] Suppe WF
south [saʊθ] Süden; Süd-; südlich
sow [səʊ] säen WF
space [speɪs] Weltraum U5: 74
Spain [speɪn] Spanien
Spanish ['spænɪʃ] spanisch; Spanisch; Spanier, Spanierin(nen) U5: 66
speak [spiːk] (I spoke, I've spoken) sprechen; **speak to** sprechen mit
speaker ['spiːkə] Redner, Rednerin WF; Sprecher, Sprecherin U5: 66
special ['speʃl] besondere, besonderer, besonderes
special offer [speʃl'ɒfə] Sonderangebot
speed [spiːd] Geschwindigkeit WF
speed limit ['spiːdlɪmɪt] Geschwindigkeitsbegrenzung WF U6
spell [spel] buchstabieren
spelling ['spelɪŋ] Rechtschreibung Next: 9
spend [spend] (I spent, I've spent) **1** ausgeben; **2** verbringen U5: 68
spent [spent] (→ spend)**: I spent** **1** ich gab aus, ich habe ausgegeben; **2** ich verbrachte, ich habe verbracht U5: 68; **I've spent** ich habe ausgegeben/verbracht U5: 156
spider ['spaɪdə] Spinne
splitting up [splɪtɪŋ'ʌp] Trennung WF
sponsored ['spɒnsəd] gesponsert
sport [spɔːt] Sport, Sportart; **play sports** Sport treiben
sports centre ['spɔːtssentə] Sportzentrum
sporty ['spɔːti] sportlich
spring [sprɪŋ] Frühling
squash [skwɒʃ] Squash
squid [skwɪd] Tintenfisch WF
stable ['steɪbl] Stall WF
stack [stæk]**: stack shelves** Regale auffüllen WF
stage [steɪdʒ] Bühne U5: 66; **on stage** auf der Bühne U5: 66
stall [stɔːl] (Verkaufs-)Stand U2: 24
stamp [stæmp] Stempel
stand [stænd] (I stood, I've stood) stehen; **I can't stand them** ich kann sie nicht ausstehen
star [stɑː] **1** Stern WF; **2** Star *(berühmte Persönlichkeit)*
start [stɑːt] **1** anfangen, beginnen; **I started to run** ich begann zu rennen; **start a programme** eine Sendung ins Leben rufen; **2** Start, Anfang
state [steɪt] (Bundes-)Staat, Land Next: 7
station ['steɪʃn] Bahnhof; **at Exeter Station** im Bahnhof Exeter
statue ['stætʃuː] Statue; **Statue of Liberty** ['stætʃuːəv'lɪbəti] Freiheitsstatue U1: 10
stay [steɪ] bleiben; übernachten
steal [stiːl] (I stole, I've stolen) stehlen U1: 14
step [step] Stufe
stew [stjuː] Eintopf WF
stole [stəʊl] (→ steal)**: I stole** ich stahl, ich habe gestohlen U1: 144
stolen ['stəʊlən] (→ steal)**: I've stolen** ich habe gestohlen U1: 144
stop [stɒp] **1** anhalten, stoppen; stehen bleiben; **2** Halt; Haltestelle Next: 6
store [stɔː] (AE) Laden, Geschäft Next: 9
story ['stɔːri] Geschichte
strawberry ['strɔːbəri] Erdbeere WF
street [striːt] Straße
stress [stres] betonen
strict [strɪkt] streng
strong [strɒŋ] stark WF
student ['stjuːdnt] (AE) Schüler, Schülerin U3: 38
studio ['stjuːdiəʊ] Studio U2: 28
stupid ['stjuːpɪd] dumm, blöd
subject ['sʌbdʒɪkt] **1** (Schul-)Fach; **2 Subject: ...** Betreff: ... WF
suburb ['sʌbɜːb] Vorort
subway ['sʌbweɪ] (AE) U-Bahn Next: 9
such [sʌtʃ]**: There's no such thing.** So etwas gibt es nicht.
suddenly ['sʌdnli] plötzlich
sugar ['ʃʊgə] Zucker WF
summary ['sʌməri] Zusammenfassung

summer ['sʌmə] Sommer
sun [sʌn] Sonne
Sunday ['sʌndeɪ, 'sʌndi] Sonntag
sung [sʌŋ] (→ sing): **I've sung** ich habe gesungen
sunglasses ['sʌnglɑ:sɪz] Sonnenbrille WF
sunny ['sʌni] sonnig
super ['su:pə] super, toll
supermarket ['su:pəmɑ:kɪt] Supermarkt
sure [ʃʊə] sicher
surf [sɜ:f] surfen U2: 29
surfboard ['sɜ:fbɔ:d] Surfbrett U2: 28
surfer ['sɜ:fə] Surfer, Surferin U2: 24
surfing ['sɜ:fɪŋ] Surfen, Wellenreiten WF
surfing gear ['sɜ:fɪŋgɪə] **1** Surfkleidung, -klamotten; **2** Surfausrüstung U2: 29
surprise [sə'praɪz] Überraschung
surprised [sə'praɪzd] überrascht WF U6
survey ['sɜ:veɪ] Umfrage, Untersuchung
swam [swæm] (→ swim): **I swam** ich schwamm, ich bin geschwommen
sweet [swi:t] süß WF
swept [swept]: **she swept** sie fegte WF
swim [swɪm] (I swam, I've swum) schwimmen
swimmer ['swɪmə] Schwimmer, Schwimmerin
swimming ['swɪmɪŋ] Schwimmen; **go swimming** schwimmen gehen
swimming pool ['swɪmɪŋpu:l] Schwimmbad
Switzerland ['swɪtsələnd] Schweiz
symbol ['sɪmbl] Symbol

T

table ['teɪbl] **1** Tisch; **2** Tabelle WF
table tennis ['teɪbltenɪs] Tischtennis
take [teɪk] (I took, I've taken) nehmen; bringen; einnehmen WF; **Take a jacket.** Nimm/Bring eine Jacke mit. **take photos** Fotos machen, fotografieren U2: 29; **Can I take a message?** Kann ich (ihm/ihr) etwas ausrichten? U2: 32
take off [teɪk'ɒf]: **I take off my jacket** ich ziehe meine Jacke aus
taken ['teɪkən] (→ take): **I've taken** ich habe genommen
talent contest ['tælәntkɒntest] Talentwettbewerb WF
talk [tɔ:k]: **1 talk (to)** reden (mit), sprechen (mit), sich unterhalten (mit); **2** Vortrag
talk show ['tɔ:kʃəʊ] (AE) Talkshow U5: 71
tall [tɔ:l] groß *(bei Personen)*
taxi ['tæksi] Taxi
tea [ti:] Tee
teach [ti:tʃ] (I taught, I've taught) beibringen WF U6; **I'd teach you to ride** ich würde dir das Reiten beibringen WF U6; **Who can teach me?** Wer kann es mir beibringen? WF
teacher ['ti:tʃə] Lehrer, Lehrerin
team [ti:m] Team, Mannschaft
techno ['teknəʊ] Techno *(Musikrichtung)* U1: 21
technology [tek'nɒlədʒi] Technik, Technologie
teen, teenager [ti:n, 'ti:neɪdʒə] Teenager
telephone line ['telɪfəʊnlaɪn] Telefonnetz WF
tell (about) [tel] (I told, I've told) erzählen (von); sagen
tennis ['tenɪs] Tennis
tent [tent] Zelt U4: 56
tepee ['ti:pi:] Tipi WF
terrible ['terəbl] schrecklich, furchtbar
test [test] Test, Klassenarbeit, Prüfung
text [tekst] **1** Text; **2** SMS
text bullying ['tekstbʊliŋ] SMS-Terror
text message ['tekstmesɪdʒ] SMS (Textnachricht)
textile technology ['tekstaɪltek'nɒlədʒi] Textilgestaltung WF
than [ðæn, ðən]: **faster than** schneller als
thank [θæŋk]: **Thank you.** Danke (schön).
Thanks. [θæŋks] Danke.
that [ðæt] **1** das; der, die, das (da); **2** dass; **3** der, die, das *(in Relativsätzen)*; **that evening** an diesem Abend; **That's OK.** Schon gut./Bitte. **That's why ...** Deshalb ..., Darum ...; **That's two pounds, please.** Das macht zwei Pfund, bitte.
the [ðə, ði] der, die, das; **The next day ...** Am nächsten Tag ...
theatre ['θɪətə] Theater U1: 11
their [ðeə] ihr, ihre
them [ðem] ihnen, sie
theme park ['θi:mpɑ:k] Themenpark U5: 74
then [ðen] dann
there [ðeə] da, dort; dahin, dorthin; **there's (= there is)** da ist, es gibt/ist; **there are** da sind, es gibt/sind; **there was/were** da war(en), es gab/war(en)
these [ði:z] die (hier); diese
they [ðeɪ] sie; **they're (= they are)** sie sind
thing [θɪŋ] Ding, Sache; **the right/best/... thing** das Richtige/Beste/...; **There's no such thing.** So etwas gibt es nicht.
think [θɪŋk] (I thought, I've thought) denken, nachdenken; finden; **think of** denken an; **What do you think of ...?** Was hältst du von ...? **they thought of making Leavenworth a German town** sie kamen darauf, aus Leavenworth eine deutsche Stadt zu machen WF
this [ðɪs] dies (hier), das (hier); diese, dieser, dieses; **this evening/...** heute Abend/...
those [ðəʊz] diese, jene, die (da)
thought [θɔ:t] (→ think): **I thought** ich dachte, ich habe gedacht
thousand ['θaʊznd] tausend
threw [θru:] (→ throw): **I threw** ich warf, ich habe geworfen U3: 42
thriller ['θrɪlə] Thriller WF
through [θru:] durch, hindurch
throw [θrəʊ] **1** (I threw, I've thrown) werfen U3: 42; **2** Wurf U3: 40; **free throw** Freiwurf U3: 40
thrown [θrəʊn] (→ throw): **I've thrown** ich habe geworfen U3: 150
Thursday ['θɜ:zdeɪ, 'θɜ:zdi] Donnerstag
ticket ['tɪkɪt] Eintrittskarte; Fahrkarte, Flugschein
tied [taɪd]: **it was tied** es war unentschieden WF
till [tɪl] bis WF
time [taɪm] Zeit; Uhrzeit; **at that time** damals WF; **(for) a long time** lange U2: 28; **What time is it?** Wie spät ist es?
timetable ['taɪmteɪbl] Stundenplan
tip [tɪp] **1** Tipp; **2** Trinkgeld WF
tired ['taɪəd] müde
title ['taɪtl] Titel

to [tuː, tu, tə] **1** zu, nach; an; **fall to the ground** auf den Boden fallen; **go to bed** ins Bett gehen; **I've been to France.** Ich bin (schon einmal) in Frankreich gewesen. **it's 24–18 to North** es steht 24:18 für North U3: 42; **Jamie says goodbye to Tess.** Jamie sagt Tess auf Wiedersehen. **they help you to read** sie helfen dir zu lesen; **things to do** Sachen, die man machen kann; **to change things** um Dinge zu verändern U1: 14; **To finish, ...** Um zum Ende zu kommen, ...; **Welcome to London.** Willkommen in London. **2** bis; **It's five to ten.** Es ist fünf vor zehn.
tobacco [tə'bækəʊ] Tabak WF
today [tə'deɪ] heute
together [tə'geðə] zusammen
told [təʊld] (→ tell): **I told** ich erzählte, ich habe erzählt; **I've told** ich habe erzählt
tomato, tomatoes [tə'mɑːtəʊ, tə'mɑːtəʊz] Tomate, Tomaten U1: 12
tomorrow [tə'mɒrəʊ] morgen
tongue twister ['tʌŋtwɪstə] Zungenbrecher
too [tuː] **1** auch; **2 too old** zu alt; **Too bad!** Schade! U3: 42
took [tʊk] (→ take): **I took** ich nahm, ich habe genommen
top [tɒp] Spitze, oberes Ende U1: 10; **at the top** ganz oben (auf), auf der Spitze U1: 10
topic ['tɒpɪk] Thema
touch [tʌtʃ] berühren, anfassen U3: 40
tough [tʌf] hart, zäh, stark
tour [tʊə] Tour; Rundgang, Führung U1: 11
tourist ['tʊərɪst] Tourist, Touristin
tourist office ['tʊərɪstɒfɪs] Touristeninformation, Fremdenverkehrsbüro
towards [tə'wɔːdz] auf ... zu, in Richtung
tower ['taʊə] Turm
town [taʊn] Stadt
town centre ['taʊnsentə] Stadtzentrum, Stadtmitte
toy [tɔɪ] Spielzeug
track [træk] **1** Weg, Pfad; **2** Bahn, Laufbahn
tractor ['træktə] Traktor WF U6
tradition [trə'dɪʃn] Tradition U4: 64
traffic ['træfɪk] Verkehr
traffic jam ['træfɪkdʒæm] (Verkehrs-)Stau WF
traffic light ['træfɪklaɪt] (Verkehrs-)Ampel
trail [treɪl] Pfad, Weg WF U6
train [treɪn] **1** trainieren; **2** Zug, Eisenbahn
trainer ['treɪnə] **1** Trainer; **2** Sportschuh
tram [træm] Straßenbahn
translate [træns'leɪt] übersetzen
trash [træʃ] (AE) Müll, Abfall WF
trash can ['træʃkæn] (AE) Mülltonne WF
travel ['trævl] **1** reisen, fahren; **2** Reise-, Reisen U1: 17
traveller ['trævələ] Reisende/r; Landfahrer/in
tray [treɪ] Tablett U3: 46
treasure hunt ['treʒəhʌnt] Schatzsuche
treat [triːt] Genuss, besonderes Vergnügen
tree [triː] Baum U4: 52
trick [trɪk] Streich WF
trip [trɪp] Ausflug, Reise
trouble ['trʌbl] Unruhe U4: 64; **I'm in big trouble** ich stecke in großen Schwierigkeiten
trousers ['traʊzəz]: **jogging trousers** Jogginghose WF
true [truː] wahr
truly ['truːli]: **Yours truly, ...** (AE) Mit freundlichen Grüßen ... U4: 63
trumpet ['trʌmpɪt] Trompete WF
try [traɪ] versuchen, (aus)probieren
T-shirt ['tiːʃɜːt] T-Shirt
tube [tjuːb] Reifenschlauch WF U6; **the tube** die (Londoner) U-Bahn
tubing ['tjuːbɪŋ] *Benutzung eines Reifenschlauchs als Floß* WF U6
Tuesday ['tjuːzdeɪ, 'tjuːzdi] Dienstag
tuna ['tjuːnə] Thunfisch WF
tunnel ['tʌnl] Tunnel
Turkey ['tɜːki] Türkei
turn (to the left) [tɜːn] sich (nach links) drehen U2: 29; **turn left/right (into Market Street)** nach links/rechts (in die Market Street) abbiegen
turn off [tɜːn'ɒf] ausschalten
turn on [tɜːn'ɒn] einschalten
TV [tiː'viː] Fernsehen; Fernsehgerät
twilight ['twaɪlaɪt] Dämmerung, Zwielicht WF
type [taɪp] Typ WF; **types of music** Musikrichtungen WF
typical ['tɪpɪkl] typisch WF U6

U

umbrella [ʌm'brelə] Schirm U5: 67
uncle ['ʌŋkl] Onkel U4: 57
uncool [ʌn'kuːl] nicht cool U2: 36
under ['ʌndə] unter
underground ['ʌndəgraʊnd] **1** unterirdisch; **2** U-Bahn Next: 9
underground station ['ʌndəgraʊndsteɪʃn] U-Bahnhof
underground train ['ʌndəgraʊndtreɪn] U-Bahn-Zug
underline [ʌndə'laɪn] unterstreichen
underlined [ʌndə'laɪnd] unterstrichen
understand [ʌndə'stænd] (I understood, I've understood) verstehen
understood [ʌndə'stʊd] (→ understand): **I understood** ich verstand, ich habe verstanden
undressing ['ʌndresɪŋ] Ausziehen WF
uniform ['juːnɪfɔːm] (Schul-)Uniform
unit ['juːnɪt] Lektion
up [ʌp]: **it's (= it was) up to me** es lag an mir WF; **What's up?** Was gibt's?
us [ʌs] uns
use [juːz] benutzen, verwenden
useful ['juːsfl] nützlich U2: 35
user ['juːzə]: **user's guide** Bedienungsanleitung WF
usually ['juːʒuəli] meistens, normalerweise, gewöhnlich

V

vacation [və'keɪʃn] (AE) Ferien, Urlaub WF
valuable ['væljuəbl] wertvoll WF
vegetable ['vedʒtəbl] (ein) Gemüse
vehicle ['viːəkl] Fahrzeug WF
venue ['venjuː] Veranstaltungsort WF
verb [vɜːb] Verb, Zeitwort
verse [vɜːs] Strophe
very ['veri] sehr
video ['vɪdiəʊ] Videofilm, Video
video game ['vɪdiəʊgeɪm] Videospiel U3: 47
viewer ['vjuːə] Fernsehzuschauer, -zuschauerin WF
Viking ['vaɪkɪŋ] Wikinger, Wikinger-
village ['vɪlɪdʒ] Dorf
violence ['vaɪələns] Gewalt, Gewalttätigkeit U1: 14

visit ['vɪzɪt] besuchen
visitor ['vɪzɪtə] Besucher/in, Gast
visitor centre ['vɪzɪtəsentə] Besucherzentrum U4: 55
voice [vɔɪs] Stimme U5: 69
volleyball ['vɒlibɔ:l] Volleyball
vote [vəʊt]: **vote for the winner** über den Gewinner/die Gewinnerin abstimmen WF

W

wagon ['wægən] Planwagen WF U6; **wagon train** Zug von Planwagen WF U6
wait (for) [weɪt] warten (auf); **I can't wait for it.** Ich kann es kaum erwarten. **Let's wait and see.** Warten wir's ab. **wait in line** (AE) Schlange stehen U2: 28
waiter ['weɪtə] Kellner WF
waitress ['weɪtrəs] Kellnerin WF
wake up [weɪk'ʌp] (I woke up, I've woken up) aufwachen U5: 70
Wales [weɪlz] Wales
walk [wɔ:k] gehen, laufen; **walk dogs** Hunde ausführen WF
walker ['wɔ:kə] Spaziergänger/in, Wanderer, Wanderin
walking ['wɔ:kɪŋ] Spazierengehen, Wandern
walking shoe ['wɔ:kɪŋʃu:] Wanderschuh
wall [wɔ:l] Wand; Mauer U4: 55
want [wɒnt] wollen; **want to go** gehen wollen
war [wɔ:] Krieg WF
warm [wɔ:m] warm
was [wɒz, wəz] war; **wasn't (= was not)** war nicht; **they thought it was a good idea** sie dachten, es wäre eine gute Idee; **it was called** es wurde genannt WF U6
Washington State [wɒʃɪŋtən'steɪt] der Bundesstaat Washington U4: 52
waste [weɪst] verschwenden; **a waste of time** Zeitverschwendung
watch [wɒtʃ] **1** beobachten, sich anschauen; zusehen; **Watch me!** Pass auf! **watch TV** fernsehen; **2** (Armband-)Uhr WF
water ['wɔ:tə] Wasser
wave [weɪv] Welle U2: 29
way [weɪ] Weg; **way of life** Lebensweise WF
we [wi:] wir; **we're (= we are)** wir sind
wear [weə] (I wore, I've worn) tragen, anziehen
weather ['weðə] Wetter
webcode ['webkəʊd] Webcode
website ['websaɪt] Website
wedding ['wedɪŋ] Hochzeit U1: 21
wedding day ['wedɪŋdeɪ] Hochzeitstag
Wednesday ['wenzdeɪ,'wenzdi] Mittwoch
week [wi:k] Woche
weekend ['wi:k'end] Wochenende
welcome ['welkəm]: **Welcome to London.** Willkommen in London. **we aren't welcome** wir sind nicht willkommen; **You're welcome.** Nichts zu danken; Bitte schön. U5: 75
well [wel] **1** gut; **Well done!** Gut gemacht! U3: 42; **2** **Well, ...** Nun/Tja, ...
Welsh [welʃ] walisisch; Walisisch; Waliser, Waliserin(nen)
went [went] (→ go): **I went** ich ging, ich bin gegangen
were [wɜ:] waren; warst; wart; **weren't (= were not)** waren/warst/wart nicht
west [west] Westen; West-; westlich
western ['westən] Western WF
wet [wet] nass, feucht
wetsuit ['wetsu:t] Surf-/Tauch-(schutz)anzug U2: 29
whale [weɪl] Wal
whale watching ['weɪlwɒtʃɪŋ] Walbeobachtung U4: 53; **go whale watching** auf Walbeobachtungstour gehen U4: 53
what [wɒt] **1** was; **What a ...!** Was für ein/eine ...! **What about you?** Und du?/Was ist mit dir? **What are they in German?** Wie heißen sie auf Deutsch? **What time is it?** Wie spät ist es? **What's that?** Was ist das? **What's your name?** Wie heißt du? **What's up?** Was gibt's? **2** welche, welcher, welches
whatever [wɒt'evə]: **whatever the weather** egal, wie das Wetter ist; **you can do whatever you feel** du kannst tun, wonach dir gerade ist WF
wheelchair ['wi:ltʃeə] Rollstuhl; **he's in a wheelchair** er sitzt im Rollstuhl
when [wen] **1** wann; **2** wenn; **3** als
where [weə] wo; wohin; **Where are you from?** Woher kommst du?
whether ['weðə] ob
which [wɪtʃ] welche, welcher, welches
white [waɪt] weiß; **white bread** Weißbrot U1: 12; **white people** Weiße U1: 14
who [hu:] **1** wer; **2** der, die, das *(in Relativsätzen)*
why [waɪ] warum, weshalb; **That's why ...** Deshalb ..., Darum ...
wide [waɪd] breit
wife [waɪf] Ehefrau WF
wild [waɪld] wild; wild lebend
wildfire ['waɪldfaɪə] Großflächenbrand WF U6
will [wɪl]: **I'll (= I will) go** ich werde gehen
win [wɪn] (I won, I've won) gewinnen
window ['wɪndəʊ] Fenster
winner ['wɪnə] Gewinner/Gewinnerin, Sieger/Siegerin
winter ['wɪntə] Winter
wishes ['wɪʃɪz]: **Best wishes, ...** Viele Grüße ...
witch [wɪtʃ] Hexe
with [wɪð] mit; bei
without [wɪ'ðaʊt] ohne
woke up [wəʊk'ʌp] (→ wake up): **I woke up** ich wachte auf, ich bin aufgewacht U5: 156
woken up [wəʊkən'ʌp] (→ wake up): **I've woken up** ich bin aufgewacht U5: 156
woman, women ['wʊmən, 'wɪmɪn] Frau, Frauen
won [wʌn] (→ win): **I won** ich gewann, ich habe gewonnen; **I've won** ich habe gewonnen
won't [wəʊnt]: **I won't (= will not) go** ich werde nicht gehen
wonder ['wʌndə] sich fragen WF
wood [wʊd] Wald
word [wɜ:d] Wort; **words (of a song)** (Lied-)Text
wore [wɔ:] (→ wear): **I wore** ich trug, ich habe getragen
work [wɜ:k] **1** arbeiten; funktionieren; **2** Arbeit
work experience [wɜ:kɪk'spɪəriəns] Berufserfahrung U4: 63; **do work experience** ein Berufspraktikum machen WF

worker ['wɜːkə] Arbeiter, Arbeiterin
world [wɜːld] Welt; **in the world** auf der (ganzen) Welt
World Trade Center [wɜːld'treɪdsentə] Welthandelszentrum WF
worried ['wʌrid]: **I'm worried (about)** ich mache mir Sorgen (um), ich bin beunruhigt (wegen)
worry (about) ['wʌri] sich Sorgen machen (um)
worse [wɜːs] schlechter; schlimmer
worst [wɜːst] schlechteste/r/s; schlimmste/r/s
would [wʊd]: **I'd (= I would)** ich würde U1: 22; **I'd like to go/...** Ich möchte gehen/...; **I wouldn't (= would not) like to go/...** Ich möchte nicht gehen/...; **Would you like ...?** Möchtest du/Möchten Sie ...?
Wow! [waʊ] Wow! Wahnsinn!
write [raɪt] (I wrote, I've written) schreiben
writer ['raɪtə] Schriftsteller/in
written ['rɪtn] (→ write): **I've written** ich habe geschrieben
wrong [rɒŋ] falsch; **What's wrong?** Ist etwas nicht in Ordnung?
wrote [rəʊt] (→ write): **I wrote** ich schrieb, ich habe geschrieben

Y

ya [jə]: **How ya doin'?** (AE) Wie geht's? WF
yeah [jeə] ja *(besonders in wörtl. Rede)*
year [jɪə] Jahr; Jahrgangsstufe; **a 13-year-old girl** ein 13-jähriges Mädchen; **What year are you in? - I'm in year 7.** In welcher Jahrgangsstufe bist du? - Ich bin in der 7. Stufe.
yearbook ['jɪəbʊk] Jahrbuch WF
yellow ['jeləʊ] gelb
yes [jes] ja
yesterday ['jestədeɪ, 'jestədi] gestern
yet [jet]: **not ... yet** noch nicht
YMCA [waɪemsiː'eɪ] CVJM WF
you [juː] **1** du; ihr; Sie; **2** dir, euch, Ihnen; dich, euch, Sie; **you're (= you are)** du bist; ihr seid; Sie sind; **I said you'd be in the shop tomorrow.** Ich habe gesagt, du wärst morgen im Laden.
young [jʌŋ] jung; **young kids** kleine Kinder U2: 36
your [jɔː] dein, deine; euer, eure; Ihr, Ihre
yours [jɔːz]: **Yours truly, ...** (AE) Mit freundlichen Grüßen ... U4: 63
yourself [jɔː'self] dir/dich (selbst); selbst U5: 69; **a picture of yourself** ein Bild von dir
youth club ['juːθklʌb] Jugendklub

Z

zone [zəʊn] Zone WF

Alphabetische Liste der Wörter aus den Bänden 1–4 (Deutsch – Englisch)

* = unregelmäßiges Verb; siehe auch *List of irregular verbs*, S.197/198

A

abbiegen: nach links/rechts (in die Hill Street) abbiegen turn left/right (into Hill Street)
Abend evening
Abendessen dinner
abends in the evening; *(mit Uhrzeit)* p.m.
aber but
Abfall litter
abholen pick up
ablesen *read out
Abneigung dislike
abreisen *leave
Absatz paragraph
abschreiben copy
abseits der Straße off-road
Abspielgerät player
Absprache arrangement; **eine Absprache treffen** *make an arrangement
Achterbahn roller coaster
Actionfilm action film
Adjektiv adjective
Adresse address
Adverb adverb
Afrika Africa
Ahnung: ich habe keine Ahnung I have no clue
Akademie academy
Akte file
Aktivität activity
Alarmanlage alarm
albern silly
Alkohol alcohol
alle all (the); *(jeder)* everybody
allein alone
alles everything
allgemein general
Alphabet alphabet
alphabetisch alphabetical
als **1** as; **2** *(Wann?)* when; **schneller als** faster than
also so
alt old
Alter age
am: am 5. August on August 5th; **am Morgen/...** in the morning/...; **Am nächsten Tag ...** The next day ...; **am selben Ort** in the same place; **am Strand** on the beach; **am Telefon** on the phone; **am Wochenende** (AE) on the weekend; **24 Stunden am Tag** 24 hours a day
American Football American football
Amerika America
Amerikaner/in American
amerikanisch American; **amerik. Ureinwohner/in** Native American
Ampel traffic light
an **1** *(bei)* at; **2** *(nach)* to; **3** *(in der Nähe von, neben)* by; **4** *(eingeschaltet)* on; **an den Armen** by his arms; **an der Küste** on the coast; **an der Tafel** on the board; **an Schultagen** on school days; **denken an** *think of
anbieten offer
andere other; **ein anderer/anderes, eine andere** another
andere/r/s, anders (als) different (from)
andererseits: Einerseits ... Andererseits ... On the one hand, ... On the other hand, ...
(sich) ändern change; **er änderte seinen Namen in ...** he changed his name to ...
Anfang start
anfangen start
anfassen touch
Angebot offer
angeln fish; **Angeln** fishing
angenehm: Einen angenehmen Aufenthalt. Enjoy your stay.
Angst: ich habe Angst I'm frightened
ängstlich nervous
Anhänger/in fan
anhalten stop
anhören: sich anhören sound; **sich die CD anhören** listen to the CD
ankommen arrive
Anlegestelle pier
Anruf phone call; **Danke für den Anruf.** Thanks for calling.
anrufen phone; call
anschauen: sich den Film anschauen watch the film
Anschlagbrett noticeboard
Anschreiben cover letter
ansehen: (sich) das Bild ansehen look at the picture
Ansicht scene
Ansichtskarte postcard
Antwort answer; **u.A.w.g.** (= um Antwort wird gebeten) RSVP
antworten answer
Anweisung order; **Anweisungen geben** Giving orders
Anzahl number
Anzeige advert
anziehen *(tragen)* *wear
Anzug: Surf-/Tauch(schutz)-anzug wetsuit
Apfel apple
Apfelwein cider
April April
Arbeit work; job
arbeiten work
Arbeiter/in worker
Arbeitgeber/in employer
Arbeitsgemeinschaft *(Klub)* club
Arbeitsstelle job
Arm arm
arm poor; **Du Arme/r!** Poor you!
Artikel article
Asiat/in; asiatisch Asian
Asien Asia
Assistent/in assistant
Astronaut/in astronaut
auch too
auf on; *(auf ... hinauf/herauf)* onto; **auf das Haus zu** towards the house; **auf dem Bild** in the picture; **auf dem Land** in the country; **auf dem Parkplatz** in the car park; **auf dem Schulhof** in the playground; **auf den Boden fallen** *fall to the ground; **auf der (ganzen) Welt** in the world; **auf der Straße** in the street; **auf Deutsch** in German; **auf die Straße (hinaus)** into the street; **Auf Wiedersehen.** Goodbye.
Aufenthalt: Einen angenehmen Aufenthalt. Enjoy your stay.
Aufgabe job
aufgeben *give up
aufgehen *(sich öffnen)* open
aufgeladen: es ist aufgeladen it's charged up
aufgeregt excited
aufheben pick up
aufhören (mit) finish
aufmachen open
aufpassen auf look after; **Pass auf!** Watch me!
aufregend exciting
aufstehen *get up

aufstellen: ein Zelt aufstellen *put up a tent
aufwachen *wake up
Auge eye
Augenblick: Einen Augenblick. Just a minute.
August August; **20. August** August 20th
aus 1 from; *(hinaus/heraus)* out; *(aus ... hinaus/heraus)* out of; 2 *(zu Ende)* over; **aus der Schule zurück** back from school
Ausbildung education
Ausdruck phrase
ausdrucken print out
Ausflug trip
ausfüllen fill in
ausgeben *spend
ausgestorben extinct
ausleihen *(mieten)* rent
ausprobieren try
ausrichten: Kann ich (ihm/ihr) etwas ausrichten? Can I take a message?
Ausrüstung equipment; gear
ausrutschen slip
ausschalten turn off
aussehen look; **Wie sieht sie aus?** What does she look like?
Aussprache pronunciation
Ausstattung equipment
ausstehen: ich kann sie nicht ausstehen I hate them; I can't stand them
Ausstellung exhibition
aussuchen pick
Austausch- exchange
Ausweispapiere papers
auswendig: Lerne es auswendig. Learn it by heart.
Auszeichnung award
ausziehen: ich ziehe meine Jacke aus I *take off my jacket
Auto car
Autobahn *(in den USA)* freeway
Autofahrer/in driver
Autogramm autograph

B

Baby baby
Bad, Badezimmer bathroom
Badminton badminton
Bahn *(Laufbahn)* track
Bahnhof station; **im Bahnhof Exeter** at Exeter Station
bald soon
Ball 1 ball; 2 *(Tanzveranstaltung)* dance
Banane banana
Band *(Musikgruppe)* band
Bande gang
Bank *(Sparkasse)* bank
Bär bear
Baseball baseball
Basketball basketball
Batterieladegerät charger
Bauer/Bäuerin farmer
Bauernhof farm
Baum tree
Bayern Bavaria
beängstigend frightening
beantworten answer
bedeuten *mean
Bedeutung meaning
beeilen: Beeil dich! Hurry up!
beenden finish
Befehl order; **Befehle erteilen** Giving orders
Befehlsform imperative
begeistert excited
beginnen start; **ich begann zu rennen** I started to run
Begleitbrief (AE) cover letter
behalten *keep
behilflich: Kann ich Ihnen behilflich sein? Can I help you?
bei 1 *(an)* at; 2 *(mit)* with; **bei Tim (zu Hause)** at Tim's house
beibringen *teach; **ich würde dir das Reiten beibringen** I'd teach you to ride; **Wer kann es mir beibringen?** Who can teach me?
Beispiel example
beitreten: einem Klub beitreten join a club
bekommen *get
belebt busy
Belgien Belgium
beliebt popular
benutzen use
beobachten watch
bereit ready
Berg mountain
Bericht report
berichtigen correct
Beruf job; **Beruf, Berufs-** career
Berufserfahrung work experience
berühmt famous
berühren touch
beschäftigt busy
Beschäftigung activity; *(im Freien)* outdoor activity
beschreiben describe
Beschreibung description
beschweren: sich beschweren complain
Besichtigungen sightseeing
besondere/r/s special
Besprechung *(Rezension)* review
besser better
beste/r/s best; **am besten** best
besuchen visit
Besucher/in visitor
Besucherzentrum visitor centre
betonen stress
Betreff: ... Subject: ...
Betrieb business
Bett bed
beunruhigt: ich bin beunruhigt (wegen) I'm worried (about)
Bevölkerung(szahl) population
bevor before
(sich) bewegen move
bewerben: sich bewerben (um/bei) apply (for/to)
bewölkt cloudy
bezahlen *pay
bezeichnen call
Bezirk district
Biber beaver
Bier beer
Bild picture
bilden: Gruppen bilden make groups
Bildung education
billig cheap
bin: ich bin I'm (= I am)
bis 1 to; 2 *(zeitlich)* till; **bis zum 15. Oktober** by October 15th; **Bis dann.** See you. **Bis morgen/...** See you tomorrow/...
bist: du bist you're (= you are); **Bist du schon einmal ...? - Ja./Nein.** Have you ever ...? - Yes, I have./No, I haven't.
bitte please; **Hier, bitte.** Here you are. **Bitte.** *(Schon gut.)* That's OK. **Bitte schön.** *(Nichts zu danken.)* You're welcome.
bitten um ask for
blau blue
bleiben stay
Bleistift pencil
blöd stupid
Blödsinn nonsense
Blog blog
Bloggen blogging
Blogger/in blogger
blond blonde
bloß only
Board *(Brett)* board
Boden floor; ground; **am Boden zerstört** devastated
Boot boat
böse (auf) angry (with)
Bote/Botin courier
Brand fire
brauchen need
braun brown
breit wide

Brett board; **Schwarzes Brett** noticeboard
Brief letter
Brieffreund/in penfriend
bringen *bring; *take; **in die richtige Reihenfolge bringen** *put in the right order
Brite/Britin British
britisch British
Broschüre brochure
Brot bread; **belegtes Brot** sandwich
Brötchen roll
Brücke bridge
Bruder brother
Buch book
buchen book
Bücherei library
Buchhandlung, Buchladen bookshop
Buchstabe letter
buchstabieren spell
Büffel buffalo, buffaloes
Bühne stage; **auf der Bühne** on stage
Bundesstaat state; **der Bundesstaat Washington** Washington State
Burg castle
Bürgersteig pavement; (AE) sidewalk
Bus bus
Busfahrer/in bus driver
Bushaltestelle bus stop

C

Café cafe; (AE) diner
Camping camping
Campingplatz (AE) campground
CD CD
Cent cent
Clique gang
Coach coach
Cola cola
Computer computer
cool cool; **nicht cool** uncool
Cousin/e cousin
Cowboy cowboy
CVJM YMCA

D

da: da(hin) there; **da ist** there's; **da sind** there are; **da war/waren** there was/were; **da drüben** over there; **Ich bin wieder da!** I'm back!
dagegen: Haben Sie etwas dagegen, wenn ich mich hier hinsetze? Do you mind if I sit here?
daheim at home
daher so
damals at that time
Dame: Sehr geehrte Damen und Herren, ... Dear Sir/Madam, ...
daneben treffen/gehen miss
Dänemark Denmark
Danke (schön). Thank you./Thanks.
danken: Nichts zu danken. You're welcome.
dann then
darauf: ich freue mich darauf, von Ihnen zu hören I'm looking forward to hearing from you
darum that's why
das the; *(das da)* that; *(das hier)* this; *(in Relativsätzen)* that; who; **Das ist ...** That's ...
dass that; **Tut mir leid, dass ich ...** I'm sorry I ...
dasselbe the same
Datum date
Definition definition
dein/e your
Delfin dolphin
denken (an) *think (of); **daran denken** remember
der the; *(der da)* that; *(in Relativsätzen)* that; who
derselbe the same
deshalb that's why
Detektiv/in detective
deutsch; Deutsch; Deutsche/r German
Deutschland Germany
Dezember December
Dialog dialogue
dich you; *(dich selbst)* yourself
Dichter/in poet
die the; *(die da; Einzahl)* that; *(die da; Mehrzahl)* those; *(die hier; Mehrzahl)* these; *(in Relativsätzen)* that; who; **Männer, die Spiele spielen** men playing games
Dienstag Tuesday
dies (hier) this
diese *(Mehrzahl)* these; *(diese da)* those
diese/r/s this; **an diesem Abend** that evening
dieselbe the same
Ding thing
dir you; *(dir selbst)* yourself; **ein Bild von dir** a picture of yourself
Discgolf disc golf
Discjockey (DJ) DJ
Disko club
Dollar dollar ($)
Dolmetschen interpreting
Donnerstag Thursday
Doppelzimmer double room
Dorf village
dort(hin) there
draußen *(im Freien)* outdoors
drehen: sich drehen turn; **sich nach links drehen** turn to the left
drinnen *(in der Halle)* indoors
Droge drug
drüben: da/dort drüben over there
drücken push
du you
Dubliner/in Dubliner
dumm silly; stupid
Düne dune
durch *(hindurch)* through
durchdrehen panic
durcheinander bringen *(mischen)* mix up
dürfen can; **nicht dürfen** mustn't
DVD DVD
DVD-Player DVD player

E

Ecke: an der Ecke 10. Straße und Ocean Drive at 10th Street and Ocean Drive
egal, wie das Wetter ist whatever the weather
Ehemaligentreffen homecoming
Ei egg
eifersüchtig (auf) jealous (of)
eigen: mein eigenes Zimmer my own room
Eigenschaftswort adjective
eigentlich really
ein/e a; an; *(Zahl)* one
eine/r/s one; **eines Tages** one day
einerseits: Einerseits ... Andererseits ... On the one hand, ... On the other hand, ...
einfach easy; **einfache Gegenwart** simple present; **einfache Vergangenheit** simple past
Einfall idea
einfügen *put in
eingeschaltet on
einige some
Einkaufen shopping
einkaufen gehen *go shopping

Einkaufszentrum shopping centre; (AE) mall
einladen (zu) invite (for)
Einladung invitation
einnehmen *take
einpacken pack
einrichten establish
einsam lonely
einschalten turn on
Eintrag entry
Eintrittskarte ticket
Eintrittspreis entrance fee
Einwanderer/Einwanderin immigrant
Einzelzimmer single room
Eis *(Speiseeis)* ice cream
Eisenbahn train
Eisenbahnstrecke railway line
elektrisch electric
Elektrizität electricity
elektronisch electronic
Eltern, Elternteil parents, parent
E-Mail e-mail
E-Mail-Freund/in e-pal
Empfangschef/-dame receptionist
empfehlen recommend
Ende end; **oberes Ende** top; **Um zum Ende zu kommen, ...** To finish, ...; **zu Ende** over
Energie energy
eng narrow
Engländer/in(nen): er ist Engländer he's English
England England
englisch; Englisch English
entlang along; **die Straße entlang** along the street
entschuldigen: sich entschuldigen *say sorry; **Entschuldigen Sie, ...** Excuse me, ...
(sich) entspannen relax
entwerfen design
Enzyklopädie encyclopedia
er he; *(nicht bei Personen)* it
Erdkunde geography
erfahren: etwas über London erfahren learn about London
Erfahrung experience
Ergebnis result
erinnern: sich erinnern (an) remember
erklären explain; **ihr etwas erklären** explain something to her
eröffnen establish
erraten guess
erschüttert devastated
erst only
erste/r/s first; **erste Hilfe** first aid
erstens firstly
Erwachsene/r adult
erwarten: Ich kann es kaum erwarten. I can't wait for it.
erzählen (von) *tell (about)
erzielen *(Punkte)* score
es it; **es ist/gibt** there's; **es sind/gibt** there are; **es war(en)/gab** there was/were
essen *eat; **ein Eis essen** *have an ice cream; **zu essen geben** *feed
Essen food; *(zubereitet)* meal
Etikett label
etwas something; **etwas anderes** something different; **etwas Schokolade** some chocolate
euch you
euer/eure your
Euro euro (€)
Europa Europe
Europäer/in; europäisch European
Experte/Expertin expert

F

Fabrik factory
Fach *(Schulfach)* subject
Fachmann/-frau expert
Fahne flag
„Fahrattraktion" *(im Vergnügungspark)* ride
fahren *go; *(ein Auto/einen Bus)* *drive; *(reisen)* travel; **Mountainboard/Quad/Rad fahren** *ride a mountain board/quad/bike
Fahren: Quadfahren/Trikkefahren/... quad/Trikke/... riding
Fahrer/in driver
Fahrgeschäft ride
Fahrkarte ticket
Fahrrad bike
Fahrrad fahren *ride a bike
Fahrt ride
Fair Play fair play
fallen *fall; **auf den Boden fallen** *fall to the ground
falls if
falsch wrong; false
Familie family
Familienname family name
Fan fan
fantastisch fantastic
Farbe colour
fast almost; nearly
Fastfood fast food
Favorit/in favourite
Februar February
Federball(spiel) badminton
Federmäppchen pencil case
fehlend: die fehlenden Wörter the missing words
Feier celebration
Feinkostgeschäft und -imbiss (AE) deli
Feld field
Fels rock
Felsen *(Klippe)* cliff
Fenster window
Ferien holiday/s
fernsehen watch TV
Fernsehen, Fernsehgerät TV
Fernsehkarriere career in TV
Fernstraße (AE) highway
fertig ready
Fest; Festival festival
Festbeleuchtung illuminations
feucht wet
Feuer fire
Feuerwerk fireworks
Figur *(Person)* character
Film film; (AE) movie
Finanz-, finanziell financial
finden *find; *think
Fisch, Fische fish
fischen fish; **Fischen** fishing
fit fit
Fitnessstudio gym
Flagge flag
Fleisch meat
fliegen *go
flogen: sie flogen they flew
Flug flight
Flughafen airport; **am Flughafen Exeter** at Exeter Airport
Flugschein (plane) ticket
Flugzeug plane
Fluss river
Folge result
folgen follow
Förderunterricht extra classes
Form form
Formular form
fort away
Foto photo; picture; **Fotos machen** *take photos
Fotoapparat camera
Fotograf/in photographer
fotografieren *take photos
Fotosession, Fotoshooting photo shoot
Foul foul
Frage question; **eine Frage stellen** ask a question
Fragebogen questionnaire
fragen ask
Frankreich France

Franzose(n)/Französin(nen); französisch; Französisch French
Frau, Frauen woman, women; *(Anrede allgemein)* Ms; *(Anrede für verheiratete Frauen)* Mrs
Freak freak
frei free; **im Freien** outdoors; **Beschäftigung im Freien** outdoor activity
Freiheit freedom
Freiheitsstatue Statue of Liberty
Freitag Friday
Freiwurf free throw
Freizeit free time
Fremdenverkehrsbüro tourist office
fressen *eat
freuen: ich freue mich darauf, von Ihnen zu hören I'm looking forward to hearing from you; **ich freue mich für sie** I'm happy for her
Freund/in friend; *(feste/r Freundin/Freund)* boyfriend/girlfriend
freundlich friendly; **Mit freundlichen Grüßen ...** (AE) Yours truly, ...
Friseur/in hairdresser
froh happy
Früchte fruit
früh early
Frühling spring
Frühstück breakfast
frühstücken *have breakfast
(sich) fühlen *feel
führen *go; *lead
Führer/in *(für Sehenswürdigkeiten)* guide
Führung *(Rundgang)* tour
Füller pen
funktionieren work
für for; **es steht 24:18 für North** it's 24–18 to North
furchtbar terrible
furchterregend frightening
Fuß, Füße foot, feet
Fußball football; soccer
Fußboden floor
füttern *feed

G

Gälisch Gaelic
Gang **1** *(Bande)* gang; **2** *(Fahrrad/Auto/...)* gear; **3** *(Korridor)* passage
ganz: das ganze Wochenende all weekend; **die ganze Zeit** all the time
gar nichts nothing
Garten garden
Gärtner/in gardener
Gast visitor
Gebäude building
gebaut: sie wurden gebaut they were built
geben *give; **Gib Tim das Buch.** Give the book to Tim. **eine Party geben** *have a party; **Was gibt's?** What's up?
Gebiet district
Gebirge: im Gebirge in the mountains
geboren: ich wurde ... geboren I was born ...
Gebrauchsanweisung instructions
Geburtstag birthday
gedacht: ich habe das (immer wieder) gedacht I've been thinking that
Gedicht poem
gefährlich dangerous
gefallen: Es gefällt mir. I like it. **Wem gefällt es am besten?** Who likes it best? **alles, was jungen Männern gefällt** everything for young men to enjoy
Gefängnis prison; **im/ins Gefängnis** in prison; **ins Gefängnis kommen** *go to prison
Gefühl feeling
gefühlsbetont emotional
gegen against
Gegend area; *(Viertel)* neighbourhood
Gegenstand object
Gegenteil opposite
gegenüber (von) opposite
Gegenwart: einfache Gegenwart simple present
gehen *go; walk; **ans Telefon gehen** answer the phone; **sie geht zur Schule** she's at school; **Wie geht's?** How are you?/(AE) How ya doin'?
Gehör hearing
Gehsteig pavement
Geist ghost
gekommen: sie waren gekommen they had come
Gelände: im Gelände off-road
Geländer railings
gelangen *get
gelangweilt bored
gelb yellow
Geld money
Gemüse vegetable/s
genug enough
Genuss treat
geöffnet open
Geografie geography
Gepäckabfertiger/in baggage handler
gerade just
Gerät machine
Geräusch noise; sound
gern: gern haben like; **Ich laufe (nicht) gern.** I (don't) like walking. **Ich lese sehr gern.** I love reading.
Geschäft business; *(Laden)* shop; (AE) store
geschehen happen
Geschenk present
Geschichte **1** *(Erzählung)* story; **2** *(Schulfach)* history
Geschichtsverein Historical Society
geschickt: es hatte geschickt it had sent
geschlossen closed
Geschwindigkeitsbegrenzung speed limit
Geschwister brothers and sisters
gesetzt: sie hat eine Anzeige in die Zeitung gesetzt she has put an advert in the newspaper
Gesicht face
Gespenst ghost
gesponsert sponsored
Gespräch conversation; dialogue
gestern yesterday
gesund healthy
Getränk drink
Gewalt(tätigkeit) violence
Gewinn prize
gewinnen *win; **im Lotto gewinnen** *win the lotto
Gewinner/in winner
gewöhnlich usually
gezeigt: es wurde ihm gezeigt he was shown
Gitarre guitar; **Gitarre spielen** play the guitar
Glas glass
glauben believe
gleich: der/die/das gleiche the same
Gleis railway line
Glück: Viel Glück! Good luck!
glücklich happy
Glückliche/r: Der/Die Glückliche! Du Glückliche/r! Lucky thing!
Glückwunsch: Herzlichen Glückwunsch! Congratulations! *(zum Geburtstag)* Happy birthday!
Golf golf
Grab grave
Grad degree
Gras grass

Graubrot brown bread
Grauwal grey whale
Grenze border
grillen grill
groß big; *(bei Personen)* tall
großartig great
Großbritannien Britain
Großeltern grandparents
Großflächenbrand wildfire
Großmutter *(Oma)* grandma
Großstadt city
Großvater *(Opa)* grandad
grün green
Grund reason
Gruppe group
Grüße: Mit freundlichen Grüßen ... (AE) Yours truly, ...; **Viele Grüße ...** Best wishes, ...; **(Viele) Liebe Grüße ...** (Lots of) Love, ...
grüßen: Grüße Dawn, bitte. Say hi to Dawn, please.
gut good; fine; *(schon gut)* OK; **gut in** good at; **gut kennen/...** know/... well; **Gut gemacht!** Well done! **Gute(n) Abend/ Morgen/Nacht.** Good evening/ morning/night. **Guten Tag.** Hello. **Wie geht's? – Danke, gut.** How are you? – I'm fine, thanks.
Guthaben credit

H

Haar, Haare hair
haben *have; **ich habe** (AE) I got; **Ich habe Geburtstag.** It's my birthday. **Welche Farbe hat dein Zimmer?** What colour is your room?
Hähnchen *(Brathähnchen)* chicken
halb: halb zwei/... half past one/...; **dreieinhalb** three and a half
Halbzeit half-time
Halle: in der Halle indoors
Hallo. Hello./Hi.
Halloween Halloween
Halt stop
halten *hold; *keep; **sich an die Spielregeln halten** play by the rules; **Halt den Mund!** Shut up! **Was hältst du von ...?** What do you think of ...?
Haltestelle stop
Hamburger hamburger
Hamster hamster
Hand hand
handeln: Der Text handelt von ... The text is about ...
Handy mobile (phone); (AE) cell-phone
Handzeichen hand signal
Happy End happy ending
hart hard; tough
Hase rabbit
hassen hate
hast: Hast du schon einmal ...? – Ja./Nein. Have you ever ...? – Yes, I have./No, I haven't.
hätte: Ich hätte gern ... I'd like ...; **Wenn ich das Geld hätte, ...** If I had the money, ...
Hauptstadt capital
Haus house; **nach Hause gehen** *go home; **zu Hause** at home; **bei Tim zu Hause** at Tim's house; **Gehen wir zu mir nach Hause.** Let's go to my house.
Hausarrest: ich habe Hausarrest I'm grounded
Hausaufgaben homework
Hausaufgabenheft homework diary
Häuserblock block
Haustier pet
Haut skin
Havanna Havana
heben: Heb(t) die Hand. Put up your hand.
Heft book
Heim home
heimatlos homeless
Heimweh haben *feel homesick
heiß hot
heißen: Ich heiße Sarah. I'm Sarah. **Wie heißt du?** What's your name? **Wie heißen sie auf Deutsch?** What are they in German?
Heizkörper radiator
hektisch busy
Held/in, Held(inn)en hero, heroes
helfen help
Helfer/in helper
Helm helmet
Hemd shirt
herausfinden *find out
herbeiführen *bring about
herbeirufen call
Herbst autumn
hereinkommen *come in
Herr *(Anrede)* Mr; **Sehr geehrte Damen und Herren, ...** Dear Sir/ Madam, ...
herstellen *make; produce
herüber across
herumhängen *hang out
herunterladen download
herzlich: Herzlichen Glückwunsch! Congratulations! *(zum Geburtstag)* Happy birthday!
heute today; **heute Morgen/...** this morning/...
Hexe witch
hier(her) here; **Hier, bitte.** Here you are. **Hier spricht Sarah.** It's Sarah.
Hilfe help; **erste Hilfe** first aid
himmelhoch sky-high
hinab/herab down
hinaus/heraus out
hinein in; **hineingehen** *go in; **hineinkriechen** crawl in
hinten: hinten im Buch at the back of the book
hinter behind; **hinter einem Ball her** after a ball
Hintergrund background
hinüber across
hinunter/herunter down
hinzufügen *put in
Hirsch, Hirsche deer
hispanisch; Hispano-Amerikaner/in Hispanic
Hit hit
Hobby hobby
hoch high
Hochhaus skyscraper
hochheben pick up
Hochsprung (the) high jump
Hochzeit wedding
Hochzeitstag wedding day
Hockey hockey
Hof *(Bauernhof)* farm
hoffen hope
Hoffnung hope
höflich polite
holen *get
hören *hear; *(sich anhören)* listen to
Horror horror
Hose: kurze Hosen shorts
Hot Dog hot dog
Hotel hotel
House house
Hüfte hip
Hügel hill
Huhn chicken
Hund dog
hundert hundred
Hunger: Ich habe Hunger. I'm hungry.
hungrig hungry
Hurling hurling
hurra rufen cheer

I

ich I; **Dies bin ich.** This is me.
Idee idea
if-Satz if-clause

ihm, ihn him; *(nicht bei Personen)* it
ihnen them
Ihnen you
ihr 1 *(Wer?)* you; 2 *(Wem?)* her; *(nicht bei Personen)* it
ihr/e 1 *(Einzahl)* her; *(nicht bei Personen)* its; 2 *(Mehrzahl)* their
Ihr/e your
illegal illegal
im: im April in April; **im Bahnhof Exeter** at Exeter Station; **im Bus** on the bus; **im Fernsehen** on TV; **im Internet** on the Internet; **im Jahre 1971** in 1971; **im Norden** in the north; **im Sonderangebot** on special offer; **im Urlaub** on holiday; **im Winter** in winter
Imbissstube *(Café)* (AE) diner
immer always
immergrün evergreen
Immigrant/in immigrant
Imperativ imperative
in in; at; *(in ... hinein/herein)* into; **in Dartmoor** on Dartmoor; **in den Urlaub fahren** *go on holiday; **in der Fairfield Road** in Fairfield Road; **in der Nacht** at night; **in der Schule** at school; **in die Mannschaft kommen** *get on the team; **in einer Reservation** on a reservation; **In welcher Jahrgangsstufe bist du? - Ich bin in der 7. Stufe.** What year are you in? - I'm in year 7. **ins Bett gehen** *go to bed; **eine Sendung ins Leben rufen** start a programme; **Willkommen in London.** Welcome to London. **Ich bin (schon einmal) in Frankreich gewesen.** I've been to France.
Indianer/in Indian; *(amerik. Ureinwohner/in)* Native American
indianisch Indian
Infinitiv infinitive
Informationen, Informations- information
Insel island
insgesamt all in all
interessant interesting
Interesse interest
interessiert (an) interested (in)
international international
Internet Internet; **im Internet** on the Internet
Internet-Kiosk Internet kiosk
Ire(n)/Irin(nen); irisch; Irisch Irish
irgendetwas anything
irgendwelche any
Irland Ireland
irre (AE) awesome
ist is
Italien Italy

J

ja yes; *(besonders in wörtl. Rede)* yeah
Jacke jacket
jagen hunt
Jäger/in hunter
Jahr year; **ein 13-jähriges Mädchen** a 13-year-old girl
Jahrbuch yearbook
Jahreszeit season
Jahrgangsstufe year; **In welcher Jahrgangsstufe bist du?** What year are you in?
Jahrmarkt funfair
Januar January
Jeans jeans
jede/r/s each; every
jeder *(alle)* everybody
jemals ever
jemand somebody
jene *(Mehrzahl)* those
jetzt now
joggen jog
Jogger/in jogger
Jogging jogging
jubeln cheer
Judo judo
Jugendklub youth club
Jugendliche/r kid
Juli July
jung young
Junge boy
Juni June
Junior-Ranger junior ranger

K

Kajakfahren kayaking
Kalifornien California
kalt cold
Kamera camera
kämpfen *fight
Kanal canal
Kanu canoe; **Kanufahren** canoeing
Kappe cap
Karneval carnival
Karriere career
Karte card; *(Landkarte)* map
Karteikarte file
Kartoffel, Kartoffeln potato, potatoes
Kartoffelchips crisps; (AE) potato chips
Käse cheese
Kassierer/in cashier
Kasten box
Katze cat
kaufen *buy
Käufer/in shopper
Kaufhaus department store
kein/e no; not ... any
kennen *know; **kennen lernen** *meet; **Schön, dich/Sie kennen zu lernen.** Nice to meet you.
kicken kick
Kilometer kilometre
Kilt *(Schottenrock)* kilt
Kind, Kinder child, children; kid, kids
Kinderheim children's home
Kino cinema
Kirche church
Kirmes funfair
Kiste box
Klamotten gear
Klapphandy flip phone
Klasse class; **9. Klasse** (AE) grade 9
Klassenarbeit test
Klassenlehrer/in class teacher
Klassenzimmer classroom
Klavier piano
Kleider, Kleidung clothes; *(Klamotten)* gear
klein little; short; small; **kleine Kinder** young kids; **„Klein-Italien"** Little Italy
Kletterer/Kletterin (rock) climber
klettern climb; **auf einen Hügel klettern** climb a hill; **Klettern** (rock) climbing
Klingelton ringtone
klingen sound
Klippe cliff
Klub club
Knopf button
Koch/Köchin cook
kochen cook
Kolumbien Colombia
komisch funny
kommen *come; *(gelangen)* *get; **Ich komme aus London.** I'm from London. **Er kommt zu spät.** He's late. **ins Gefängnis kommen** *go to prison; **sie kamen darauf, aus Leavenworth eine deutsche Stadt zu machen** they thought of making Leavenworth a German town

Komödie comedy
König king
Königin queen
können can
konnte: ich konnte (nicht) I could(n't)
könnte: ich könnte (nicht) I could(n't)
Kontext context
kontrollieren check
Konzert concert
Kopf head
kopieren copy
Korb *(Basketball)* hoop
Korbwurf shot
Korridor passage
korrigieren correct
kosten: Was kostet/kosten ...? How much is/are ...?
kostenlos free
Kräcker cracker
Kraft energy
Krähe crow
krank ill; **krank werden** (AE) *become sick
Krankenhaus hospital
Krankheit illness
kriechen crawl
Krieg war
Küche kitchen
Kuchen cake
Kuh cow
kümmern: sich kümmern um look after; **sich um Taschen kümmern** *deal with bags
Kumpel buddy
Kunst art
Kurier/in courier
kurz short; **kurz (be)vor** just before
(sich) küssen kiss
Küste coast; *(Strand)* seashore; **an der Küste** on the coast

L

lächeln smile
lachen laugh
Lachs salmon
Ladegerät charger
Laden shop; (AE) store
Ladendieb/in shoplifter
lag: es lag an mir it's (= it was) up to me
Lagerfeuer campfire
lagern camp
Lampe lamp; light
Land **1** land; **2** *(ländliche Gegend)* country; **auf dem Land** in the country; **3** *(Staat)* state
Landfahrer/in traveller
Landkarte map
Landwirtschaftsschau county fair
lang: 14 Jahre lang for 14 years
lang/e long
lange (for) a long time; **lange bleiben** stay for long
Langhaus longhouse
langsam slow
langweilen: ich langweile mich I'm bored
langweilig boring
Laptop laptop
Lärm noise
lassen: stehen/liegen lassen *leave; **Lasst uns aufhören.** Let's finish.
Lauch(stange) leek
Laufbahn **1** *(Bahn)* track; **2** *(berufliche Laufbahn (im Fernsehen))* career (in TV)
laufen *run; walk; **Laufen** running
Läufer/in runner
laut loud
leben live
Leben life
Lebenslauf (AE) résumé
Lebensmittel food
Lebensweise way of life
„Lebewohl-Biegung" Farewell Bend
legen *put
Lehrer/in teacher
leicht easy
Leichtathletik athletics
leid: Tut mir leid. I'm sorry./Sorry.
Leider ... I'm afraid ...
leihen: sich einen Füller (aus)leihen borrow a pen
leisten: erste Hilfe leisten *give first aid
Lektion unit
lernen learn; **Lerne es auswendig.** Learn it by heart.
lesen *read
Leser/in reader
Lesetagebuch reading log
Lesewoche reading week
„Letterboxing" letterboxing
letzte/r/s last
letztendlich in the end
Leute people; **Hallo Leute.** (AE) Hi you guys.
Lexikon encyclopedia
Licht light
Lichtschalter light switch
lieb: Liebe/r ... Dear ...; **(Viele) Liebe Grüße ...** (Lots of) Love, ...
Liebe love
lieben love
Liebesfilm, Liebesroman romance
Lieblings- favourite
Lied song
Limonade fizzy drink; (AE) soda; *(Zitronen-)* lemonade
Lineal ruler
Linie line
Link link
links left; **auf der linken Seite** on the left; **links (von Ihnen)** on your left
Lippe lip
Liste list
Loch hole
los: es war viel los there was lots of activity
loslassen release
Lotterie: in einer Lotterie gewinnen *win a lottery
Lotto lotto
lügen lie
lustig funny
Luxemburg Luxembourg

M

machen *do; *make; **ein Picknick machen** *have a picnic; **Das macht zwei Pfund, bitte.** That's two pounds, please. **Es macht Spaß.** It's fun. **Ich mache Hausaufgaben.** I *do my homework. **Mach dir Notizen.** *Make notes. **Mach(t) / Machen Sie nur.** Go ahead. **sie macht Urlaub** she's on holiday **Was machst du (da)?** What are you doing?
Macht power
Mädchen girl
Mahlzeit meal
Mai May
Make-up make-up
Mama mum; (AE) mom
manchmal sometimes
Mann, Männer man, men
männlich male
Mannschaft team
Marke brand
Marshmallow marshmallow
März March
Maschine machine
Mathe(matik) maths
Mauer wall
Medien: die Medien the media
Medizin-; medizinisch medical
Meer sea; ocean
mehr more
Meile mile

mein/e my
meinen *mean
Meinung opinion; **meiner Meinung nach** in my opinion; **Ich bin derselben Meinung (wie du).** I agree (with you).
meiste/n: der/die/das meiste, die meisten most
meistens usually
Mekka Mecca
Mensch person; **Menschen** people
Metal metal
Meter metre
Mexiko Mexico
mich me
Michigansee Lake Michigan
mieten rent; *(Fahrrad/Kanu/...)* hire
Milch milk
Million million
Mindmap mind map
Minute minute
mir me
mischen mix up
mit with; **mit dem Rad/Bus/Auto/...** by bike/bus/car/...
mitbringen *take
Mitglied in einem Klub werden join a club
mitnehmen *take
Mittagessen lunch
Mittagspause lunch break; lunchtime
Mittagszeit lunchtime
Mitteilung message
Mittwoch Wednesday
„Mobber/in" bully
Mobbing bullying
Möbel furniture
Mobiltelefon mobile (phone); (AE) cellphone
Modell model
modern modern
mögen like; **sehr mögen** love; **Ich möchte (gehen/...)** I'd like (to go/...); **Ich möchte nicht gehen/...** I wouldn't like to go/...; **Möchtest du/Möchten Sie ...?** Would you like ...?
Moment moment; **im Moment** at the moment
Monat month
Mond moon
Monster monster
Montag Monday
Moor *(Hochmoor)* moor
morgen tomorrow
Morgen morning; **Montagmorgen** Monday morning
morgens in the morning; *(mit Uhrzeit)* a.m.
Motel motel
Motorrad motorbike
Mountainbike mountain bike
Mountainbikefahren mountain biking
Mountainboard mountain board
Mountainboardfahren mountain boarding
MP3-Player MP3 player
müde tired
Mund mouth; **Halt den Mund!** Shut up!
Muschel seashell
Museum museum
Musik music
Musiker/in musician
Musikinstrument musical instrument
Muslim/in Muslim
müssen *have to; must; **du müsstest** you should; **(ich) muss einen Ort finden** gotta find me a place
mutig brave
Mutprobe dare
Mutter mother
Mutti mum; (AE) mom

N

nach **1** *(Wann?)* after; **nach der Schule** after school; **fünf nach zehn** five past ten; **Viertel nach elf** quarter past eleven; **2** *(zu)* to; **nach Hause gehen** *go home
Nachbar/in neighbour
nachdem after
nachdenken *think
Nachfüllung refill
Nachmittag afternoon
nachmittags in the afternoon; *(mit Uhrzeit)* p.m.
Nachname family name
Nachricht(en) news; *(Mitteilung)* message
nachsprechen repeat
nächste/r/s: der nächste Flughafen the nearest airport; **nächste Woche** next week
Nacht night
nachts at night
Nähe: in der Nähe von by; near
Name name
nass wet
Nationalpark national park
natürlich of course
Naturwissenschaft science
neben by; next to
nehmen *take; **Ich nehme ...** *(Bestellung)* I'll have ...
neidisch (auf) jealous (of)
nein no
nennen call; name
nerven: Eltern nerven! Parents are a pain!
nervös nervous
nett nice
Netz network
neu new
Neuigkeit(en) news
nicht not; **Iss nicht.** Don't eat.
nichts nothing; not ... anything
nie never
Niederlande Netherlands
niemals never
niemand nobody
nirgendwo(-hin/-her) not ... anywhere
noch: noch ein/e/er/s another; **noch einmal** again; **noch nicht** not ... yet; **noch nie** never
Nomen noun
Nord- north; northern
(im) Norden (in the) north
Nordirland Northern Ireland
nördlich north; northern
Nordwesten: der Nordwesten the north-west
normalerweise usually
Notiz note
November November
Nummer number
nun now; **Nun, ...** Well, ...
nur only
nützen: ein Ball nützt nichts a ball's no good
nützlich useful

O

ob if; whether
obdachlos homeless
oben: ganz oben (auf) at the top
Oberschule *(in den USA)* high school
Objekt object
Obst fruit
oder or
offen open
(sich) öffnen open
oft often
ohne without
Ohr ear
okay OK
Oktober October

Öl oil
olympisch: die Olympischen Spiele the Olympics
Oma grandma
Onkel uncle
online online
Opa grandad
Orange orange
ordnen organize
Ordnung: in Ordnung OK; **Ist alles in Ordnung bei dir?** Are you OK? **Ist etwas nicht in Ordnung?** What's wrong?
organisieren organize
Orkan hurricane
Ort place
Osten; Ost- east
Österreich Austria
östlich east
Ozean ocean

P

paar: ein paar some
packen pack
Paddeln canoeing
Panik: in Panik geraten panic
Papa dad
Papiere papers
Park park
Parkplatz car park
Partner/in partner
Party party
passieren happen
Passiv passive
Pause break
Pence pence (p)
Person person; *(Figur)* character
Pfad track; trail
Pferd horse
Pfund *(brit. Währung)* pound (£)
Picknick picnic
Pier pier
pink pink
Pionier/in pioneer
Pirat/in pirate
Pizza pizza
Plan plan; *(Karte)* map
planen plan
Planer/in planner
Planwagen wagon
Platz place; *(Spielfeld)* court
plötzlich suddenly
Polen Poland
Polizei- police
Polizist/in police officer
Pommes frites chips
Pony pony
Popcorn popcorn
Pop(musik) pop
Porree(stange) leek
Portfolio portfolio
Post(amt) post office
Poster poster
Postkarte postcard
Präposition preposition
präsentieren present
Preis **1** *(Kaufpreis)* price; **2** *(Gewinn)* prize; **3** *(Auszeichnung)* award
preiswert cheap
pro per; **24 Stunden pro Tag** 24 hours a day
probieren try
Problem problem
produzieren produce
Projekt(arbeit) project
Protektor protector
protestieren protest
Prozent per cent
Prüfung test
Puma (AE) cougar
Punk(musik) punk
Punkt point
Punktzahl score

Q

Quad quad (bike)
Quiz quiz

R

Rabe raven
Rad *(Fahrrad)* bike; **Rad fahren** *ride a bike
Radfahren cycling
Radiergummi rubber
Radio radio
Ranch ranch
Ranger ranger
Rap(musik) rap
Rapper/in, Rapsänger/in rapper
Rasen grass
Rat advice
raten guess
Ratte rat
rauchen smoke
Räucherlachs smoked salmon
Raum room
Raumpfleger/in cleaner
raus: Ich muss hier raus. I have to get out of this place.
Rechner computer
Recht right; **Du hast Recht.** You're right.
rechts right; **auf der rechten Seite** on the right; **rechts (von Ihnen)** on your right
Rechtsanwalt, -anwältin lawyer
Rechtschreibung spelling
reden (mit) talk (to)
Redner/in speaker
Regal, Regale shelf, shelves
Regel rule
Regisseur/in director
regnen rain
Reifenschlauch tube
Reihe *(Serie)* series
Reihenfolge order
(sich) reimen (auf) rhyme (with)
Reise trip; **Reise-** travel
reisen travel; **Reisen** travel
Reisende/r traveller
reiten *ride; **Reiten** horse riding
rennen *run
reparieren fix
Reservat(ion) reservation
reservieren (lassen) book
Restaurant restaurant
retten save
Rettungssanitäter/in paramedic
Rezension review
Rhein Rhine
Rhythmus rhythm
richtig right; **das Richtige/Beste/...** the right/best/... thing
Richtung: in Richtung Haus towards the house
Rindfleisch beef
Rodeo rodeo
Rolle role
Rollen(spiel)karte role card
Rollstuhl wheelchair; **er sitzt im Rollstuhl** he's in a wheelchair
Rom Rome
romantisch romantic
rosa pink
rot red
Rubrik heading
rufen call; *(laut rufen)* shout
Rugby rugby
ruhig quiet
Rundgang tour

S

Sache thing; **Sachen, die man machen kann** things to do
Saft juice
sagen *say; *tell; **ihr etwas sagen** say something to her; **Jamie sagt Tess auf Wiedersehen.** Jamie says goodbye to Tess.

Salat salad; *(Kopfsalat)* lettuce
sammeln collect
Samstag Saturday
samstags on Saturdays
Sandwich sandwich
Sänger/in singer
Satz sentence
sauber clean
Schade! Too bad!
Schaf, Schafe sheep
Schatzsuche treasure hunt
schauen look
Schauspieler/in actor
Scherz joke
Scheune barn
schicken *send
Schiedsrichter/in referee
schießen *shoot; *(Tor)* score
Schiff boat; ship
Schikanieren bullying
Schild sign
Schildchen label
Schinken ham
Schirm umbrella
schlafen *sleep
Schlafzimmer bedroom
schlagen *hit
Schlange *(Warteschlange)* (AE) line; **Schlange stehen** queue (up); (AE) wait in line
schlecht bad
schlechter worse
schlechteste/r/s worst
schließen close
Schließfach locker
schließlich in the end
schlimm bad
schlimmer worse
schlimmste/r/s worst
Schloss castle
Schluss ending
Schlüssel key
schmal narrow
Schmerzen pain
schmücken decorate
schmutzig dirty
schnell fast; quickly
Schnellimbiss *(für Fisch/Pommes frites)* fish and chip shop
Schokolade chocolate
schon: schon einmal ever; **Schon gut.** *(Bitte.)* That's OK. **schon wieder** again
schön beautiful; fine; nice; **(Einen) Schönen Tag noch!** (AE) Have a nice day!
Schotte(n)/Schottin(nen) Scottish
Schottisch *(engl. Dialekt)* Scots
Schottland Scotland
Schrank cupboard
schrecklich terrible
schreiben *write
Schreibetui pencil case
schreien scream; shout
Schriftsteller/in writer
schüchtern shy
Schuh shoe
Schularbeiten homework
Schule school
Schüler/in pupil; (AE) student
Schülerkalender homework diary
Schulheft exercise book
Schulhof playground; **auf dem Schulhof** in the playground
Schultag school day
Schultasche bag
schütteln *shake; **sie schüttelt den Kopf** she shakes her head
Schützer protector
schwarz black
Schwarze black people
Schwein pig
Schweiz Switzerland
schwer hard; *(schwierig)* difficult
Schwerpunkt main point
Schwester sister
schwierig difficult
Schwierigkeiten: ich stecke in großen Schwierigkeiten I'm in big trouble
Schwimmbad swimming pool
schwimmen *swim; **Schwimmen** swimming
schwimmen gehen *go swimming
Schwimmer/in swimmer
sechziger: in den sechziger Jahren des 19. Jahrhunderts in the 1860s
See *(Binnensee)* lake
sehen look; *see
sehr very; **Sehr geehrte Damen und Herren, ...** Dear Sir/ Madam, ...
seid: ihr seid you're (= you are)
sein *be
sein/e his; *(nicht bei Personen)* its
Seite side; *(Buch, Heft)* page
selbst gemacht home-made
Selbstbeherrschung self-control
selbstsicher confident
selbstverständlich of course
senden *send
Sendung *(Radio, TV)* programme
September September
Serie series
Sessel chair
setzen: sich setzen *sit
seufzen sigh
Sheriff sheriff
Shorts shorts
Show show
Shuttle shuttle
sicher sure; *(in Sicherheit)* safe
Sicherheit: in Sicherheit safe
Sicherheitsausrüstung safety gear
Sicherheitskontrolle security check
sie **1** *(Wer?)* she; *(nicht bei Personen)* it; *(Mehrzahl)* they; **2** *(Wen?)* her; *(nicht bei Personen)* it; *(Mehrzahl)* them
Sie you
Sieger/in winner
Signal signal
sind are
Singapur Singapore
singen *sing
sitzen *sit; **er sitzt im Rollstuhl** he's in a wheelchair
Skateboard skateboard
Skateboarder/in skateboarder
Skater/in skater
Ski fahren ski
Skifahren skiing
Sklave, Sklavin slave
Skunk skunk
Smog smog
SMS text (message)
SMS-Terror text bullying
Snowboarder/in snowboarder
so **1** so; **2** like that/this; **so ein Job** a job like that/this; **So etwas gibt es nicht.** There's no such thing. **so viele/... wie** as many/... as
soeben just
Softball softball
Software software
sogar: Es war sogar besser. In fact, it was better.
sollen: Wann soll ich ...? When should I ...? **du solltest** you should
Somalia Somalia
Sommer summer
Sonderangebot special offer
Sonnabend Saturday
Sonne sun
sonnig sunny
Sonntag Sunday
Sorgen: sich Sorgen machen (um) worry (about); **ich mache mir Sorgen (um)** I'm worried (about)
spannend exciting
Spanien Spain
Spanier/in(nen); spanisch; Spanisch Spanish

spanischsprachig Hispanic
sparen save
Spaß fun; **Es macht Spaß.** It's fun.
spät, zu spät late; **Er kommt zu spät.** He's late. **Wie spät ist es?** What time is it?
später later
Spazierengehen walking
Spaziergänger/in walker
speichern *(MP3-Player)* *hold
Speiseeis ice cream
Speisekarte menu
Spiegel mirror
Spiel game; *(Wettkampf)* match
spielen play; **Gitarre spielen** play the guitar; **Spielt das Gespräch nach.** Act the dialogue.
Spieler/in player
Spielfeld court
Spielhalle amusement arcade
Spielregel: sich an die Spielregeln halten play by the rules
Spielstand score
Spielzeug toy
Spind locker
Spinne spider
Spitze top; **auf der Spitze** at the top
Spitzname nickname
Sport, Sportart sport; **Sport treiben** play sports
sportlich sporty
Sportplatz field
Sportschuh trainer; (AE) sneaker
Sportzentrum sports centre
Sprache language
Sprechanlage intercom
sprechen (mit) *speak to; talk (to); **Hier spricht Sarah.** It's Sarah.
Sprecher/in speaker
springen jump
Squash squash
Staat state
Stadt town; *(Großstadt)* city
Stadtmitte, -zentrum town centre
Stand *(Verkaufsstand)* stall
Star star
stark tough
Stärke power
Start start
statt instead of
Statue statue
stehen *stand; **es steht 24:18 für North** it's 24–18 to North; **Wie steht's?** What's the score?
stehen bleiben stop
stehlen *steal
Stein *(Fels)* rock
Stelle place
stellen *put
Stempel stamp
sterben die
Stimme voice
Stinktier skunk
stoppen stop
Strand beach; *(Küste)* seashore; **am Strand** on the beach
„Strandbuggy" dune buggy
Strandpromenade boardwalk
Straße road; street
Straßenbahn tram
streiten: sich streiten *fight
streng strict
Strom electricity
Strophe verse
Stubenarrest: ich habe Stubenarrest I'm grounded
Studio studio
Stufe step; *(Jahrgangsstufe)* year; **Ich bin in der 7. Stufe.** I'm in year 7.
Stuhl chair
Stunde hour; *(Unterrichtsstunde)* lesson
Stundenkilometer kilometres per hour
Stundenplan timetable
suchen look for
Suchmaschine search engine
Süden; Süd-; südlich south
super super
Supermarkt supermarket
Surf(schutz)anzug wetsuit
Surfausrüstung surfing gear
Surfbrett surfboard
surfen surf; **Surfen** surfing
Surfer/in surfer
Surfkleidung, -klamotten surfing gear
Symbol symbol
Szene scene

T

Tabelle table
Tablett tray
Tafel board
Tag day
Tagebuch diary
Talkshow chat show; (AE) talk show
Tante aunt
tanzen dance; **tanzen gehen** *go dancing
Tänzer/in dancer
Tanzveranstaltung dance
tapfer brave
Tasche bag; *(Kleidung)* pocket
Taschengeld pocket money
Tasse cup; **eine Tasse Tee** a cup of tea
Taste button
Tatsache fact
taub deaf
Tauch(schutz)anzug wetsuit
Tausch- exchange
tausend thousand
Taxi taxi
Team team
Technik technology
Techno techno
Technologie technology
Tee tea
Teenager teenager, teen
Teil part
teilen: sich ein Zimmer teilen share a room
Teilzeit, Teilzeit- part-time
Telefon phone; **am Telefon** on the phone; **ans Telefon gehen** answer the phone
telefonieren phone
Telefonnotiz phone message
Tennis tennis
Termin *(Verabredung)* appointment
Terminkärtchen appointment card
Terror: SMS-Terror text bullying
Test test
teuer expensive
Text text; *(Liedtext)* words (of a song)
Theater theatre
Thema topic
Themenpark theme park
Tier animal; *(zahmes Tier, Haustier)* pet
Tierhandlung pet shop
Tierrechte, Tierschutz- animal rights
Tipi tepee
Tipp tip
Tisch table
Tischtennis table tennis
Titel title
Tja, ... Well, ...
Tochter daughter
toll cool; great; super; (AE) awesome
Tomate, Tomaten tomato, tomatoes
Tor gate
töten kill
Tour tour
Tourist/in tourist

Touristeninformation tourist office
Tradition tradition
tragen *(anziehen)* *wear
Trainer trainer
trainieren train; practise
Traktor tractor
Traum dream
träumen dream
traurig sad
treffen, sich treffen (mit) *meet; **eine Absprache treffen** *make an arrangement
Treffpunkt: ein Treffpunkt a place to meet
treten kick
trinken *drink; **eine Cola trinken** *have a cola
trocken dry
Trubel: es gab viel Trubel there was lots of activity
Tschechische Republik Czech Republic
Tschüs. Bye.
T-Shirt T-shirt
tun *do; *(an einen Platz tun)* *put
Tunnel tunnel
Tür door
Türkei Turkey
Turm tower
Turnhalle gym
Tut mir leid. I'm sorry./Sorry.
Tüte bag
Typ type
typisch typical
Tyrann bully

U

U-Bahn underground; (AE) subway; **die (Londoner) U-Bahn** the tube
U-Bahnhof underground station
U-Bahn-Zug underground train
üben practise
über **1** above; **2** *(über die Straße)* across (the road); **3** about; **über die Sprechanlage** on the intercom
überall(-hin, -her) everywhere
überfliegen scan
übernachten stay
überprüfen check
überrascht surprised
Überraschung surprise
Überschrift heading
übersetzen translate
übrig: ich habe nicht viel dafür übrig I'm not keen on it
Übung exercise
Uhr clock; **um acht/zwanzig Uhr** at eight o'clock
Uhrzeit time
um: um acht/zwanzig Uhr at eight o'clock; **um Dinge zu verändern** to change things
umbringen kill
Umfrage survey
Umgebung environment
umschreiben *rewrite
Umstandswort adverb
umsteigen change
Umwelt environment
umziehen move
Unabhängigkeitstag Independence Day
und and; **Und du?** What about you?
unentschieden: es war unentschieden it was tied
Unfall accident
ungefähr about
ungesetzlich illegal
Uniform uniform
Unruhe trouble
uns us
unser/e our
Unsinn nonsense
unter under
unterhalten: sich unterhalten (mit) *have a chat (with); talk (to)
Unterhaltung conversation
unterirdisch underground
Unterrichtsstunde lesson
unterstreichen underline
unterstrichen underlined
Untersuchung *(Umfrage)* survey
unterwegs on the road
unwahr false
Urlaub holiday/s; **in den Urlaub fahren** *go on holiday; **sie macht Urlaub, sie ist im Urlaub** she's on holiday

V

Vater father
Vati dad
Verabredung appointment
verabschieden: sich von ... verabschieden *say goodbye to ...
Veränderung change
Verb verb
verbieten prohibit
Verbindung link
verboten prohibited
verbrachte: ich verbrachte I spent
Verbrechen crime
verbringen *spend
verdienen earn
Verein club
verfolgen follow
Vergangenheit past
vergessen *forget; *(stehen/liegen lassen)* *leave
Vergleich comparison
vergleichen compare
Vergnügen: besonderes Vergnügen treat
Verhältniswort preposition
verheiratet married
verirren: sich verirren *get lost
(sich) verkaufen *sell
Verkäufer/in shop assistant; (AE) sales clerk
Verkehr traffic
Verkehrssicherheit road safety
verlassen *leave
Verlaufsform der Gegenwart/Vergangenheit present/past progressive
verlegen embarrassed
verletzen *hurt; **ich habe mir die Hand verletzt** I hurt my hand
verlieren *lose
vermieten hire
vermissen miss
verschieden different
verschwenden waste
verspätet late
verstehen *understand; **..., verstehst du?** ..., you see.
versuchen try
verwenden use
Video(film) video
Videospiel video game
viel lots of; much; **eine viel befahrene Straße** a busy road; **Viel Glück!** Good luck!
viele lots of; many; **Viele Grüße ...** Best wishes, ...
vielleicht maybe
Viertel neighbourhood
Viertel vor/nach eins quarter to/past one
Visagist/in make-up artist
Vogel bird
Volk people; **das Volk der Makah** the Makah people
Volleyball volleyball

vollständig complete
von **1** of; **2** from; **3** *(vom/von ... herab/herunter)* off; **4** *(durch)* by
vor **1** *(Wo?)* in front of; **2** *(Wann?)* before; **vor zwei Jahren** two years ago; **fünf vor zehn** five to ten
vorbei *(zu Ende)* over; **am Haus vorbei** past the house
Vordergrund foreground
vorhaben plan
vorlesen *read (out); **ihr etwas vorlesen** read something to her
Vorlieben und Abneigungen likes and dislikes
Vormittag morning
vormittags *(mit Uhrzeit)* a.m.
Vorname first name
Vorort suburb
Vorschrift rule
vorsichtig careful
Vorsingen audition
Vorsitzende/r chairperson
Vorsprechen audition
vorstellen: sich (etwas) vorstellen imagine
Vortrag talk
vorziehen prefer

W

Wachfrau/-mann security guard
wachsen *grow
wählen pick
Wahnsinn! Wow!
wahr true
Wal whale
Walbeobachtung whale watching; **auf Walbeobachtungstour gehen** *go whale watching
Wald wood; *(Waldgebiet)* forest
Wales Wales
Waliser/in(nen); walisisch; Walisisch Welsh
Wand wall
Wanderer, Wanderin walker; hiker
wandern hike
Wandern walking
Wanderschuh walking shoe
Wandschrank (AE) closet
wann when
war was
wäre: sie dachten, es wäre eine gute Idee they thought it was a good idea
waren, warst, wart were
warm warm
wärst: Ich habe gesagt, du wärst morgen im Laden. I said you'd be in the shop tomorrow.
warten (auf) wait (for); **Warten wir's ab.** Let's wait and see.
Warteschlange (AE) line
warum why
was what; **Was für ein/e ...!** What a ...! **Was für Sendungen?** What kind of programmes? **Was gibt's?** What's up? **Was ist das?** What's that? **Was ist mit dir?** What about you?
waschen: du kannst dich waschen you can get yourself clean
Wasser water
Webcode webcode
Website website
weg away
Weg way; *(Pfad)* track; trail
weggehen (von) *leave
wehtun *hurt
weiblich female
Weihnachten Christmas
weil because
weinen cry
weiß white
Weißbrot white bread
Weiße white people
weit far
weitere **1** *(mehr)* more; **2** *(andere)* other
welche/r/s what; which; **Welche Farbe hat dein Zimmer?** What colour is your room?
Welle wave
Wellenreiten surfing
Welt world; **auf der (ganzen) Welt** in the world
Weltraum space
weniger less
wenn if; when
wer who
werden *become; **ich werde gehen** I'll (= I will) go; **ich werde nicht gehen** I won't (= will not) go; **ich werde gewinnen, ich gewinne** I'm going to win; **Ich werde Ranger.** I'm going to be a ranger. **Erste/r werden bei ...** *come first in ...
werfen *throw; *shoot
weshalb why
Westen; West- west
westlich west
Wettbewerb competition
Wetter weather
Wettkampf match
wichtig important
wie **1** how; **Wie geht's?** How are you? **Wie heißen sie auf Deutsch?** What are they in German? **Wie heißt du?** What's your name? **Wie nennt/bezeichnet man ...?** What do you call ...? **Wie spät ist es?** What time is it? **wie man uns findet** how to find us; **ich sehe, wie sich ihr Mund bewegt** I see her mouth moving; **2** *(so wie)* like; **wie das Buch ist** what the book is like; **Wie sieht sie aus?** What does she look like? **Träume, in denen ich wie ... bin** dreams of being like ...
wieder again; **Ich bin wieder da!** I'm back!
Wiedersehen. Bye.
Wiese field
Wikinger Viking
wild wild
willkommen: wir sind nicht willkommen we aren't welcome; **Willkommen in London.** Welcome to London.
Winter winter
wir we
wirklich really
Wirtschaft economy
wissen *know
Witz joke
wo where
Woche week
Wochenende weekend
woher: Woher kommst du? Where are you from?
wohin where
wohnen live
Wohnung flat; (AE) apartment
Wohnwagen *(Standwohnwagen)* mobile home
Wohnzimmer living room
Wolke cloud
Wolkenkratzer skyscraper
wollen want; **gehen wollen** want to go
wonach: du kannst tun, wonach dir gerade ist you can do whatever you feel
Wort word
Wörterbuch, -verzeichnis dictionary
Wortnetz, Wörternetz network

Wow! Wow!
wunderschön beautiful
wurde: es wurde genannt it was called
würde: ich würde I'd (= I would)
Wurf throw
Wurst, Würstchen sausage
Wurzel root
wütend (auf) angry (with)

Z

zäh tough
Zahl number
zahlen *pay
zahmes Tier pet
Zahnarzt/-ärztin dentist
Zeichen sign; signal
zeichnen *draw
zeigen *show
Zeile line
Zeit time
Zeitschrift magazine
Zeitung newspaper
Zeitverschwendung a waste of time
Zeitwort verb
Zelt tent
zelten camp
Zeltplatz (AE) campground
Zentrum centre
Ziffer number
Zimmer room
Zitat quote
Zoohandlung pet shop
zu **1** to; **sie helfen dir zu lesen** they help you to read; **zu Fuß** on foot; **zu Hause** at home; **2** for; **3** **zu alt** too old; **zu spät** late; **4** *(geschlossen)* closed
zuerst first
zufälligerweise war es ... (it) so happened to be ...
Zug train; **Zug von Planwagen** wagon train
Zuhause home
zuhören listen
zujubeln cheer
Zukunft future
zum: zum Frühstück/Mittagessen for breakfast/lunch
zumachen close
Zungenbrecher tongue twister
zuordnen match
zur: sie geht zur Schule she's at school; **Er kommt zu spät zur Schule.** He's late for school.
zurück back
zurückrufen call/phone back
zurufen: sie ruft ihm etwas zu she shouts something at him
zurzeit at the moment
zusammen together
Zusammenfassung summary
Zusammenhang context
zusehen watch
zustimmen: Ich stimme (dir) zu. I agree (with you).
zuversichtlich confident
Zweitsprache: Englisch als Zweitsprache English as a Second Language
zwingen: keiner kann mich dazu zwingen, dies zu essen nobody can make me eat this; **wenn man mich zwänge** if they made me
zwischen between

Girls/Women

Adrienne [eɪdri'en]
Alexa [ə'leksə]
Alice ['ælɪs]
Amanda [ə'mændə]
Angela ['ændʒələ]
Ashley ['æʃli]
Brianna [bri'ænə]
Britany ['brɪtəni]
Britney ['brɪtni]
Caitlin ['keɪtlɪn]
Calina [kə'li:nə]
Candice ['kændɪs]
Destiny ['destɪni]
Halma ['hælmə]
Janet ['dʒænɪt]
Jazmin ['dʒæzmɪn]
Katherine ['kæθrɪn]
Kaylee ['keɪli]
Kimberley ['kɪmbəli]
Lana ['lɑ:nə]
Laura ['lɔ:rə]
Leanne [li'æn]
Mariela [meəri'elə]
Natalie/Nattalie ['nætəli]
Pauline ['pɔ:li:n]
Rita ['ri:tə]
Sancha ['sæntʃə]
Sophie ['səʊfi]
Stephanie ['stefəni]
Sue Li [su:'li:]

Families

Bailey ['beɪli]
Brodess ['brəʊdes]
Cortez [kɔ:'tez]
Dunn [dʌn]
Garcia [gɑ:'si:ə]
Greene [gri:n]
Harris ['hærɪs]
Howard [haʊəd]
Hughes [hju:z]
Jones [dʒəʊnz]
Kennedy ['kenədi]
Moore [mɔ:]
Nguyen [nu:'jen]
Ramirez [rə'mɪərez]
Stone [stəʊn]
Wilson ['wɪlsən]

Boys/Men

Bob [bɒb]
Damon ['deɪmən]
Diego [di'eɪgəʊ]
Dylan ['dɪlən]
Frank [fræŋk]
Hassan ['hɑ:sən]
Joel [dʒəʊəl]
Joseph ['dʒəʊzɪf]
Josh [dʒɒʃ]
Kenichi [kə'nɪtʃi]
Kyle [kaɪl]
Lanh [læn]
Lee [li:]
Luke [lu:k]
Mack [mæk]
Miguel [mɪ'gel]
Pete [pi:t]
Ramon [rə'mɒn]
Richard ['rɪtʃəd]
Robert ['rɒbət]
Steph [sti:v]
Taylor ['teɪlə]
Thomas ['tɒməs]
Toby ['təʊbi]
Tyrell [taɪ'rel]

Tipp:
Auf S.196 gibt es noch mehr Namen.

People

Abi Russell ['eɪbi'rʌsəl]
Akon ['eɪkɑ:n]
Alicia Keys [ə'li:ʃə'ki:z]
Ben Gordon [ben'gɔ:dən]
Beyoncé [bi:ɒn'seɪ]
Calvin Klein ['kælvɪn'klaɪn]
Carlos Oliva ['kɑ:lɒsə'lɪvə]
Carmelo Anthony [kɑ:'meləʊ'æntəni]
Courtney Long ['kɔ:tni'lɒŋ]
Eddie Murphy ['edi'mɜ:fi]
Elizabeth Urban [ɪ'lɪzəbəθ'ɜ:bən]
Gerard Way ['dʒerɑ:d'weɪ]
Geronimo [dʒə'rɒnɪməʊ]
Goyathlay [gɔɪ'æŋklɑ:]
Gwen Stefani ['gwenste'fɑ:ni]
Harriet Tubman ['hæriet'tʌbmən]
Jennifer Lopez ['dʒenɪfə'ləʊpez]
Jesse James ['dʒesi'dʒeɪmz]
Justin Timberlake ['dʒʌstɪn'tɪmbəleɪk]
Kelly Clarkson ['keli'klɑ:ksən]
Lady Sovereign ['leɪdi'sɒvrɪn]
Lil' Kim [lɪl'kɪm]
Little Steven ['lɪtl'stɪ:vn]
Madonna [mə'dɒnə]
Malcolm X ['mælkəm'eks]
Marc Anthony [mɑ:k'æntəni]
Notorious B.I.G. [nəʊ'tɔ:riəs'bɪg]
Robin Hood ['rɒbɪn'hʊd]
Robin Thicke ['rɒbɪn'θɪk]
Scarlett Johansson ['skɑ:lətdʒəʊ'hænsən]
Sean Penn [ʃɔ:n'pen]
Shakira [ʃə'ki:rə]
Wyclef Jean ['waɪkləf'dʒi:n]

NAMES

Places

Anacortes [ænə'kɔ:tes]
Arizona [ærɪ'zəʊnə]
Bandon ['bændən]
Berlin [bɜ:'lɪn]
Calle Ocho [kʌjeɪ'ɒtʃəʊ]
Central Park [sentrəl'pɑ:k]
Chambers Street ['tʃeɪmbəzstri:t]
Chicago [ʃɪ'kɑ:gəʊ]
Chinatown ['tʃaɪnətaʊn]
Cleveland ['kli:vlənd]
Commercial Avenue [kə'mɜ:ʃəl'ævənju:]
Costa Rica [kɒstə'ri:kə]
Crater Lake [kreɪtə'leɪk]
Deschutes County [də'ʃu:ts'kaʊnti]
Disneyland ['dɪznilænd]
Dulles Airport ['dʌləs'eəpɔ:t]
Ellis Island [elɪs'aɪlənd]
Empire State Building [empaɪə'steɪtbɪldɪŋ]
Epcot ['epkət]
Everglades ['evəgleɪdz]
Fidalgo Island [fɪ'dælgəʊ'aɪlənd]
Florida ['flɒrɪdə]
Fort Laramie [fɔ:t'lærəmi]
Fort Lauderdale [fɔ:t'lɔ:dədeɪl]
Friday Harbor ['fraɪdi'hɑ:bə]
Glendale ['glendeɪl]
Grand Canyon [grænd'kænjən]
Grand Central [grænd'sentrəl]
Greenville ['gri:nvɪl]
Ground Zero [graʊnd'zɪərəʊ]
Harlem ['hɑ:ləm]
Hobuck Beach ['həʊbʌk'bi:tʃ]
Hollywood Boulevard ['hɒliwʊd'bu:ləvɑ:d]
Hurricane Ridge ['hʌrɪkəɪn'rɪdʒ]
Independence [ɪndɪ'pendəns]
Leavenworth ['levənwəθ]
Lincoln Center ['lɪŋkən'sentə]
Los Angeles [lɒs'ændʒɪli:z]
Madison Square Garden ['mædɪsən'skweə'gɑ:dn]
Manhattan [mæn'hætən]
Maryland ['meərilænd]
Miami [maɪ'æmi]
Millennium Park [mɪ'leniəmpɑ:k]
Missouri [mɪ'zʊəri]
Neah Bay ['ni:ə'beɪ]
Nebraska [nə'bræskə]
New Jersey [nju:'dʒɜ:zi]
New York City [nju:jɔ:k'sɪti]
Anacortes [ænə'kɔ:tes]
Ohio [əʊ'haɪəʊ]
Olympic National Park [ə'lɪmpɪk'næʃnəl'pɑ:k]
Omaha ['əʊməhɑ:]
Oregon ['ɒrɪgən]
Panther Parkway ['pænθə'pɑ:kweɪ]
Pennsylvania [pensɪl'veɪniə]
Philadelphia [fɪlə'delfiə]
Port Angeles [pɔ:t'ændʒɪli:z]
Portland ['pɔ:tlənd]
Port Townsend [pɔ:t'taʊnzend]
Puerto Rico [pwɜ:təʊ'ri:kəʊ]
Richmond ['rɪtʃmənd]
Roche Harbor ['rəʊtʃ'hɑ:bə]
Santa Monica ['sæntə'mɒnɪkə]
Sears Tower ['sɪəztaʊə]
Seattle [si'ætl]
Snake River ['sneɪk'rɪvə]
South Carolina ['saʊθkærə'laɪnə]
Tennessee [tenə'si:]
Times Square ['taɪmz'skweə]
Tropical Park ['trɒpɪkəl'pɑ:k]
United Center [jʊ'naɪtɪdsentə]
Venice ['venɪs]
Vietnam [vjet'næm]
Washington Square [wɒʃɪŋtən'skweə]
West Palm Beach [westpɑ:m'bi:tʃ]
Yellowstone ['jeləʊstəʊn]
Yosemite [jəʊ'semɪti]

Other names

Amy's Place ['eɪmiz'pleɪs]
Chicago Bulls [ʃɪ'kɑ:gəʊ'bʊlz]
Daddio's Pizza ['dædiəʊz'pi:tsə]
Greenpeace ['gri:npi:s]
Makah [mə'kɑ:]
My Chemical Romance [maɪ'kemɪkəlrəʊ'mæns]
Odeon Cinema ['əʊdiən'sɪnəmə]
Peter Pan ['pi:tə'pæn]
Radio Cascades ['reɪdɪəʊkæs'keɪdz]
San Juan Safaris [sæn'hwɑ:nsə'fɑ:riz]
Segway ['segweɪ]
Spinreel Dunes ['spɪnri:l'dju:nz]
Sullivan High ['sʌlɪvən'haɪ]
Sunset Motel ['sʌnsetməʊ'tel]
The Chorus [ðə'kɔ:rəs]
The Pirates of the Caribbean [ðə'paɪrətsɒvðəkærɪ'bi:ən]
The Pixies [ðə'pɪksiz]
The Splash Mountain [ðə'splæʃ'maʊntən]
The Starbury One [ðə'stɑ:bəri'wʌn]
Warner Brothers ['wɔ:nəbrʌðəz]
Wikipedia [wɪkɪ'pi:diə]
Within Temptation [wɪ'ðɪntemp'teɪʃn]

Tipp:
Auf S.195 gibt es noch mehr Namen.

IRREGULAR VERBS

Infinitive form (Grundform)	Simple past form (Einfache Vergangenheit)	Present perfect form (Vollendete Gegenwart)	
be	I was, you were, she was	I've been	sein
have	I had	I've had	haben
do	I did	I've done [dʌn]	tun, machen
become	I became	I've become	werden
bring	I brought	I've brought	bringen
buy	I bought	I've bought	kaufen
come	I came	I've come	kommen
deal	I dealt [delt]	I've dealt [delt]	sich kümmern
draw	I drew	I've drawn	zeichnen
drink	I drank	I've drunk	trinken
drive	I drove	I've driven ['drɪvn]	fahren
eat	I ate [et]	I've eaten	essen
fall	I fell	I've fallen	fallen
feed	I fed	I've fed	füttern
feel	I felt	I've felt	(sich) fühlen
fight	I fought	I've fought	kämpfen; sich streiten
find	I found	I've found	finden
forget	I forgot	I've forgotten	vergessen
get	I got	I've got	bekommen; holen
give	I gave	I've given	geben
go	I went	I've gone [gɒn]	gehen; fahren
grow	I grew	I've grown	wachsen
hear	I heard [hɜːd]	I've heard [hɜːd]	hören
hit	I hit	I've hit	schlagen
hold	I held	I've held	halten
hurt	I hurt	I've hurt	verletzen
keep	I kept	I've kept	halten, behalten
know	I knew	I've known	wissen; kennen
lead	I led	I've led	führen
leave	I left	I've left	verlassen; (liegen) lassen
lose	I lost	I've lost	verlieren
make	I made	I've made	machen
mean	I meant [ment]	I've meant [ment]	meinen; bedeuten
meet	I met	I've met	treffen; kennen lernen
pay	I paid	I've paid	zahlen, bezahlen
put	I put	I've put	stellen, legen, tun
read	I read [red]	I've read [red]	lesen, vorlesen
ride	I rode	I've ridden	(Rad/Quad) fahren
run	I ran	I've run	rennen
say	I said [sed]	I've said [sed]	sagen
see	I saw	I've seen	sehen
sell	I sold	I've sold	verkaufen
send	I sent	I've sent	senden
shake	I shook	I've shaken	schütteln
shoot	I shot	I've shot	schießen; werfen
show	I showed	I've shown	zeigen

IRREGULAR VERBS

Infinitive form (Grundform)	Simple past form (Einfache Vergangenheit)	Present perfect form (Vollendete Gegenwart)	
sing	I sang	I've sung	singen
sit	I sat	I've sat	sitzen; sich setzen
sleep	I slept	I've slept	schlafen
speak	I spoke	I've spoken	sprechen
spend	I spent	I've spent	ausgeben; verbringen
stand	I stood	I've stood	stehen
steal	I stole	I've stolen	stehlen
swim	I swam	I've swum	schwimmen
take	I took	I've taken	nehmen; bringen
tell	I told	I've told	erzählen; sagen
think	I thought	I've thought	(nach)denken; finden
throw	I threw	I've thrown	werfen
understand	I understood	I've understood	verstehen
wake up	I woke up	I've woken up	aufwachen
wear	I wore	I've worn	tragen, anziehen
win	I won	I've won	gewinnen
write	I wrote	I've written	schreiben

Lösungen (S.144–156)

S.144: Test yourself 1: financial, salmon, lettuce, prison, violence, opposite, message; **2:** false; busy; brown bread; lose; **3:** 1 top; 2 theatre; 3 dinner; 4 menu; 5 salmon; 6 lettuce; **4:** 1 I'll have a beef sandwich and some water, please. 2 Most tourists come here to go skiing. 3 I have to finish the article by Thursday.
Do you remember? a) amusement arcade, block, church, cinema, district, hospital, museum, post office, theatre; b) brochure, guide, holiday, sightseeing, tour, tourist, traveller, trip

S.147: Test yourself 1: movies; comedies; models; messages; drugs; **2:** 1 stall; 2 camera; 3 audition; 4 entry; **3:** 2 romance; 3 jog; 4 meaning; 5 useful; 6 uncool; **4:** 1 What kind of films do you like best? 2 We jogged through a field for a long time. 3 We took lots of photos on holiday.
Do you remember? a) diary; b) invitation; c) break; d) dialogue

S.150: Test yourself 1: fix; hit; kick; leave; miss; panic; shoot; throw; touch; **2:** 1 Well done! 2 Good luck! 3 Too bad!
Do you remember? 1 rules; 2 point; 3 sign; 4 gear

S.153: Test yourself 1: 2 illness; 3 fish; 4 European; 5 cleaner; 6 cook; **2:** 1 My mum is looking forward to meeting you. 2 After driving to London, I was really tired. 3 I have to look after my little cousins.
Do you remember? a) forest, island, lake, mountain, ocean, river, sea; b) camping, cycling, fishing, hiking, hunting, kayaking, skiing, swimming, walking

S.156: Test yourself 1: female; in front of; sadly; slow; moon; loud; **2:** 1 piano; 2 lie; 3 astronaut; 4 employer; **3:** 1 award; 2 umbrella; 3 deaf; 4 key; 5 alarm; 6 power
Do you remember? a) concert, guitar, musical instrument, musician, piano, singer, song, sound, stage, title; b) above, behind, between, in front of, into, near, onto, opposite, through, towards

Bildquellen

Alamy, Abingdon (S.8 Kenichi / Vova Pomorttzeff, Kaylee / Dynamic Graphics Group / IT Stock Free; S.9.2 / Barry Mason, 3 / Mark Hamilton, 4 / Philip Scalia, u-re / Sylvia Cordaiy Photo Library Ltd; S.10.1 / AA World Travel Library, 3 / Black Star, 5 / Sylvia Cordaiy Photo Library Ltd; S.11 mittig / Alex Segre, o-re / Ambient Images; S.17 Greenville / James Schwabel, Britney / Stockdisc Classic, re / Mark Baigent; S.22 re / David Young-Wolff; S.24 o-re / EuroStyle Graphics, u-li / Glow Images, u-re / LHB Photo; S.25 E / flonline, F / Peter Jordan, G / LHB, H / dreamtours; S.34 mi-li / archivberlin; S.44 Bild 4 / Rodolfo Arpia; S.45 oben / Dennis MacDonald; S.46 li / Steve Skjold ; S.47 u-re / Judith Collins; S.48 D / Charles Ridgeway; S.53 u-re / Jeff Greenberg; S.56 Mi / imagebroker; S.59 / Jeff Greenberg; S.62 li / Steve Skjold, re / Ace Stock Ltd; S.66C / Jeff Greenberg; S.67F / Stock Connection Blue; S.68 li / Steve Skjold; S.70 unten / geogphotos; S.71 li / Ken Weingart, re / Ingram Publishing (Superstock Limited); S.73 / David Levenson; S.78 oben / David R Frazier Photolibrary Inc, Mitte / Jim West; S.81 u-re / Index Stock; S.82 li / Digital Vision, re / Buzzshotz; S.83 o-li / Andre Jenny, S.84 / Stan Rohrer; S.85 oben / William S.Kuta; S.92 o-re / America, u-re / Dennis McDonald, Mitte/ Jupiter Images / Comstock Images; S.101 re / Vlad; S.102.2/ Visions of America LLC, Bild 4 / James Nesterwitz; S.104a / TNT Magazine, b / David Ball, e / Chuck Eckert; S.110 o-re / Brian Atkinson; S.113a / David J. Green–Lifestyle, c / Formcourt, d / Thinkstock, e / Caro; S.118 / Patrick Blake; S.119 / Digital Vision; S.122 / North Wind Picture Archives); **Associated Press**, New York (S.103); **Avenue Images**, Hamburg (S.32 unten / Image Source; S.44 Bilder 1 & 2 / Image 100, Bild 6 / Radius Images; S.46 re / Blend Images; S.50 / ImageSource; S.52 o-li / Index Stock; S.55 beaver / Alaska Express; S.56 oben / Bananastock; S.66A / Stockbyte; S.67E / Index Stock; S.83 u-li / Index Stock; S.88 / Index Stock; S.104 C & D / Index Stock; S.112 / BrandX; S.113b / Digital Vision, f / Radius Images); **Annette Bondzio-Abbit**, Bielefeld (S.74 oben); **Steve Berentsen**, Anacortes (S.53 o-li; S.60.1); **Bridgeman Art Library**, Berlin (S.57 / William Page; S.80 Peter Newark American Pictures); **Anna Catania**, Berlin (S.36); **Corbis**, Düsseldorf (S.14 / Bettman; S.15 / Bettmann; S.44 Bild 3 / moodboard; S.53 o-re / Kevin Schafer; S.66B / Tim Mosenfelder & D / Buddy Mays; S.67G / Nathan Benn; S.76 re / Reuters; S.104F / Angelo Hornak; S.108 / Michael S.Lewis; S.122 unten / Richard Cummins; S.123 li / Louie Psihoyos ;S.124 / Bettmann; S.125 oben / Bettmann, u-li); **Corel Library** (S.47 skull; S.126 pasta, soup, stew); **George Delgado**, New York (S.41 oben; S.42–43; S.106); **Denver Public Library**, USA (S.81 o-li & re / Colorado Historical Society & Denver Art Museum); **Frank Donoghue**, Nenagh (S.53 u-li; S.54 u-re; S.56 unten; S.60.2 & 3; S.88a& b; S.101 star; S.111 o-li); **EUP-Images**, Brussels (S.120 & 121 / Gorm K. Gaare); **F1Online**, Frankfurt (S.92 mi-re / Wildgruber); **Gundula Friese**, Berlin (S.12 o-re; S.19); **Getty Images**, München (S.41 unten; S.67H; S.68re / WireImage; S.69 / Scott Gries; S.70 oben / SW Productions; S.72 / Tom Sadler; S.76 li; S.105; S.115 unten / Donald Kravitz; S.117 unten / Hulton Archive; S.123 re); **Helicopter Flight Services Inc.**, New York (S.17 unten); **IFABilderteam**, München (S.11 Bild 9); **Ingram Publishing**, Cheshire (S.12 tomato & lettuce); **Interfoto**, München (S.98 o-re /Archiv Friedrich); **invitationconsultants.com** (S.20 o.li); **Jupiter Images**, Ottobrunn / München (S.53 o-mi / Tom Brakefield); **Kennedy Space Center**, Florida (S.74 unten); **The Kobal Collection**, London (S.100 / Polygram); **LA Youth** (S.34 o-li); **Los Angeles Magazine**, Los Angeles (S.26 unten); **Lower Manhattan Development Corporation**, New York (S.98 Freedom Tower); **Makah Museum**, Neah Bay (S.61 unten); **Mauritius Images**, Mittenwald (S.10 o-mi / Pixtal); **Christine Maxwell**, Berlin (S.47.3 T-shirt; S.48 Bilder 2,3,4 & B; S.49 unten); **Robert Nadolny**, Berlin (S.52–53 Hintergrund); **National Parks Service Photo**, Washington DC (S.52 bear; S.54 fire, bear); **New York City Transit**, New York (S.13); **Guy Noffsinger**, Los Angeles (S.28; S.29; S.32 o-re); **Vaughan Oliver**, London (S.34 u-li); **Oregon Parks & Recreation Department**, Salem (S.54 o-re; S.59 o-li); **Photofusion**, London (S.48C / Brian Mitchell); **Photographers Direct**, UK (S.25I /Buddy Mays; S.52 u-re / Francis Caldwell; S.109 / Merrilyn McDonald; S.111 o-re / Steve MacAulay); **Photolibrary**, London (S.92 u-li / ImageS.com); **Picture Alliance**, Frankfurt / Main (S.78 u-li & re / dpa; S.97.1 / dpa / dpaweb, 2 / Schroewig / Cyberimage, 3 / dpa, 4 / Schroewig / Cyberimage, 5 / dpa-Report); **Redferns**, London (S.115 oben / gna); **Reuters**, Berlin (S.64 / Anthony Bolante); **Rex Features**, London (S.16 / David Fisher); **San Juan Safaris**, Friday Harbor, WA (S.61 o & mi); **Salt & Light Ministries, Inc.**, N. Bend, (S.116); **Santa Monica Pier Restoration Corporation**, Santa Monica, (S.26 oben); **Segway** (S.31); **Shutterstock**, New York (S.8 Emily / Cathleen Clapper, Luke / Galina Barskaya, Shanna / Lorelyn Medina; S.9.1 / Jan Vancura, 5 / 6169758076, 4 / Luca Flor; S.10 licence plate, u-li / Luca Flor; S.11.6 / Donald R. Swartz; S.12 u-li / Sharon D, bagel / Olga Lyubkina; S.17 li / Albo; S.18 bags / prism_68, tooth / Timashov Sergiy; S.22 li / Lorelyn Medina; S.24 o-li / Susan McKenzie; S.34 o-re / Edyta Pawlowska, witch / Simone van den Berg, u-re / ene; S.44 Bild 5 / kristian sekulic, Bild 6 / Larry St. Pierre; S.47 Bild1 / maxstockphoto, Bild 2 / Stocksnapper, Bild 4 / JoLin, Bild 5 / Jessica Bilen, u-li / Scott Waldren; S.48 A / Jenny Solomon; S.49 oben / J. Helgason; S.52 deer / Mike Rogal, cougar / Tony Campbell; S.53 Mi-li / Hiep Nguyen; S.55 deer / Andrew Taylor, unten / Jamie cross; S.58.1 / red06, 2 / Fernando Jose Vasconcelos Soares, 3 / Slobodan Djajic, 4 / Kirsty Pargeter, 5 / Elisabeth Perotin, 6 / Grzegorz Japol; S.63 oben / Rafa Irusta, unten / Chris Turner; S.77 li / Peter Albrektsen, re / Lisa F. Young; S.80 oben / Najin; S.83 o-re / Eric Patterson, u-re / Robynrg; S.85 unten / Tyler Olsen; S.87 / Anita Patterson Peppers; S.92 o-li / Jinglebeez Photo Gallery, mittig-li / Natalia Bratlavsky; S.94 oben / Jan Carbol, u-li / Miguel Angel Salinas Salinas, u-re / Andryianava Alena; S.95 oben / Heath Doman, unten / Szymon Apanowicz; S.96 / Scott A. Maxwell; S.98 Mi-li / Natalia Bratlavsky, re / Marcin Wasilewski; S.99 / Emin Kuliyev; S.102.1 / Roger Dale Pleis, 3 / Stephen Finn, 5 / Dana Bartekoska; S.106A / Graca Victoria, B / Morgan Lane Photography, C / Joszef Szasz-Fabian, D / Anubhav Suri, E / lev dolgachov, F / vnlit; S.111 unten / Martine Oger; S.114 / Yuri Arcurs; S.117 oben / Ronald Sherwood, Mitte / Jamie Cross; S.126 pork / Colour, lamb / Robyn Mackenzie, squid / Pawel Strykowski, bacon / VanHart, tuna / Karin Lau, plums / Isidore Milic, strawberries / bhathaway, pears / Olga Shelego, cherries / JoLin, melon / Stefano Tiraboschi, cauliflower /Jow Gough, beans / Sally Scott, pepper / Marc Dietrich, mushrooms / arnaud weisser, broccoli / LockStockBob, rice / Elena moiseeva, biscuits / Gabi Garcia; S.127 western / Jim Parkin, scifi / Antonis Papantoniou, newspapers / 4736202690, magazines / Tan Wei Ming, detective / Peter Hansen, scales / Le Loft 1911; S.128 shorts / Johanna Goodyear, glove / Byron W. Moore, helmet / Panagiotis Mouzakis, boots / oddech, referee / george green, cheerleader / Jaimie Duplass, goalkeeper / Vova Pomortzeff, athletics / Petur Asgeirsson, kick / Shawn Pecor, throw / Rena Schild, court / Albo, racket / Denis Pepin, net / Elena Eliseeva, pool / Billy Lobo H; S.129 PE / Jerry Sharp, art / Amanda Flagg, textiles / Susanne Karlsson, environment / Cathy Keifer, orchestra / WizData Inc., chess / PhotoCreate, arts and crafts / Jyothi Joshi, judo / Tito Wong; S.130 oben / Andresr, u-li / Nikolay Okhitin, u-re / Joe Gough; S.131 accordion / Alexei Novikov, bass guitar / Jaimie Duplass, clarinet / Kiselev Andrey Valerevich, drums / iofoto, electric guitar / Robynrg, keyboard / Peter Albrektsen, piano / Brian Chase, recorder / Thomas M Perkins, saxophone / Kiselev Andrey Valerevich, trumpet / photobank.ch, goose / Zaichenko Olga, milking machine / Nitipong Ballapavanich, tractor / Olga Zaporozhskaya, combine harvester /Gilmanshin, barn / David Scheuber, stable / Jakez, sow / Chepko Danil Vitalevich, feed / Rtimages; S.141 / Stephen Aaron Rees; S.142 / David Dea; S.145 / Tatiana Sayig; S.151 / James Steidl; S.155 / Lynne Barrows; S.156 / Najin; S.157 sign / Julien, frisbee-golf / Jason Maehl); **Stills Online**, Hamburg (S.128 jogging trousers); **Stockdisc** (S.106 u-re pencil case); **Sullivan High School**, Chicago (S.38, S.39, S.45 unten; S.106 Mitte; S.107); **Ullstein Bild**, Berlin (S.98 WTC / Reuters); **US Postal Service** (S.125 u-re); **Silvia Wiedemann**, Berlin (S.60, 124 map)
Umschlag: George Delgado, New York

Lied- und Textquellen

S.31: *Das Oxford Schulwörterbuch* © Oxford University Press, 2007; S.34: *L.A. Youth*, Los Angeles; S.40: *YMCA*, T: Belolo, Henri © Scorpio Music. Für D/A/CH: Roba Music Verlag GmbH; S.70/71: *A life without music* © 2007 Elizabeth Urban.

New Highlight
Band 4

Im Auftrage des Verlages herausgegeben von
Frank Donoghue, Nenagh, Irland

Erarbeitet von
Frank Donoghue, Nenagh, Irland • Rebecca Robb Benne, Otterup, Dänemark

Verlagsredaktion
Susanne Döpper (Projektleitung) • Silvia Wiedemann (verantwortliche Redakteurin)
Christine Maxwell (Bildredaktion)

Anhang
Redaktionsbüro Birgit Herrmann, Freudenstadt

Beratende Mitwirkung
Hans Bebermeier, Bielefeld • Hartmut Bondzio, Bielefeld • Annette Bondzio-Abbit, Bielefeld •
Gisela Feldmann, Haltern • Prof. Dr. Liesel Hermes, Karlsruhe • Ingrid-Barbara Hoffmann, Böblingen •
Dagmar Höffner, Ingelheim • Barbara Hohkamp, Stuttgart • Petra Klein, Runkel • Martina Kriebel, Brigachtal
Inge Kronisch, Flensburg • Christa Lüdemann, Hannover • Konstanze Stöckermann-Borst, Leimen •
Ellen Wiegard-Kaiser, Bielefeld • Herbert Willms, Herford • Gunhild Wolf, Unna

Illustration/Grafik
Adrian Barclay, Bristol • John Batten, London • Dr. Volkhard Binder, Berlin • Carlos Borrell, Berlin •
Klaus Ensikat, Berlin

Umschlaggestaltung
Leonardi.Wollein, Berlin

Layoutkonzept
Christoph Schall

Layout und technische Umsetzung
Klein & Halm Grafikdesign, Berlin

www.cornelsen.de

1. Auflage, 5. Druck 2013

Druck: Stürtz GmbH, Würzburg

ISBN 978-3-464-34462-0 – broschiert
ISBN 978-3-464-34346-3 – gebunden

Inhalt gedruckt auf säurefreiem Papier aus nachhaltiger Forstwirtschaft.